AN
ESSAY
CONCERNING
Computer Understanding

In Four BOOKS

John G. Gorman
John W. Gorman

First printing   November 2011
Printed   December 2011

ABOUT THE COVER

The cover design, modeled on the cover of his 1691 *An Essay Concerning Human Understanding* is a salute to John Locke, 17th century scholar, physician and empiricist philosopher. Readers of the *Essay* is always in awe of his brilliant analytical approach to a theory of ideas and to introspection into the operations of the mind. Locke's use of *relations, modes* and *substance* were inspirational in the authors' development of the ideas presented in this book.

DEDICATION

To Julia

CONTENTS

ACKNOWLEDGEMENTS

Our sincere thanks to Tony Cooper whose remarkable skills in writing software code that is able to parse long complex English sentences, and for the book design of *An Essay Concerning Computer Understanding*. Tony and one of us (JGG) have worked on various computer projects together for four decades, from the early hospital blood bank management system installed at Lenox Hill hospital in the 1970s, through the Tracker database editor and viewer to the present Mensa language understanding software. Tony has extraordinary skills in making complex ideas work most elegantly and reliably in software, and his contributions of many truly nimble features to Mensa have been crucial to its success. We also thank sister and aunt Jocelyn Morris for her careful reading of the book and encouraging discussion of the ideas contained.

PROLOGUE

The focus of this essay is to document our effort to develop an orthography of human thought and language that is computer friendly. Our goal has been to develop a system whereby human thought can be stored in a computer in all its subtlety and processed by the computer in a manner on a level with the human mind. And where one can interact with the computer in unrestricted natural language. This has required an understanding of exactly how expressions work

For over 40 years the goal of our language understanding project has been to work towards modeling the human mind in a computer. Developing a machine capable of understanding human thought and natural language has been a leading edge objective of computer science since Alan Turing first proposed the Turing Test in 1950. Much has been written about HAL, the iconic character in 2001: *A Space Odyssey*, a 1968 science fiction film directed by Stanley Kubrick, written by Kubrick and Arthur C. Clarke, as the gold standard in this field.[1][2]Achieving this echelon is recognized as the holy grail of computer and cognitive science today.

Enormous investments of time and money have been committed to computer understanding. Intense efforts have resulted in schemes like RDF, OWL, CYC and IBM's current Watson project, which are still works in progress. After 60 years this enterprise is well funded, ongoing, with great hopes, but there is still no guarantee of success. It is proving to be a very difficult task. There is still is no clear roadmap.[3] Language understanding is made difficult because the literal meaning of an utterance is very often not the intended meaning of that utterance. Any utterance has to be interpreted with many considerations in mind. Workers in the field generally acknowledge that there are still three breakthroughs required: breakthroughs in Knowledge Representation, breakthroughs in Natural Language Theory, and breakthroughs in Language Understanding Software.[4]

Inspired by HAL our project was embarked upon in the late 1960s and we have consistently pursued it since. We have developed a data structure capable of recording human thought in detail, which captures nuances in full to exactly the same level as language, and working software that can communicate with it in ordinary conversation. We call it *Mensa* technology, We believe it is unique. The discipline the computer imposed was essential.

---

1   *2001: A Space Odyssey*, a 1968 science fiction film directed by Stanley Kubrick, written by Kubrick and Arthur C. Clarke

2   *HAL's Legacy, 2001's Computer as Dream and Reality*, edited by David G. Stork, foreword by Arthur C. Clarke. See Chapter 8 by Roger Shank, Chapter 9 by Douglas Lenat,

3   Wilks, Y. *Is there progress on talking sensibly to machines*, Science Vol. 318, Nov'07, pp. 927-928

4   Etzioni, O, *Search needs a shake-up*, Nature, 476, 25–26, 2011

During this 40 year project there was no epiphany, no "Eureka moment", except perhaps for the day that our parser program successfully parsed a long sentence for the first time, taking into account the contribution of every word and punctuation mark. Insights came slowly and incrementally with each new insight usually leading to a new perspective on old insights. The underlying theory and understanding, and practice, steadily became simpler and more robust.

And, help came from a close study of John Locke's classic *Essay Concerning the Human Understanding* (1692) without which the essential foundation ideas would never have occurred to us. The cover design of our book, modeled closely on the cover of his 1691 *Essay*, is a salute to John Locke, 17th century scholar, physician and empiricist philosopher. As our dog-eared, marked-up, multi-highlighted paperback copy of the *Essay* is read and reread, John Locke's sense of humor comes through, his occasional tongue in cheek remark evoking an eerie feeling that he is talking warmly to one across three centuries, sharing his thoughts and feelings in person. Yet, one is always in awe of his brilliant analytical approach to a theory of ideas and introspection into operations of the mind so startlingly modern as to inspire computer software that works today.

This has required an understanding of exactly how expressions work in general. We have discovered that language expressions operate exactly like algebraic expressions. The exact same parser program that will parse a language expression will evaluate an arithmetic expression. As will be explained, our system relies on a very simple parsing algorithm with access to a *Mensa* table of relations between pairs of concepts. Blessed with the superb programming skills of our colleague Tony Cooper, who wrote the current software code, we have practical working software and a database structure which enables a computer to process and interact with pre-installed knowledge at the same intellectual level as the human mind.

In an effort to truly understand how a language expression addresses a particular concept, we have not been able to resist exploring some very seductive side tracks. Because of the close ties language has to thought we entertain what language can tell us about neuroscience, about consciousness. We explore what insights can be derived from the history of the invention of writing and from the invention of algebra.

.

We propose that, in the brain, each idea is represented by a "grandmother' neuron in the left temporal cortex, and that a language expression addresses its particular neuron by defining a path to it by using the same principle that a tennis tournament uses to pick a champion; in the same way that a mathematician evaluates an algebraic expression; in the same way that a telephone switchboard rings a particular phone out of tens of millions upon input of a numerical expression, a series of decimal digit symbols.

The human mind is considered to comprise three integrated systems- the *cognitive*, the *emotive* and the *conative*.[5] We have concentrated mostly on modeling the cognitive. However we have also spent some effort on the mind's conative volitional system in that our computer programs can make quite apposite responses to text inputs. And our programs can initiate actions on their own. For example, in our examination program the computer asks set questions and then grades answers given in natural language for correctness. On the other hand we have done little towards modeling the mind's emotive system; evaluating importance of concepts; detecting when things don't add up. It is necessary but not sufficient to understand the meaning of a language expression. One also has to feel the truth of it. This aspect of our project represents a future challenge but one with marvelous possibilities for our software tools and we see some promising first approaches.

One very important point of distinction between this project and current efforts in computational linguistics should be made. Science writer and novelist Richard Powers points out, *"Open-domain question answering has long been one of the great holy grails of artificial intelligence."*[6] Having the advantage of being unencumbered by knowledge we have not ventured along the ambitious and difficult path of present statistics based Natural Language Processing (NLP). In contrast we are *closed-domain*, and only knowledge that has been pre-encoded in the database is dealt with. But dealt with with very precise understanding of what complex language text means. All the sentences that our parser will encounter have been pre-parsed. For this reason, we have no need to manually tag words for parts of speech to help assess the particular POS a word may have in any instance; no need to train our parser on large text corpora; no need

---

5   For background on these three mental systems, Google "conation" and browse the results page.

6   Powers, R, New York Times, The Opinion Pages, 2/5/11

to use statistics to fathom the particular sense a word may have in any instance.

Because our databases are composed under the supervision of a human mentor the intended meaning of each sentence is determined precisely. When the author intends double meaning, they can be recognized and both meanings can be recorded (along with a value for how funny or trite they may be). In this way our system can be made fully aware of and precisely record double meaning, humor, spin, arguments, cause and effect, metaphor, analogy, simile, allegory, irony, satire, sarcasm, puns, subtext and allusions, metonymy, personification, rhetorical questions and more for what they are because they have been identified and prerecorded by the human mentor.

We have avoided trying to program any processes that require the computer to "think" except for a one-off diversion described in Book III, Chapter I where we had the computer do intricate abstract logic faster and more accurately than humans. Otherwise, all of the thinking is done by a human mentor and our programs and databases simply record the product of that thinking. We have found it very difficult to get people to understand that ours is a fundamentally less ambitious approach to language understanding, but nevertheless is very useful and practical.

Even though our language system is closed domain it is freely scalable. Millions of concepts can be installed and answers for myriad questions can be made available. Both sensitivity and specificity of question answering in our system are 100%, better than Watson's 90% sensitivity and specificity for his one word answers, and well above Google's perhaps 70% sensitivity and less than 10% specificity for first page search results. One might say that, while supremely useful, Google is like a box of chocolates – one never knows what one is going to get. On the other hand, to make it worthwhile for him to interact with our system a user must have reasonable expectations or know or be told that the answer is there, because only information that has been precoded is available. Think of it this way, whereas search engines do "search" we do "find".

Writing this monograph the realization has come up again and again that the ideas presented will not be accessible to a reader who lacks background in linguistics, psychology, philosophy, cognitive science and software theory and practice. One ultra quick and efficient way to raise background to a sufficient level while reading this monograph is to browse topics in Google or Wikipedia. It is not the task of this monograph to teach neuroscience or linguistic theory, so from time to time we regularly suggest search terms in footnotes to search on Google or Wikipedia for necessary background. Not only will very pertinent information be provided but also useful citations. We encourage the reader to make use of these suggested search terms so as to find this monograph much more accessible.[7]

The purpose of this *essay* is to put new spin on some aspects of the current conceptual framework for cognition and linguistics, which makes it possible for a computer to deal with meaning. As Ferdinand de Saussure said *"Everyone, left to his own devices, forms an idea about what goes on in language which is very far from the truth."* As Albert Szent-Györgi said *"Research is to see what everybody else has seen, and to think what nobody else has thought."* As Leo Tolstoy said *"Truth, like gold, is to be obtained not by its growth, but by washing away from it all that is not gold."* Yes, there is a need for some new innovative ideas but also a need to escape from some of the old ones. We have begun to think that when we get agreement and nodding heads we are teaching same old same old. That immediate pushback from a person well versed the field means that we are on to something. For example, we expect major pushback against our claim in Book II Chapter V that only a small minority of English finite sentences have *SVO* form and that most have *subject-seam* form.

In setting down all of the essential ideas in this essay and arranging them in order, providing needed background material has proved a difficult task. There have been many changes of order and emphasis. In Dwight Bolinger's words *"One builds one's house, and the children come, triplets and quadruplets, and an entire room has to be added, and not always in the most harmonious place."*[8]

---

7   To make "I'm feeling lucky" available, turn Google Instant off in Web Search Help reached with search string "Web search help"
8   Dwight Bolinger, Degree Words, Mouton, The Hague Paris, 1972. p20.

INTRODUCTION

John Locke in his famous classic, An Essay Concerning Human Understanding, argued that concepts are tangible entities that are experienced clearly in the mind. Leibniz used symbols to represent mental concepts. An expression is an ordered list of symbols. Language and the mind use the powerful symbolic methods of algebra to model the world. We have found the lexicals and grammaticals of language ordered in expressions are a symbolic system that can be well managed in a computer.

In 1691, John Locke in his famous *An Essay Concerning Human Understanding*, a masterpiece of introspection, argued that an observer holds clear ideas in his conscious mind, as tangible entities that can be recognized, experienced, identified and described.

> *"The coldness and hardness which a man feels in a piece of ice being as distinct ideas in the mind as the smell and whiteness of a lily; or as the taste of sugar, and smell of a rose. And there is nothing can be plainer to a man than the clear and distinct perception he has of those simple ideas"*   Essay II, xii,5

Locke goes on to claim that a complex mental concept is a construct of simple mental concepts that can be assembled into formal structures that represent complex ideas.

> *"Secondly, there are others compounded of simple ideas of several kinds, put together to make one complex one;- v.g. beauty, consisting of a certain composition of colour and figure, causing delight to the beholder; theft, which being the concealed change of the possession of anything, without the consent of the proprietor, contains, as is visible, a combination of several ideas of several kinds: and these I call mixed modes."*   Essay II, xii,5

John Locke viewed clear ideas as tangible entities in the mind and believed there were only three kinds of ideas, R*elations, Modes* and *Substance*.[1] Locke regarded the *relations* between ideas to be just as clear as the ideas they relate. Locke's view of clear concepts as tangible *entities* and *relations* in the mind led us to the idea that we could give each clear concept a unique symbolic identifier, which the computer could treat and operate upon like an algebraic symbol. We see symbols as mnemonic containers and shapers of meaning. However, representing mental concepts with symbols is not a new idea. Leibniz in 1676 used symbols for concepts in his unfinished "algebra of thought" project and they are the basis of modern symbolic logic.

However, the best tip we got from John Locke was his idea that *relations* were just as tangible in the mind as *entities*. Locke's insight was that a *relation* is a concept in its own right, just as clear in our minds as any

---

1   Locke's *Substances* are mental concepts whose structure is strictly governed by the way things are structured in the real world. His simple and complex *Modes* are mental concepts free of this restriction and limited only by the imagination.

other concept. Besides being containers and shapers of meaning, certain grammatical symbols stand for *relations* between concepts. So, assigning a unique symbolic identifier to each *relation* concept was perhaps the watershed idea of our entire project. We have come to believe that *relations* are perhaps the most important class of concept, an idea we will discuss at length in this essay.

Our approach has been based upon studying algebraic expressions to understand exactly how they work and then on applying the principles learned to language expressions. Then, to closely study how language symbols are manipulated, ordered, put in *relations*. By studying language closely from an algebraic point of view we have been able to draw out the principles of the mind's symbolic system and develop both a coherent theory of how it works, as well as being able to get computer programs to process language symbols, to emulate human thought and the way the world is. The best *prima facie* demonstration we have for this idea is that our computer program (askme.exe), which can parse an algebraic expression to determine its value, can evaluate a language expression to determine its precise meaning.

Anyhow, in our system, we stay very close to language to model the world in a computer, mostly using the very same symbols. Like language, we treat all three of the elements of a language expression, lexical words, grammaticals and punctuation marks exactly like the symbols of an algebraic expression. We found that language symbols and expressions and algebraic symbols and expressions work in exactly the same way. This raised the hope that an uncomprehending computer could be programmed to mimic human thought by manipulating symbols according to the methods of algebra. We believe that this hope has been fulfilled.

Language is an extraordinarily powerful orthography of human thought. Natural language is able to encode a comprehensive and nuanced model of the world. Leonard Talmy has best described how language comprises lexical words and free and bound grammatical elements that have different functions.[2] Lexical words, nouns and adjectives, verbs and adverbs, are an open class that is being regularly augmented. Grammatical particles, pronouns, prepositions, noun suffixes, verb inflections, punctuation marks,

---

2   Leonard Talmy, *Towards a Cognitive Semantics*, Volume I, The MIT Press, Cambridge, 2003, p22.

etc. are entries responsible for the structure of concept. They are a closed class with no new entries. A key purpose of this essay is to fully understand the exact role grammaticals and punctuation marks play in defining the structure of mental concepts. It appears that the main function of lexicals is to enrich grammaticals to form more complex grammaticals.

In the chapter on invariance, we describe how our parser can detect whether a sentence does or does not express a particular concept even if it is worded in any one of billions of different ways. The parser rejected any sentence, even one using the same words, that did not express the concept correctly or used bad grammar. This exercise also showed that a computer can be programmed to mindlessly perform highly abstract logic better and faster than humans.

The Meaning of Meaning

Each language symbol, driven by its mnemonic value by social consensus, stands for a particular mental concept and at the same time for a particular real or imaginary thing. Language manipulates symbols, to mirror operations of the mind that reflect goings on in the world. So we have the famous triangle of Ogden and Richards'.

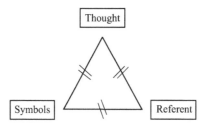

Fig. I.1   The Famous Triangle of Ogden and Richards

In their classic work, *The Meaning of Meaning*, they argue that the symbols (words), the referent (the thing) and the thought, (concept) are in a three-way correspondence.[3] This triangle is encapsulated in the finite sentence, a language expression that always involves an observer, attention and consciousness. Every finite sentence is an equation with the equals sign

---

3   Ogden C K and Richards I A, *The Meaning of Meaning*, Harcourt, Brace, Jovanovich, San Diego, 1989, p.11

being between the thoughts in the observer's mind and the reality he is observing.

Spoken language was not an invention of mankind; it emerged by a process of Darwinian evolution about 200,000 years ago as the human line evolved.[4] Children do not have to be taught to speak.[5] On the other hand, children do have to be taught to read and write. Written language is a man made invention developed painstakingly only over the last 5000 years. In parallel and somewhat independently, scholars developed algebra over much the same time period.[6] Using symbols, mankind has developed algebraic methods, expressions and equations. The necessary adaptations of algebraic variables in different contexts, make algebra, and language too, capable of modeling the real world with awe-inspiring power.

Another realization was that lexical words themselves are comprised of a combination of phonemes, graphemes and morphemes that cue us in mnemonically to the meaning of the lexical. The idea became stronger and stronger in our minds as we pursued this project that language is a vast mnemonic system. De Saussure famously has claimed that the association of phonemes and morphemes with their meaning is arbitrary, that any word can be picked to mean a particular concept. And, many linguists have followed his belief. It is clearly not true. We have noticed that once one has an idea of just what each phoneme does, e.g. sounds like *t to for er en em ed ch* etc, one can often see why a word was chosen to mean what it does just by analyzing its combination of mnemonic *phonemes* and *graphemes*.[7]

We have also noticed to our dismay that advancing the idea that phonemes and graphemes are highly mnemonic for the meaning of words and giving examples induces immediate pushback from most people. We are criticized for extrapolating from coincidence rather than using sound science. Nevertheless, we have sprinkled examples of likely mnemonics throughout this essay in the hope that the idea will catch on. Gentle reader,

---

4   Nicholas Wade, *Before the Dawn*, The Penguin Press, New York, 2006,p.30
5   Stanislas Dehaene, *Reading in the Brain*, Viking, New York, 2009, pp 131-140.
6   Google "Melissa Snell The History of Algebra" I'm feeling lucky
7   Google "grapheme" I'm feeling lucky

we beg your indulgence when you come across an example of matching sound and letter shape to meaning.

Relations

A theory of *relations* features centrally in this essay. We will show that the set of specific *relations* between the concepts of a system is the key to their organization. A coherent set of *relations*, which we call a *relationship*, can build a very complex mental structure. We could not foresee the huge role that *relations* play in the construction of concepts where words focus meaning on each other, in Dwight Bolinger's words *"in fevered competition and intervention ... language is at war with itself"*.[8]

We argue that *grammaticals,* including punctuation marks, are containers of meaning that can be filled with conceptual content emitted by adjacent relative concepts. We have also found it necessary to treat punctuation marks as full-fledged *grammaticals*. Natural language key word processing systems that remove these "stop words' and punctuation marks and employ statistically-based key word and key phrase search rashly discard essential contributors to meaning. While key word search is very powerful, it will never be adequate to recover the full meaning of language. It's like a detective trying to solve a crime, having thrown most of the valuable clues away.

Another critical idea is that grammaticals, as a set, divide into two distinct functioning groups. One group of grammaticals serve as containers and shapers of meaning, *relatives*, while the other group regulates the flow of meaning between the containers and shapers, *relations*. This insight engenders appreciation for the amazing power of both language and algebraic expressions to record how a cluster of related concepts can be fitted together into a precisely structured *relationship*. They record how concepts that are party to an expression influence each other so that each one adapts its sense to fit in. Once related, there is a flow of meaning between concepts that causes them to adapt their sense to the context they happen to be in in any one instance. In a *relation* two relatives adapt to each other in a certain way and they may well retain their adaptation after being released from the *relation*. Recording these post-relational adaptations by relabeling grammaticals is a critical step.

---

8   Dwight Bolinger, *Degree Words*, Mouton, The Hague . Paris, p.20

Expressions

An expression, an ordered list of symbols that stand for concepts, brings together all the concepts mentioned into a congruent structure, a single unitary complex concept that can be identified by a single compact symbol. In this essay we call such a complex unitary symbol the **it** concept (bolded). Symbol order is key; in language expressions the order in which the symbols, words, are arranged is essential to establishing the right meaning. As Tom Stoppard says " ... *words are (sacred). They deserve respect. If you get the right ones in the right order, you might nudge the world a little ... "*[9]

In an expression symbols fall naturally into pairs so that an expression can also be viewed as a list of binary *relations* or interactions between adjacent terms in the list; each interaction being a mathematical or mental operation. This pairing of adjacent symbols enables expressions to model concepts as directed binary trees of Graph Theory.[10] These realizations enable an alternative orthography for language expressions: a simple table of the operations specified by the expression, which is much more computer friendly than text because it also includes operations that are implied by but are not explicit in text expressions. We call this table a *Mensa table*.

A language expression, and its *Mensa table* correlate, can be viewed as defining the path to be taken to reach a particular concept among millions of concepts extant in the mind and billions of other possible concepts that can be defined by a language expression. Think of it this way. Let each row of a *Mensa* table indicate which road is to be taken at each of a series of binary forks along a *path*. The metaphor of a tennis tournament is apt with the winner's path to victory being determined by who wins the match in each round. We use the metaphor of a *single-elimination tournament*, tennis, golf, bridge, to get a true understanding of how expressions are parsed to single unitary concepts.[11] Parsing is a powerful technique used by the brain to enable an expression to address one neuron out of millions.

Grammar - Rules of Syntax

Every type of expression, from decimal numbers to postal addresses, has its own idiosyncratic *grammar* or *rules of syntax*. It is necessary to

---

9   Tom Stoppard, *The Real Thing*, Act II, Scene V, HENRY and ANNIE.
10 Google "Graph Theory"
11 Google "single elimination tournament"

understand these rules in each case to successfully parse the expression. As language first appeared two hundred thousand years ago in lock step with the emergence of modern human intelligence, evolution made sure the rules of syntax for language expressions would be as simple and transparent as possible.[12] Children attain complete command of them by the age of five without instruction. The rules of grammar state that the first symbol of each expression wins the tournament, that symbol order causes symbols to fall naturally into pairs, that the first mentioned symbol in each pair wins the match to survive into the next round, that grammatical symbols trump lexical symbols, that punctuation mark symbols trump grammaticals and thereby get byes to quarter final, semifinal or grand final matches. By "putting two and two together" using syntax a parser can "figure out" exactly what a language expression means.

Grammar requires that the contribution to meaning of every grammatical and punctuation mark in an expression is taken into account when deriving the meaning of a language text. One missing word or word order that is bad grammar will prevent an expression from being parsed to a single concept. Our parser is able to detect such errors, however slight - we make sure of that.

Flow-of-Meaning Trees and Mensa tables

So, we developed a table of mental operations with a special format we call *Mensa*, the *Fifth Medium* of knowledge or *M5*, and a *flow-of-meaning -tree* graph which graphically illustrates mental processes, We have annexed the word *Mensa* because it means table in Latin and connotes mental activity, and coined two new words, *ment* and *endit*, to describe the two types of *flow-of-meaning -trees* that parse to a single **it** concept, and thereby make sense of an expression.[13] We will illustrate these with many examples.

A *Mensa* table precisely mirrors what the mind has to do to connect element concepts into a larger whole. Once a computer is given access to a corresponding *Mensa* table it can "understand" perfectly the meaning of any string of words that makes sense. Because it is a simple table of

---

12   " .. but not simpler", Albert Einstein
13   John Locke: "I beg pardon; it being unavoidable in discourses, differing from the ordinary received notions, either to make new words, or to use old words in somewhat a new signification; the later whereof, in our present case, is perhaps the more tolerable of the two."   Essay II, XII, 4

connections between pairs of computer memory addresses, a *Mensa* table, can capture the exact structure of complex systems of knowledge. To appreciate the ideas presented in this monograph, it is important for the reader to follow the meaning flow illustrated in *flow-of-meaning-trees* and *Mensa* tables to understand clearly how they work since these two concept modeling tools allow a computer to model mental processes and language:

Here is the format we have developed for rows of the *Mensa table* to enable them to represent operations of both algebraic and language expressions that reflect parallel operations of mind. In each row two concepts mate and beget an offspring concept. This creates an ability to translate English expressions into exactly equivalent *Mensa* tables and capture the full knowledge encoded in language. Thereby, any knowledge that can be stored in language can be stored in *Mensa* to an equal degree of nuance. And once concepts are stored in its *Mensa* memory, it can be processed by a remarkably simple computer algorithm. With basically five lines of code a computer can determine exactly which concept a human is expressing in ordinary language. And, like text corpora, the amount of knowledge that can be stored in a *Mensa* database is infinitely scalable. There is no limit.

Interestingly, studies of the brain activity that occurs during thought and language processing, using electrodes, functional MRI, diffusion MRI electroencephalography and , suggest strongly that concepts are mapped locally and topographically in the brain and that individual "grandmother" neurons are assigned as identifiers of individual sensory patterns. A sensory pattern is a concept and we believe that all concepts even complex concepts have their own "grandmother neuron". That "grandmother neuron" fires whenever its concept is sensed, words that mean it are read or heard, or the concept is imagined. Observed relations are sensory patterns and therefore concepts. And when a *relation* is observed, no doubt the specific neuron with a receptive field for that *relation* fires. And *relations* between concepts are modeled by physical connections between neurons. By connecting neurons assigned to concepts the human brain can physically model human thought. In our computer model of this system we emulate the brain's physical topography by assigning a physical row in our *Mensa* database that corresponds to the physical neuron that represents each mental concept, with pointers to related rows representing connections.

There are five innovations without which this project could not have been done.

1.   *Mensa* tables - *Fifth Medium* (*M5*)
2.   *Flow-of-meaning-trees* - *ments*
3.   *Grammaticals* standing for both *entities* and *relations*
4.   Parser algorithm
5.   Achieving *invariance* to expressions with the same meaning

Because of our ability to record highly intellectual thought, with full control of both syntax and semantics, there is the prospect for making important advances in linguistic theory and cognitive science. There are great opportunities for research doing hands on experiments with computer models of declarative knowledge. As for practical applications: the first interface will be communication with the Internet in natural language.[14] And we foresee many other applications for our technology

To access the new ideas embodied in this essay it is essential for the reader to fully understand how *flow-of-meaning-trees* and *Mensa tables* function to define the construction of complex concepts, and how essential they are for our parser software to parse expressions and finite sentences. *Mensa* tables are a critical element of our system of encoding human thought and language. We strongly suggest you work through a number of the many examples given. Even better, follow Wilbur Wright's advice: *"If you really wish to learn then you must mount the machine and become acquainted with its tricks by actual trial"* and heed Richard Feynman's belief *"What I cannot build, I do not understand."* Build some *Mensa* tables for yourself.

---

14 Tim Berners-Lee *The Semantic Web*, Scientific American, May 2001.

BOOK I
CHAPTER I

Making Sense of the World

As an observer senses a part of the world he looks at a cluster of sensory patterns, each sensory pattern representing something out there in the world. The observer's mind makes sense of the raw sensory data it perceives by assigning a neuron and a symbol to each observed sensory pattern and connects the neurons to relate the symbols to each other to form a single congruent relationship of symbols. To make the picture complete the mind often has to fill in the relationship with related concepts that are implied but not observed. The observer's brain makes sense of the raw sensory data it sees by assigning a cortical neuron to each observed sensory pattern and connecting the neurons to form a single congruent network.

A n observer's mind and brain sensing a local section of the world perceives a localized cluster of objects and activities. Any local cluster of world entities and activities usually forms a congruent physical system, with each party thing adapting to fit with all the others. Like the parts of an automobile, **it** is the way the world fits together. And, each individual observed thing is modeled in his mind as a clear mental concept, as described by John Locke. The mind has to muster that cluster of concepts, each matching something observed out in the world, and organize them into a structured relationship so they adapt to with each other and mirror "the way **it** is out there". By assembling neighboring sensory inputs that fit - they are **of-it** - together into a congruent whole the mind constructs a rich graphic geometric-space model of the world that is experienced live in consciousness.

That the overall structure of a complex system of related concepts can be captured by a bare listing of the relations between pairs of its individual parts is clearly illustrated by the famous "Dry Bones" song of the Delta Rhythm Boys.

> *"The head-bone connected to the neck-bone,*
> *the neck-bone connected to the back-bone*
> *the backbone connected to the thigh-bone*
> *the thighbone connected to the knee-bone*
> *the kneebone connected to the leg bone*
> *the leg bone connected to the foot bone"*

This song lyric, a bare list of six (n-1) relations between seven (n) "concepts", not only provides a correct picture of the overall structure of the human body but positions each part in its correct place. Such lists of relations between adjacent components are a simple and powerful method for mustering a collection of items, putting them in correct relation with each other and precisely defining the whole complex structure they form together.[1]

In the brain, every recognized thing in the observer's view with a distinctive sensory pattern activates a particular cortical neuron, or local network of

---

1   But this lyric is not a good example for illustrating how concepts put in relation adapt their sense to fit with their neighbors and into the structure. One remarkable aspect of the bringing together of concepts into juxtaposition in a context is that they adapt to fit with each other.

neurons, in his cerebral cortex. This neuron, the one with a receptive field for that sensory pattern, has been termed a "grandmother neuron".[2]

When an observed or imagined sensory pattern fires its assigned grandmother neuron, the sensory pattern is experienced vividly in consciousness, rich with qualia, colorful, auditory, tactile, fragrant and tasty, along with feelings and evaluations. It "makes sense". This results from anterograde and retrograde projections from the grandmother neuron to innumerable neurons in both cortical hemispheres that have connections to the primitive limbic nuclei where consciousness resides.[3] But when an observed scene is experienced in consciousness, it is not just neurons firing in the brain – they mirror what is real and operating out there in the world of the observer - the corresponding thing exists in the real world of his view. The ability to experience vivid sensations in consciousness evolved hundreds of millions of years ago, well before the human line split off from the mouse. All the higher animals share graphic consciousness with us. And, ironically, consciousness is not involved in mediating the more intellectual levels of human thought.

We are constantly trying to make sense of the world around us. Frank Wilczek sees this effort, in his inspiring book *The Lightness of Being*, as *"a struggle to find patterns and meaning in the seemingly random, strange and cruel world we live in"*.

> *"Constructing profoundly simple theories of physics ... The goal is to find the shortest possible message-ideally, a single equation-that when unpacked produces a detailed, accurate model of the physical world. .... Nature's data set seems far from arbitrary. We've been able to make short codes that describe large parts of reality fully and accurately. More than this: in the past, as we've made our codes shorter and more abstract, we've discovered that unfolding the new codes gives expanded messages, which turn out to correspond to new aspects of reality .... When Newton encoded Kepler's three laws of planetary motion into his law of universal gravity, explanations of the tides, the precession of the equinoxes, and many other tilts and wobbles tumbled out."*

When an observer looks out at the world, he sees only part of the picture. He sees what is in plain sight; just a sample of what is going on is seen

---

2   Google "grandmother neuron"

3   Damasio A R, *The Brain Binds Entities and Events by Multiregional Activation from Convergence Zones*, Neural Computation, 1. 123-132, 1989.

literally. To know what it means, a viewer has to mentally construct the rest of the whole picture by calculation aided by memory and imagination. To make the picture complete the mind has to fill in concepts that are not observed. An observer builds a bigger mental picture by looking at signs or clues that tell him what he can't see directly.

Art critic Peter Schjeldahl says it well:

> *"We know now, from brain science, that seeing is not a direct register of what meets our eyes but a fast mental construction that squares sensations with memory and desire: what we believe and wish reality to be."*

> *Peter Schjeldahl, The New Yorker, November 29, 2010 p.46*

NYU Philosopher Thomas Nagel also says it well:

> *It is obvious, without the need for scientific research, that vastly more of the work of the human mind is unconscious or automatic in this sense than conscious and deliberate. We do not consciously construct a visual image from sensory input or consciously choose the word order and produce the muscle movements to utter a sentence, any more than we consciously digest our food. The huge submerged bulk of the mental iceberg, with its stores of memory and acquired skills that have become automatic, like language, driving and etiquette, supplies people with the raw materials on which they can exercise their reason and decide what to think and what to do."*

> *Thomas Nagel, New York Times Book Review, March 13, 2011*

A physician, a person with previous experience and accumulated training in a field of inquiry, making a diagnosis from signs, symptoms and lab results might observe *"His fasting blood sugar is 135"*. *"That tells me the patient has diabetes"*. A detective solving a crime from a small number of clues might say: "The DNA was the most telling evidence". We try to fit what we observe into a larger picture that "makes sense". To "figure out" the picture fully we have to come up with *ideas*. The word "idea" refers to the unobserved components of his world picture that have to be filled in mentally. Then, largely unconsciously, with calculations most likely performed in the frontal lobes, the human mind puts an importance value on each concept in context. The ability to figure out what's behind what is observed is an important survival faculty. The pleasure obtained from exercising it encourages us to practice it at every opportunity.

The following cartoons illustrate the constant human need to understand what a limited sampling of the world "tells" us about the bigger picture, the way **it** is.

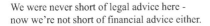

We were never short of legal advice here - now we're not short of financial advice either.

I understand you're from Chicago.

With each cartoon, the reader collects raw observations presented, detects and leverages subtle distinctions in those *signs* and fills in the rest of the picture based solely on his experience and imagination. Most viewers of the first cartoon will understand that Bernie Madoff and Raj Rajaratnam are fellow inmates.

Besides crafting a highly graphic picture of the world in consciousness, the human mind makes use of an even more powerful, parallel, non-graphic system of symbols to model the world. With the advent of language around 200,000 years ago the human mind began to use sound symbols to stand for observed concepts. In consensus with other speakers of a language, the human mind assigned phonemes, words, phrases, expressions and sentences as symbols to stand for clear mental concepts, for definite worldly things; first developing phoneme and word symbols for spoken language, much later pictographic symbols for written language. Each word has a unique compact phonetic or pictographic sensory pattern.[4]

The pictographic symbols the mind uses are the elements of language, words and punctuation marks, which, when ordered in language expressions and sentences, form a well organized ordinal numbering system for mental concepts, like ID#s or SKU barcodes. Totally in parallel the brain assigns

---

4   Stanislas Dehaene, *Reading in the Brain*, Viking, New York, 2009, pp 11-51

individual neurons and networks of neurons, and symbols and networks of symbols to match clear mental concepts. Then, the mind identifies each organized cluster of concepts with a compact higher level symbol, and a specific left inferior temporal lobe cortical neuron. Then, sensing the sound, the written word or the real thing out in the world, or imagining it, causes the neuron that *means* that concept to fire; the same higher level neuron in each case.

It is worth noting here that lexicals, nouns, adjectives, verbs and adverbs, are symbols that stand for distinctive graphic sensory patterns of real world things that are instantly recognizable when seen. The sensory patterns of noun entities like *house*, *river* or *taxi* are examples. And, verb actions have sensory patterns that are just as recognizable as noun sensory patterns. A horse can *walk, trot, canter or gallop* and all these verb action sensory patterns will be instantly recognized. They will fire the specific cortical neuron with the receptive field for that verb sensory pattern. Note that verb sensory patterns can only be recognized with the passage of time. This is the existential difference between nouns and verbs; noun sensory patterns can be seen in a photograph, verb sensory patterns require a moving picture.

How does the mind assemble a congruent "big picture"? The mind's task when it observes a scene and recognizes a group of familiar things and activities is to assemble them so they all fit together into a congruent structure. It does this by identifying the relations between pairs of them.

With many sophisticated intellectual words, like *austerity* or *postmodernism* for example, the only sensory pattern experienced in consciousness is that of the word itself. Such words do not stand for any vivid graphic sensory pattern, just for the concept. However, use of symbols allows even sophisticated intellectual concepts that do not stand for any vivid graphic sensory pattern to be dealt with proficiently by the human mind and by the computer.

Short phrases stand for more complex concepts than single words do, expressions and sentences for even more complex concepts. Sentences tell how **it** is. Paragraphs stand for a coherent unit of thought. Each complex graphic world thing or going on is represented by a binary tree of symbols, a *ment* or an *endit*, that in turn are represented by single root node symbols. Hearing or reading a word, a phrase, an expression or a sentence will fire its assigned neuron and evoke the graphic sensory pattern of the clear concept, if there is one, in consciousness. We will argue that the general method of parsing, the method of the *single elimination tournament*, is the same method that the mind and brain employs to enable an expression, which by definition is an ordered string of word symbols, to address a particular neuron out of billions. Much more on how neuron networks parse language expressions in Book I Chapter III.

Language and Art

As early as 32,000 years ago as shown by carbon-14 dated the Lascaux and Chauvet cave paintings indicate that humans realized they could create artifacts to mimic the raw sensory data coming off natural things and evoke the same conscious experience. Much later, writing was developed which emitted raw sensory data that could be processed to evoke conscious experience almost equivalent to sensing the real thing. Artifactual raw sensory data could be mapped on to concepts just as well as natural raw sensory data. This enabled language to use of binary connections between symbols to model connections between mental concepts and the brain to employ physical connections between *neurons* in the brain. Thus, language, art and the mind have the power to organize a cluster of relationships into a whole unified structure, powerfully tracking the way world things are structured into complex unified systems.

By generating a list of identified relations between these higher level symbols, a cluster of observed sensory patterns can be put together as a unit. Then, the unconscious mind can organize very large systems of graphic patterns by putting these complex units together. This method of relating unit symbols that stand for a large conceptual arrangements is very effective. The conscious graphic system and the unconscious symbolic system work together intricately to organize knowledge but the power of the symbolic system transcends the graphic conscious system of representation. Its power is astonishing. As we will see, it has the power of algebra. The use of symbols explains why humans are far more intelligent than any of the other animals. And as this very consistent and powerful symbol model tracks the way it is out there, it allows us to deal appropriately and safely with the physical world. It is the basis for our *Mensa* database tables that relate concept symbols to each other in like fashion to enable a computer to manage complex mental concepts.

Language expressions function by arranging a series of symbols into ordered pairs whereby each element symbol conveys *meaning* into its peer. Each symbol directly modifies only its next-neighbor symbol and then retires leaving the meaning enriched survivor symbol to pair with the survivor of the next pair in line in the manner of a *single-elimination tournament*. Such a list of binary operations can define a tree. Lexical "leafical" words are the leaves of the tree. Grammatical words like articles are the nodes or joints of the tree. Thereby, words, phrases expressions and paragraphs *parse* to one surviving but highly enriched symbol that represents the *sense* of the whole expression. All of the concepts mentioned in the expression are now in an organized tree relationship.

Understanding and Explaining

In interpreting language, text is the artifact we see literally. But, what we *understand* is the unitary **it** concept that the text creates in our minds as we parse the words. A *flow-of-meaning-tree* can illustrate this point. Figure 1.1.1 is the first illustration in the essay of a *flow-of-meaning-tree (FOMT)* which we make use of many times throughout the essay. *Flow-of-meaning-trees* show how meaning flows from symbol to symbol in successive rounds to contribute meaning to the unitary **it** concept of the whole expression. They show how the symbols (words) combine to "understand" the unitary meaning of the whole expression, to show how as our eyes view the text laterally, our *mind's eye* understands what is behind the text. And, fortunately for computer programming, this same flow of meaning can be defined precisely by a *Mensa* table, of which much more will be said.

In the diagram in Fig. 1,1,1 the text symbols are what we see directly. The text line is "plane" language. Can we "see through" the "plane", can we see what's *behind* the text, to the tree figure, the meaning understanding **it**? Do we *understand* the deeper *ideas* that are the *gist* behind the plane of word symbols? Do we *get **it***, or will we have to have **it** "explained" to us? The mind has to" figure **it** out" to *get* what words and phrases mean.

Although not exactly their original meaning, the terms "surface structure" and "deep structure" of sentences are apt for referring to the text and tree of this *flow-of-meaning-tree.*

Seen through the "plane" of text, the arrow heads, which are the nodes of the tree, represent what we "understand", the "ideas" that we have to come up with mentally when we put in pairs (pairse) the "clues" provided by the text. They are the *meaning* of the text. They are what we can "tell" from the text. They are what the text "tells" us as we parse the text to single unitary concept it, to "get **it**". They are what we *know*. Sometimes text is "subtle" (sub-tell), contains subtext, and sometimes "overt" (over-tell). Is **it** clear, or will **it** be a "mystery" because the ideas are shrouded in a "mist" or our mind is "foggy". It depends on *how clear* **it** is. The text is *literal*. It is *sure*. Looking at the word symbols metaphorically from a ship at sea they are the "littoral", the "shore" that we see directly. And from a ship the foreshore is the "far shore" in the sense of "far west". Do we sense pushback from the reader against the idea of such mnemonics being important in conveying meaning?

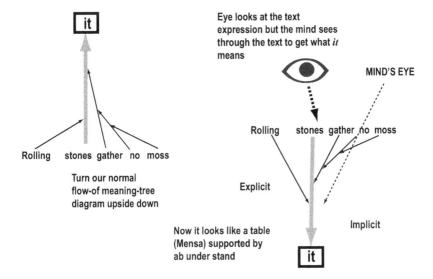

Fig 1.1.1 As our eyes observe text our mind's eye understands its meaning

So humans have had to get good at getting **it**. And good at thinking about **it**. And good at expressing and communicating **it**. Evolution has made sure that there is reward for practicing and exercising this skill, accounting for the great pleasure taken in reading, humor and in games where tactical and strategic skills can be honed more or less harmlessly.

From a small amount of data and some rules one can derive a large amount of knowledge. For example, it is possible in Sudoku, given 23 cells filled in, to fill in the remaining 58 cells by observing rules of syntax that constrain which number can be entered in each cell. Limited data plus syntax rules enable impressive compression of data, which language expressions need to employ to take advantage of because language is such a slow one dimensional communication channel.

BOOK I
CHAPTER II

Paths, Parsing and Tournaments

In this chapter we explore the idea of a path as a means of getting to a particular object among a large set of objects by specifying which of the alternate ways to take at a series of decision points along the way to its location. A path can be specified by an expression, which by definition is an ordered string of symbols. We will show that language, numbers, algebra, computers, the brain, and sports tournament organizers have all adopted this method, let's call it "pathing", to identify, organize and retrieve things in their domain. We will see that in the abstract this is the same process as parsing an expression, and is the method by which a sports tournament decides the winner.

L et's consider how an ordered string of symbols, an expression, can specify a particular *path* using an airline flight itinerary as an example of a *path*. A three digit decimal number, 724, can provide all the necessary information to specify a flight itinerary. Starting in San Diego, go to the airport, go to gate 7 and board the plane leaving from that gate, on arrival in Atlanta go to gate 2 and board, on arrival in Gatwick go to gate 4 and board, arrive in Faro, Portugal, a particular airport of the world's 1000 most active airports. This three decimal digit expression, perhaps written on a post-it, telling at each successive decision point which gate to choose can address 1000 destination airports. And, there will be 999 "roads not taken". However it will only work in a certain context, at a certain time of day, since flight schedules generally remain the same from day to day. Following these instructions at another hour would get you to an entirely different city, as would starting at a different airport. Two more terms are needed in the expression specifying the airport of origin and the time of day to arrive at the airport: *SAN 16 7 2 4*. And it could be that expression would also ensure arrival in Faro. However, a precise knowledge of flight schedules would be required to write these expressions and the *Mensa tables* that are required to parse them.

SAN 16 7 2 4		SAN 14 4 9 8	
SAN~16 = SAN16	San Diego at 4PM	SAN~14 = LAX14	Los Angeles at 2PM
SAN16~7 = ATL	Atlanta	LAX14~4 = JFK	Kennedy New York
ATL~2 = LGW	London Gatwick	JFK~9 = LHR	London Heathrow
LGW ~4 = FAO	Faro	LHR ~8 = FAO	Faro

The central principle of *pathing*, let's call it that, is that it's doing an itinerary in stages or legs directed by an expression. At the starting point, the origin, and at the location point reached as each leg is completed there is a decision to be made as to which of the alternate ways to choose for the next leg toward the next decision point. At each decision point two symbols, say ATL and gate symbol 2, are matched up, interact and ATL survives, but morphed into a new configuration, LGW. Once at ATL one is in a position to fly to LGW, which could not be done from SAN. Notice that ATL is a constructed symbol generated by taking the path, produced by the journey so far, and is matched up with symbol 2, which as the next symbol in order in the expression provides the information for where the next leg will arrive at. To gain deeper understanding of a path it is helpful to imagine staying in San Diego airport and seeing it morph before your eyes in steps into Atlanta airport, then into Gatwick and finally into Faro airport in Portugal. Also note that there are hundreds of possible paths via various intermediate airports from SAN to FAO, like the one above via LAX.

A very important point here is that the traveler does not need to know which airport he's at to make the right connection. He can get to a known destination via a bunch of unknown airports as long as they are related or connected appropriately. At each next airport he gets the only information he needs, the gate number, from the next number in the original expression. This mirrors the power of algebra using variables that are identified, related appropriately, but not given specific values. And, this is why the expression does not need to include airport details explicitly.

For another example of this idea, let's look at how a decimal number can be seen as an expression specifying a *path* to a single numeral address. Proceeding left from the decimal point, the unit digit can specify which one of ten ways to take. Then the tens digit in turn specifies one path out of ten choices allowing 100 possible paths to a number destination to be defined with two decimal digits. Then again, for each of these paths the hundreds digit specifies 10 choices. Taking the one specified by the hundreds digit identifies one out of 1000 possible paths. Upon the input of a 4 digit decimal expression, after 4 path decisions a *path* will have been taken that reached a particular one of ten thousand points. And there are 9,999 "roads not taken" leading to other points. One six digit decimal expression can address any one of a million computer memory locations. In this manner a decimal number of **n** digits can identify any one of 10^n paths, address 10^n points in a number space. A barcode expression encoding an **n** digit ordinal number can identify 10^n items. Computers readily use binary, decimal or hexadecimal numbers to address particular memory locations on hard drives by making a choice as to which way to go at a series of points or nodes, a *path*.

Also, look at it like this: one can imagine that the *point* reached in each leg lies along a one dimensional *path* and that the next digit specifies how far along to go to reach that next *point*. To measure the total distance traveled along the path specified by a four digit decimal number, *rules of syntax* are required. The following *rules of syntax* must be followed: multiply the fourth digit from the decimal point is by 1000, then add the third digit multiplied by 100 to it, then add the second digit multiplied by 10 to it and finally add the unit digit. Here arises the idea of *place value* – the meaning of a digit symbol varies by its *place* in the decimal number.[1] The total obtained, identifies the point reached by its distance in units from the origin. This distance is the *numerosity* of the decimal number expression. This is a narrow *path* and we will see later that it is the structure of a *narrative concept*.

A mathematical or software function is also an expression, comprising a function name and several arguments in a set order, which also have *place value*. However, the rules of syntax, grammar, for each function are unique to that function and may be very complex. The opposite is required the rules of syntax of language, kept as simple as possible, and exactly the same simple syntax rules apply for all language expressions.

A literal example of a series of digits serially selecting a physical path from many alternates is embodied in the old rotary telephone system. Rotary dialing a seven decimal digit telephone number is used to ring a particular phone in a *space* of 10 million phones. Although in practice it is much more complicated, a rotary phone system routes a call by sending a series of pulses or clicks to a physical rotary switch at each decision point on an outbound electrical circuit, each click indexing the switch to the next position until it reaches the right one for the intended path. These routing switches have *place value*. The physical switch is literally counting clicks. One more or one less click at any decision point, rotary switch, will result in an entirely different phone ringing. Interestingly, the idea that clicks can be counted to index meaning from one concept to the next is reminiscent of the early click languages of Southern Africa.[2] And, Roman numerals work this way in counting I pulses to index away from V 5 with IV - VI VII VIII denoting 4-8.

Paths specified by an expression are a very commonly used and practical method for identifying, locating, fetching or activating resources. For example, the bible identifies each item of information with an expression comprising three coordinates: *book, chapter* and *verse*. In computers, file managers use *path* expressions to define paths through successive folders to locate particular files. *C:/Program Files/Internet Explorer/iexplore.exe*

---

1   Google "place value"
2   Google "Click languages of Southern Africa" I'm feeling lucky

is one such example of an expression that identifies a file. A path expression not only identifies a file of interest but also tells the computer how to find it and to open or run it. The path *C:\Documents and Settings\All Users\ Start Menu\Programs\Startup\iexplore.exe* will cause a personal computer to run the file to open your browser on startup if it finds a shortcut to *iexplore.exe* in that last folder.

An Internet Universal Resource Locator (URL) or Web Address is an expression defining a path to a file on a particular computer somewhere in the world.[3] A URL expression comprises a path of six steps at each of which a choice is defined. Because millions of choices can be defined at each step each specified recursively by an expression, URLs can address an infinite number of "resources" and enable a computer to physically reach and run or fetch any particular item, be it a web page or a file on one of the world's computers. The process picks a directed single serial path out of billions of paths not taken that can be defined. These examples illustrate four key properties of expressions: a relatively terse expression can define one of billions of available paths; all of the symbols of an expression contribute essential meaning; their order matters, they have *place value*, and writer and reader must know the appropriate *grammar* or *rules-of-syntax*, for that type of expression.

Identification by Location

Cartographers can locate Los Angeles, Texas, with a coordinates expression, an ordered string of ten symbols such as *Latitude 28 27 57 N Longitude 99 0 0 W*. With agreement on syntax the symbols *longitude* and *latitude* can be left out and only eight symbols *28 27 57 N 99 0 0 W* are necessary. Each symbol has *place value*, The *Cartesian Product* of a standard syntax coordinates expression is $180*60*60*2*180*60*60*2$, which means that, if required, standard coordinates can address 1,680 billion discrete points on earth. Here again because order matters we see symbols have a *place value*. One can imagine a trip, instructed by this coordinates expression, starting from coordinates origin on the equator in the Atlantic Ocean off West Africa and traveling a specified number of arcseconds North, turning West, traveling for another specified number of arcseconds to reach Los Angeles, Texas.[4]

---

3   Google "wiki URL" I'm Feeling Lucky
4   Google "Cartesian Product"

Cartographers can also represent Los Angeles, Texas, without a label by placing a dot at a certain location on a map of Texas and it still means that town. In the same manner a physical neuron at a certain location in the brain can represent a mental concept, again without a label. In the same fashion a physical computer memory address can represent a mental concept again without a label. Identifying things by location is a very efficient and practical. Furthermore, physical connections between neurons can relate mental concepts to each other and combine them into organized networks that represent complex concepts. And the neurons and memory addresses perform these functions expertly and mindlessly, exploiting the power of algebra. And we can in practice biomimic this method of concept representation by allocating concepts to memory addresses related to each other with pointers.

Single Elimination Tournaments

Next, a word about the method of a *single elimination tournament.*[5] A *tournament* is a clever objective method that operates automatically to pick the best player. In a tournament players are put in an ordered list called a *draw* which matches players up in pairs. The winner of each match goes on to the next round, the loser goes home. In each next round survivors remain in the same order they had in the draw and are matched up accordingly again in pairs. Rounds are played until there is one survivor, who's "one" the tournament. We don't know *ex ante* who will win each match, who the champion will be, or which path the champion will take to the title. But - look at it this way - the draw, the ordered list of players in the first round, is an expression that can, well, draw a *path* that the winner will take to final victory in exactly the same manner that expressions define paths in the examples above.

And, tournaments are a very efficient because multiple pairings can be done simultaneously making it possible in the first round to start several paths in parallel, which will meet in later rounds. The principles of tournaments are relevant to many areas of society, business and government. For a clear definition of a *single-elimination tournament* and an entertaining glimpse of underlying theory and some of the issues faced by organizers, lightly browse Dmytri Ryvkin's paper, *The Predictive Power of Noisy*

---

5   Google "single elimination tournament"

Elimination Tournaments.[6] *Noise* occurs in a tournament when a lesser player eliminates a seeded player unexpectedly thus causing an error in the ranking. Noise can interfere too in parsing a language expression when a wrong partner concept survives leading to a wrong meaning being taken for the whole expression, which is often quite humorous.

To illustrate the power of the tournament method to decode an expression to determine a *path* consider the US Men's Open tennis tournament with 128 (2^7) players in the draw where there are seven rounds of matches between pairs of players. If there are **n** players there will be **n-1** matches played before a winner emerges. Matches in each round are played in parallel at the same time on multiple courts. Consider the number of different paths the winner might take to the championship. It the opponent that the eventual winner meets in each round were to be picked at random, he might be in one of 127 possible pairings in the first round, 63 in the second, 31 in the third, 15 in the fourth, 7 in the quarter finals, 3 in the semi finals and only one in the final. Thus there are 78,128,765 (127x63x31x15x7x3x1) possible paths the winner might take to become champion. But any one of 128 players can be the winner, each via any one of his possible paths so the total number of possible ways that the tournament as a whole could play out is about 10 billion (78,128,765 x128).

There are strong parallels between a language expression and a tournament. The order of the draw determines the order of precedence matches must be played. Word symbols in an expression are drawn up in order just like the tennis players in a draw. However, in language expressions not all adjacent symbols are matched up in each round. Many symbols get byes to later rounds, one sometimes even to the final round, as in a boxing championship. Symbols have to wait for the right round to take their turn in the tournament, for their time to come. Survivors of matches reach each next round modified by their match ordeal and symbols are generated to stand for their new status. This means that many next symbols matched in later rounds are new symbols generated in previous rounds. Thinking in the abstract, these symbols can be considered to represent locations reached on the paths taken by survivors who are now in a *position* to play in the next round. Path decisions are made by the outcome of each match in successive rounds of a tennis tournament where the next adjacent symbol,

---

6   For the PDF, Google "Working Paper Series (ISSN 1211-3298)   Dmytri Ryvkin" I'm feeling lucky.

the next player matched, provides the decision information required to reach the correct next point.

Rules of Syntax - Grammar

A terse expression plus *rules of syntax* (ROS) have the power to organize a large amount of knowledge. For example, by simply listing the names in the draw in a particular order - a tennis tournament *draw* is an expression - and applying one simple rule of syntax, it is possible to compose a *draw* in a particular order able to specify which one of 10 billion paths the winner of the US Men's Singles Tennis Championship has taken. Simple syntax rule: in ordering the draw list the champion of the tournament first in the draw and winner of each match first of each pair. Such an ordered draw list of players, an expression, plus one simple syntax rule, can specify the path taken by the winner, and tell at the same time how many rounds there were, how many matches were played, who played who in each match and in which round, who won each match, and who became the champion, a complete history of the tournament. How terse is that?

There is an important idea here. English grammar does largely follow this rule, that first mentioned concept of a match is always the surviving concept. However, English makes exceptions to this rule, such as putting adjective concepts before the survivor noun and expressions before the survivor punctuation symbol, making it more difficult for English speaking children to master syntax than, say, French children.

And, organizers of the tournament have other considerations. For TV and gate purposes they don't want top ranked players to knock each other out in early rounds, but rather to meet in the finals on center court. So the 16 top ranked players are seeded into separate sections of the draw so they will not meet and eliminate each other until the round of 16. And, please, no *bracketbusters*. A seeded player's chances of getting into the finals are improved because seeding makes it less likely he will be eliminated in the early rounds. His chances are affected by what tournament theory calls *noise level*: a weaker player on a good day may play well above himself or luck may play a part at a critical point resulting in a seeded player losing in an early round. This gives the top seeded players an advantage but is considered within the limits of fairness. Seeding can only go so far in influencing the outcome of a tournament. The organizers cannot make sure that a particular player will win, although they can help.

However, to get clear meaning from a language expression the author must make sure that a preselected symbol will attain the final and win, thereby traversing one path among billions to a particular point. To this end an author has to radically tilt the playing field using strong rules of syntax: *place value* counts; first mentioned symbols win; nouns beat adjectives, grammaticals beat lexicals, punctuation marks beat grammaticals; personal pronouns get a bye up to the final etc. And in many matches the author just knows from experience which symbol will win a particular match. Then, for the addressee to parse the expression correctly he must also be fluent in the rules of syntax and know from experience in certain matches which symbol will win and point will be reached.

Appreciating in the abstract the parallels between the mechanics of a tournament, the evaluation of decimal numbers, file manger paths, URLs, the solving of algebraic equations, and parsing of language expressions will be very helpful for accessing the ideas advanced in this essay. Perhaps the most important realization that has emerged from our project is for the power of *parsing*, using an analog parallel method to enable a short string of symbols to address a definite point in a very large *space*.

It is easy for a computer to compute the end locations of these paths by mathematical methods. But, how can a analog system like the brain enable an ordered string of symbols to activate a path to address one particular neuron out of billions? And how will it do it in hundreds of milliseconds? We will argue in Book I Chapter IV that the brain uses the method of *pathing* to allow a language expression to fire a particular grandmother neuron among millions in the left inferior temporal cortex.[7] The brain cannot choose mathematically between ten ways to connect to the next neuron in a path as instructed by a next symbol in an ordered input string. It has to obtain the information from the next symbol to compute the right choice at each decision point on the *path* by being creative within the limits of its biology. To *path* or *parse* a language expression, the human brain has marvelously developed the analog method of the *single elimination tournament* using binary operations between pairs of neurons in parallel, in rounds at higher and higher levels, to establish a path to a particular cortical neuron, the neuron that now will have the receptive field for that expression and also for the concept it expresses.

---

7 *Pathing* may be the phonetic mnemonic origin of the word "parsing"

BOOK I
CHAPTER III

The Neural Correlate of Expressions and Thought

The brain of an observer assigns a particular "grandmother" neuron, or local network of neurons for redundancy, to each individual sensory pattern observed. This neuron will fire whenever that pattern is experienced. It is said to have a receptive field for that sensory pattern. Since a sensory pattern is a concept, we argue that the brain assigns a physical neuron to each mental concept, including the relation concepts that lie between entity concepts. Then, the brain models a complex of sensory patterns, a cluster of concepts, by connecting these neurons into a tree network headed by a single neuron. This root neuron governs the entire involved network, which models the relationship of sensory patterns, the relationship of concepts. In parallel, the mind assigns a language symbol to each concept neuron so that spoken or written symbols can fire and control those concept neurons. In this way a language expression, an ordered string of language symbols, can fire an ordered string of concept neurons, which in turn will cause a very particular neuron out of millions to fire. We have been able to model this schema precisely in the computer.

How does the concept modeling system of the central nervous system work? The human brain contains about 100 billion neurons, some having thousands of synapses connecting with other neurons to form very elaborate networks. Recent research indicates that every recognized thing with a distinctive sensory pattern sensed by an observer activates a local cortical "grandmother" neuron, or local network of neurons for redundancy. Neurons have been shown to have *receptive fields* for unique sensory patterns. The assigned neuron with a receptive field for each object or activity, fires when the graphic sensory pattern of the entity or activity, real or art, is either observed or imagined, or when word sensory patterns meaning that concept are heard or read.[1] Thus, the brain represents each mental concept in a particular cortical neuron. Cognitive scientist Stanislas Dehaene's two books, *The Number Sense* and *Reading in the Brain* are essential reading for the reader who wants access to the underlying neuroscience and new way of thinking necessary to appreciate these ideas.[2][3]

Receptive Fields of Neurons

Studies using electrodes implanted in cortical neurons have shown that a specific "grandmother" neuron fires when a specific sensory pattern is presented to the senses. This cell specific sensory pattern is called its *receptive field*. Receptive fields have been studied most intensively in the retina, and in the visual cortex using fMRI, implanted electrodes and electroencephalography. Stanislas Dehaene in his book *Reading in the Brain,* has an excellent description of receptive fields, referencing the Jennifer Anniston neuron which fires only when a picture of the actress is presented to the retina.[45] The neurophysiology of receptive fields is well understood, particularly with regard to the brain's ability to recognize the meaning of individual written words, phrases and expressions. The *visual pathway* of the brain maintains an elaborate supportive neural network from retina via occipital cortex, left temporal cortex to left inferior frontal lobe. Interestingly, this idea of grandmother cells was anticipated famously

---

1   Google "receptive field"
2   Stanislas Dehaene, *The Number Sense*, New York 200x
3   Stanislas Dehaene, *Reading in the Brain, Viking, New York, 2009* .
4   Stanislas Dehaene, *Reading in the Brain, Viking, New York,* pp. 131-140.
5   Google "Jennifer Anniston neuron"

by art collector Louisine Havermeyer when 90 years ago she wrote *"It takes special brain cells to appreciate Degas."*

One can also usefully speculate that the *relation* between two sensory patterns is assigned its own neuron just like the sensory patterns themselves. When a relation between two sensory patterns is recognized, the neuron with its receptive field will fire too.

Neurons make use of a general principle: neurons are organized topographically, identifying entities by their location in a 2-dimensional map. In the retina and the posterior visual cortex topographic maps of neurons closely match features of the outside world. In the inner ear hair, cells in the organ of Corti are assigned topographically to respond to pitch of sound, arranged in order of frequency. The brain tells the frequency composition of sound heard by which combination of hair cells are firing.[6] The place cells of the hippocampus are another good example. They are arranged in a literal physical Cartesian plane, which constitutes a map. With a rat moving around his habitat with electrodes implanted in the place cells of the Hippocampus, neurons fire according to his location. The researchers can tell where the rat is by which cells are firing, and presumably the rat does too as he unconsciously integrates the familiar visual and locomotor cues of his environment.[7] Consider what is in your mind when you type the letter "w" on a QWERTY keyboard. There is no alphanumeric thought, the left ring finger just goes unconsciously to the "w" key and presses it. The symbols of the alphabet have been mapped to the location of the QWERTY keyboard keys represented by certain neurons ordered topographically in your brain. Thus, the brain seems to have adopted this method of having individual neurons organized topographically in physical planes, sorted to represent symbols that in turn identify concepts.

And, as explained so well by Dehaene, the further forward neurons are in the brain, the larger and more complex is their receptive field. No doubt neurons in the prefrontal cortex respond to particular highly intellectual ideas and the logical relations between them. No doubt complex individual plans and actions are encoded in individual neurons in the more anterior areas of the prefrontal cortex.

---

6   Google "Organ of Corti"
7   Google "place cells of the Hippocampus" I feel lucky

Humans can employ expressions, strings of relatively few ordered words, to capture the salient gist and purpose of complex world situations. Language is able to trigger the same neuron that responds to the real world sensory pattern of the object or its picture. The outstanding question to ponder is how a short ordered string of words, an expression, can fire a particular neuron out of millions in just hundreds of milliseconds. How does the brain map an expression of a few words onto that one particular neuron?

Let's look at some principles the brain and mind must apply to enable the mapping of a language expression onto a particular mental concept. The brain does not have the machinery to do purely mathematical operations automatically. How then? Let's grant, without going into explanations here, that each language word is represented by a cortical neuron with a receptive field for the word and that each word symbol can fire that neuron. Thus, each symbol in a language string activates its own assigned neuron, the one with a receptive field for that symbol.

Then, input of an ordered expression of, say, ten input words will fire in order the ten neurons with receptive fields for those words, another expression by definition. Let's say the axon branches of each of these activated neurons synapse to dendrites of many downstream neurons. But the neuron has to somehow decide which higher level neuron it will fire. How will the choice be made? Like a decimal number, the next symbol in the ordered expression provides this information. But how?

Each word neuron synapses to many higher level neurons. *Parsing* means that of all the follow on neurons that a word's axon branches to, it will fire the one that is already primed. So, the one that it fires is the one that the next active word neuron also synapses to. Summation of stimuli from two consecutive word neurons firing in short order will reach a threshold in just that one higher-level neuron with synapses in common, making it the one to be fired. Two neurons matched up in order will thus cause a very particular downstream neuron to fire. In *turn* this neuron will be matched up in a later round with another downstream fired in parallel by other words of the expression. And, words further along in the expression or words further back behind a comma may already have "pre-paired" so as to prime higher level neurons, having them ready to participate when their *turn* comes. This process, exactly the same process used in a single elimination sports tournament, creates a path to the final destination neuron which the ordered input string of symbols addresses. Did the brain have to fall back on the same *parsing* method developed for algebra and tournaments?

Just as a digital computer reads the next decimal number to decide which path to take, one can consider the neuron fired by the next word in order of the expression provides the information that enables the neuron before to know which higher level neuron to fire. Just like decimal numbers, neurons work in adjacent pairs, the method of the single-elimination tournament.[8]

At each decision point on a *path* information as to which way to take next has to be obtained somehow. A neuron preferentially transmits its signal up that axon branch connecting to a synapse that is post-synaptically active, This will be the one that happens to be activated by an axon branch of the neuron fired by the next symbol in the expression. One could say the neuron sees *"a light at the end of the tunnel"* along that branch.

This idea echoes the statement by Donald Hebb in his 1932 M.A. thesis:

> *"An excited neuron tends to decrease its discharge to inactive neurons, and increase this discharge to any active neuron, and therefore to form a route to it, whether there are intervening neurons between the two or not. With repetition this tendency is prepotent in the formation of neural routes" (Hebb, 1932, p. 13). 9*

The idea that certain neurons may be tuned to fire upon receiving signals in a particular order has been advanced to explain the rapid speed of reactions to patterned sensory stimuli.[10] A target neuron pre-tuned to receive signals in a given order would certainly provide some top-down help for an expression to fire it.

And, there is an interesting homology in the development of telephone switchboards, the need for the invention of the *line finder*, which automatically detects and connects to any call originating telephone that is off hook.[11] One could say the *line finder* too picks a line that has *"a light*

---

8   That's presumably why the name "parsing" (pairs-ing) has stuck.

9   Hebb, D. O. Conditioned and Unconditioned Reflexes and Inhibition. M.A. Thesis, McGill Univ. (1932).

10   Richmond B., Wiener M., *Recruitment Order: a Powerful Neural Ensemble Code*, Nature Neuroscience 7, 97, 2004

11   http://goo.gl/y7n57

at the end of the tunnel". In a plumbing analogy, water will instantly flow along a branch pipe as soon as a faucet at its end is opened.

Remarkably, it appears that evolution, the intelligent designer, came upon precisely the same binary solution that the inventors of algebra did to organize the related numbers and symbols of a language expression into a unitary congruent whole and to evaluate it. And the same principle organizers of sports tournaments invented to establish a winner. And, we came upon exactly the same principle in our *Mensa* tables to meet the same need.

The Physical Basis of a Memory

This scheme leads to Donald Hebb's theory as to how a memory can be captured in a compact physical network of neurons. A neuron network tuned to one certain concept, very sensitive to a particular string of input symbols whenever encountered again, could represent a memory physically. How could it self organize naturally? The overall neuron network appears to grow under genetic control, but Hebb's Law is a perfect mechanism for constructing actual physical neural trees by local strengthening of synapses. Hebb's Law [12] states that "neurons that fire together, wire together" by strengthening synapses that are activated simultaneously both pre- and post-synaptically. Any synapse with simultaneous or closely timed activation in presynaptic and postsynaptic neurons will change physically so as to pass signals more strongly.[13] The phenomenon of long term potentiation (LTP) results in rapid plasticity of synapses with extended residual strengthening.[14]

So, let two neurons with receptive fields for two adjacent words of an expression be fired by input of the expression. If axons of both connect to the dendrite of a common higher level neuron it will be fired. Synapses will strengthen because there is pre- and post-synaptic excitation in synapses. Relating two concepts is a matter of connecting their neurons via strengthened synapses; and a binary tree will form in the brain connecting the involved neurons, constituting a memory. And networks would form naturally and allow the brain, upon input of an ordered series of phonemic

---

12 Google "Hebb's Law"
13 Google "wiki chemical synapse"
14 Google "long term potentiation"

or graphemic symbols, to fire a very particular cortical neuron that represents the complex concept meant by the expression.

The numbers say that, with axons branching to around 30-40 next level neurons, 5 layers of neurons in the cortex would be enough for an expression to address a particular one of millions of neurons, just the number of layers observed. And, in the interest of keeping connections short neurons for commonly associated concepts and for categories of like items would become sorted topographically into nearby groups. Again as observed, neurons for *faces, animals*, *tools* etc. sort together in the left temporal cortex.

Such a complex of neurons interconnected by strengthened synapses can map an observed complex sensory pattern onto a single neuron. And often, a single word can map onto that same neuron. And the same neurons can be reused in many different networks. We expect that very high level neurons in the frontal cortex represent, have receptive fields for complex ideas and are fired by hearing or reading the corresponding complex language expressions. Then, with appropriate connections, they would be able to manage relations between very complex ideas, perform abstract logic. Expressions made up of high level symbols allow easy communication of these complex mental structures from one human to another.

How a Language Expression Addresses a Particular Neuron

So, let's conjure up an explicit example of how neurons might function to parse an expression like *"The White House"*. The lexical words of the phrase *"The White House"* are members of a very large vocabulary, which enables just the neuron with the receptive field for this phrase to be fired, singling it out from the millions of neurons with receptive fields for other phrases. The important point here is that there are millions of "roads not taken".

How a slow analog brain can make use of the tournament process to match the speed of powerful digital computers is illustrated in Figure 1.3.1, which shows input of three ordered word symbols, *"The White House"*. These three words fire the grandmother neurons with receptive fields for the sensory patterns of those particular words, Neurons 4, 5 and 6, in order. Both neuron 5 and Neuron 6 have synapses to Neuron 3, which is then activated by summation of signal. Activated Neuron 4 can then sum with Neuron 3 to fire Neuron 1, which represents the congruent meaning of the three ordered symbols. In tennis tournament terms one might say neuron 4 gets a bye to the final match.

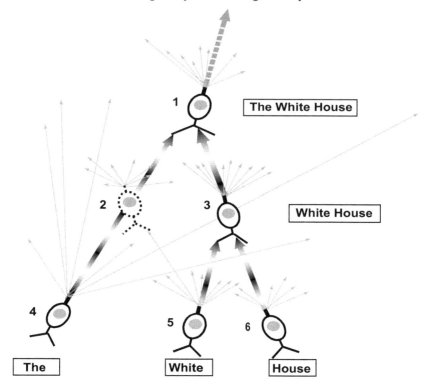

Fig. 1.3.1 Input expression "The White House" fires Neurons 4, 5 and 6 in order. Activated Neuron 5 projects to both Neuron 2 and Neuron 3 among many others, but only Neuron 3 will fire, because of summation of signal from next in order activated Neuron 6, which also projects to Neuron 3 among many others. Now, active Neuron 3 in turn fires neuron 1 already primed by Neuron 4. Neuron 2 represents one of the many neurons in the network that do not fire for lack of two simultaneous signals,

This diagram is completely congruous with the *flow-of-meaning-tree* needed to parse this three word expression.

Order of words in an expression is key to its meaning. In the above case, words are input serially; *"White"* milliseconds after *"The"* and *"House"* milliseconds after *"White"*. It is necessary for signals to reach the soma of Neuron 1 simultaneously if it is to fire. It takes finite time for signals to travel along dendrites to the neuron soma. So, for this phrase to work, axon branch of Neuron 4 must synapse distally on the dendrite tree of Neuron 1. Neuron 4 getting a bye to the final round mirrors the prerogative of determiner, personal pronoun and punctuation mark symbols. The irony is that the more compact the language symbol the more complex the meaning that it maps to. Axon branch of Neuron 5 must synapse proximally on the dendrite tree of Neuron 3 and axon branch of Neuron 6 more proximally. And axon branch of Neuron 4 more distally on dendrite tree of Neuron 1 than axon branch of Neuron 3. On this basis the phrase comprised of the same three words in the order *"House White The"* would not fire follower Neuron 1, which is sensitive to timing of the order of first spikes received from upstream neurons.

Once a neuron is primed by a signal it may remain activated for hundreds or thousands of milliseconds. If there is a threshold for a neuron to fire the activation may be just sub-threshold. Then, just part of the full word that would normally fire the neuron may be sufficient to fire an already primed neuron. For example, a pun, having enough of the syllables of the correct word, may fire the correct words neuron as well as its own, leading to double meaning. And, just imagining the word that a pun substitutes for will fire this neuron too, reinforcing the *path*. These ideas may also explain how rhyme works, by firing a neuron already activated, its rhyming intraword phoneme giving it another boosting jolt. It's a form of a synecdoche within a word. These ideas are elaborated on in Book II, Chapter VIII in the section on poetry and song.

Because the tournament process is analog and massively parallel, it is fast. Likewise, parsing is a highly parallel process. It allows a biological system with transmission speeds of feet per second to match electronic computing with speed of light transmission speeds. Algebra uses the same parsing principle. An arithmetic or algebraic expression is a string of symbols that can address one in a very large number of points simply by changing values of terms and factors.

And, in the brain, the top level target neuron of such a tree network has widespread anterograde and retrograde projections to and from both cerebral cortices and once it fires it can evoke a rich sensory experience in consciousness recruited from these myriad cortical convergence zones.[15] This may explain why, when an expression gets through to fire such a convergence zone neuron that is already widely connected by projections to both hemispheres and to consciousness, we experience sensations and feelings. One might say the language expression "makes sense".

Even with some syntactical parts-of-speech (POS) restrictions, a person with a typical 60,000 word vocabulary has a choice of thousands of words to put in most positions in a short language expression or sentence. So, even a three word expression can define billions of possible paths, many more than the number of language neurons in a highly educated individual's mind.

We do not claim that this scheme is the actual physical basis for a text expression to address a particular neuron. The real situation is undoubtedly much more complicated. However, these principles and methods lend themselves very readily to being simulated in a computer. Just as the mind assigns a particular neuron to a particular concept, we assign a particular memory address to each concept and assign pointers to connect these addresses in manner highly analogous to connections between neurons. What our experience with *Mensa* tables has shown is that all that matters is that database rows representing concepts are individualized with appropriate connections. This is all that is required for our computer parser, upon input of a particular text expression, to be able to address a particular physical computer address out of billions. This is exactly the same principle described above for the neurons. We hope these ideas may foster a mental attitude in neuroscience researchers that will guide the design of future experiments.

Our *flow-of-meaning trees* and *Mensa tables* faithfully utilize these principles and their behavior closely mimics human thought. And it may be that neurons, simply by virtue of their individual locations and connections, enable abstract computations to be done just as mindlessly in the brain as in our computer programs. Millions of years of natural selection have no doubt produced a biological neuron addressing scheme that is highly optimized; computer programmers could well find that the

---

15 Damasio A R, *The Brain Binds Entities and Events by Multiregional Activation from Convergence Zones*, Neural Computation, 1. 123-132, 1989.

main features of the single-elimination tournament were discovered by nature millions of years ago.

Consciousness

We spend our conscious lives dealing with the world around us. The subjective sensations and feelings, our will and volition, seen or felt by our innermost consciousness are very real to us. The subjective colorful, noisy, tactile, tasty and fragrant three dimensional moving-in-time world that we consciously experience exists only in the mind.[16] Consciousness resides in the primitive limbic system of the brain, thalamus, amygdala, hippocampus, home to sensations and feelings, and the closely connected nucleus accumbens, home to the dopamine reward system. It is totally based upon a physico-chemical system as shown in that it can be erased by anesthetic agents and distorted by hallucinogenic chemicals.

Paradoxically, consciousness is not the highest level of human thought; there is no reason to doubt that dogs, for example, are just as conscious as we are, feel love just as deeply as we do, and certainly experience smell sensations consciously much more richly than humans. Supported in the limbic system, the ancient brain developed consciousness more that 60 million years ago before the human line diverged from the mouse, well before language.

It is useful to think of the ancient limbic system as the general purpose CPU of the brain where volition and conscious awareness exist. And the cortex as hard disk where representations of worldly objects and concepts and relations between them are stored. Antonio Damasio's classic paper on the *binding problem* proposes that features and fragments of sensation are stored widespread in cortices of both hemispheres and connected by multiple projections from convergence zones in the temporal and frontal cortices. This paper is essential reading.[17]

These recordings can be transmitted to the limbic system via hippocampal connections to be played to consciousness there. All recordings need a player. Direct inputs from the five senses to the limbic system are played to consciousness in real time and are the source of the aforesaid cortical

16 Google "qualia" I'm feeling lucky
17 Google "binding problem" and browse results page

representations.[18] Hippocampal damage as in Alzheimer's disease thwarts this communication resulting in forgetting and inability to retrieve or store recent memories. Our *Mensa* database closely models this distributed cortical function by storing "fragments and features" in widespread addresses and allowing our parser to represent of complex concepts by connecting simple features together.

Consciousness can call upon a marvelous computer, the human frontal lobes, manipulating symbols representing complex concepts, to analyze and evaluate sensory inputs. Results of these rational analyses relayed to the limbic system can cause strong feelings of fear and joy in consciousness. Presented with, say, a subtle joke or a clever cartoon, we have to wait until our unconscious mind computes the solution and serves it up to consciousness; we "get it". Being able to understand what observed things mean to us, and able to predict what will happen as a result of whether one acts, how one acts, or a failure to act is essential for well being and survival.

Consciousness is not required to perform high level logic. This is done at an even higher levels (thicker logs) of the tree in the unconscious by manipulation of compact symbols that represent complex concepts, with the results only then being presented to consciousness. The unconscious mind is highly intelligent at managing highly intellectual concepts, working with symbols, harnessing, we will argue, the mindless but powerful methods of algebra. As described in Book III, Chapter I, in one special instance we have been able to have a computer program perform abstract logic faster and more accurately than intelligent humans trained in the field.

Recent thinking sees consciousness as a construct manufactured by the unconscious mind: that most mental operations are performed by the unconscious mind and the results presented to consciousness on a "screen" giving us the illusion that we are rational and in command and control. Electroencephalographic studies have shown that our conscious mind is not informed that we have made a decision for 750 milliseconds after it has been made in the unconscious. In discussions of consciousness the

---

18 These ideas correlate perfectly with John Locke's doctrine that there are no innate ideas

question always comes up as to who is looking at this screen, assessing the situation, feeling the feelings and issuing orders.[19]

The real mystery is why consciousness arises in a purely physico-chemical system. What are necessary network circuits? And the intriguing corollary in the context of this essay is that if these circuits could be fully analyzed and understood, and biomimicked *in silico*, would consciousness emerge there?

---

19 For the sake of recording a striking episode somewhere, one of us (JGG) witnessed Linus Pauling come to give a lecture on consciousness at Columbia University College of Physicians and Surgeons in the late 1950's. He made the following sublime statement at the beginning of his lecture: *"the only way for the mechanism of consciousness to be determined is for me to sit in an armchair and think about it"*. Pauling didn't make it but his approach may be only one that will succeed.

BOOK II
CHAPTER I

Relatives, Relations and Relationships

The mind models the world as a set of relations between concepts. According to John Locke, relations are themselves very clear concepts in our minds; fully fledged concepts in their own right that we recognize when we see them or think them. We have found that a relation concept that relates a pair of relative concepts, its subject concept and its object concept, can be represented by a unique unitary symbol like any other concept. Each relation symbol mediates exchange of meaning between two related concepts, causing them to adapt to fit each other; to become creatures of the relationship. While molded by the relation, relatives also transform the relation. Relations can be static with the relation between the relatives remaining the same whether the relation is constant or dynamic. Relations can also be recursive: relations occurring between relations, where either one of both of the relatives is itself a relation. Relations are pervasive in modeling the world, the basis for so many disparate things. Understanding and managing relation concepts is basic to modeling natural language and human thought in a computer.

T he crucial inspiration that we derived from John Locke's *An Essay Concerning the Human Understanding, Book II*, was his idea of relations. In his *Of Relations* chapter he declares that a relation consists of the mind

> "*bringing two ideas, whether simple or complex, together, and setting them by one another, so as to take a view of them at once, without uniting them into one; by which way it gets all its ideas of relations.*"
> John Locke, Essay II, XII, 1

Implicit in this observation is the idea that relations are very clear concepts in our minds and fully fledged concepts in their own right. His example in Book II of the particular relation between two four feet tall flightless birds in St. James Park is delicious:

> "*having the notion that one laid the egg out of which the other was hatched, I have a clear idea of the relation of dam and chick between the two cassowaries in St. James's Park; though perhaps I have but a very obscure and imperfect idea of those birds themselves.*"
> John Locke Essay, II, XXV

However, in Book III, Locke does show he has a good idea of what a Cassowarie is. His description of a Cassowarie tells us how simple concepts are assembled in to a unitary complex concept able to be named by a single word.

> "*Instance in Cassowaries. Were I to talk with any one of a sort of birds I lately saw in St. James's Park, about three or four feet high, with a covering of something between feathers and hair, of a dark brown colour, without wings, but in the place thereof two or three little branches coming down like sprigs of Spanish broom, long great legs, with feet only of three claws, and without a tail; I must make this description of it, and so may make others understand me. But when I am told that the name of it is cassuaris, I may then use that word to stand in discourse for all my complex idea mentioned in that description; though by that word, which is now become a specific name, I know no more of the real essence or constitution of that sort of animals than I did before; and knew probably as much of the nature of that species of birds before I learned the name, as many Englishmen do of swans or herons, which are specific names, very well known, of sorts of birds common in England.*"   John Locke Essay III 34

John Locke's emphasis in the importance of relations is key to understanding how language works. We present a very general idea of *relation* in this essay. Relations are key to modeling the world, being the basis for so many disparate things. Relations can be highly abstract or solid real things. For example, a screwdriver is the relation between the hand and the screw.

In particular, Locke notes that a relation is only between two things. In modern terms we say all relations are *binary*.

> *"a relation is a way of comparing or considering two things together, and giving one or both of them some appellation from that comparison; and sometimes giving even the relation itself a name."* [1]

Locke points out that the number of possible relations between any two things is infinite:

> *"there is no one thing, whether simple idea, substance, mode, or relation, or name of either of them, which is not capable of almost an infinite number of considerations in reference to other things: and therefore this makes no small part of men's thoughts and words"* [2]

John Locke also notes that any relative that has received meaning via its relation with a relative may acquire a lexical appellation that characterizes it as a relative and subtexts the relationship.

> *" ... one single man may at once be concerned in, and sustain all these following relations, and many more, viz. father, brother, son, grandfather, grandson, father-in-law, son-in-law, husband, friend, enemy, subject, general, judge, patron, client, professor, European, Englishman, islander, servant, master, possessor, captain, superior, inferior, bigger, less, older, younger, contemporary, like, unlike, &c., to an almost infinite number: he being capable of as many relations as there can be occasions of comparing him to other things, in any manner of agreement, disagreement, or respect whatsoever. For, as I said, relation is a way of comparing or considering two things together, and giving one or both of them some appellation from that comparison; and sometimes giving even the relation itself a name."* [3]

Just the use of such a word from John Locke's list above, like *husband, friend, or patron* implies a relationship. For example, with *husband*, a *wife* is implied; with *general* an *army* relative is implied. In the case of Locke's two birds in St. James Park, the terms *dam* and *chick* tell us everything about that complex relation. Such appellations tell us what is related, which relation it is and that the relation exists or did exist. Often, one of

---

1   John Locke, Essay II, XXV, 7
2   John Locke, Essay II, XXV, 7
3   John Locke Essay II, XXV, 7

these words serves as a metonym that means the whole relationship. For example after he tees off in a game of golf, one might say *"Kevin's in the bunker"* to refer not to the golfer but his relative, the golf ball.

John Locke led us to treat relation concepts just like relative concepts, represent them with a unique symbol and have them take part in expressions just as relative concepts do. Relation concepts receive meaning from and relay meaning to their two relatives. Put another way, when two concepts are related, they adapt to accommodate the *relationship*. Their sense as meaning flows from one to the other, in both directions via the *relation*. Idiosyncratic properties of each intermediary *relation concept* allow precise control of what meaning will flow between related concepts in a given context. *Relative concepts* party to *relationships* become creatures of the *relationship*. However, while molded by the *relationship*, they also transform the *relationship* itself – they are two different views of the same phenomenon.

The Symbols of Relationships

We have found that relation concepts, just like end concepts, can be represented by unique unitary symbols. A relationship involving concept **A** and concept **B** can be represented by a string of three symbols, A**R**B, where **R** is the symbol standing for the relation and **A** and **B** are symbols standing for the first and second relatives.[4] Since symbols can have many senses, just like words, once related, the sense of each of the three symbols shifts to fit in with the other two. Concept **A** has its sense altered by being enriched by meaning flowing into it from its relative, concept **B**, via *relation* concept **R**. The sense of concept **B** adapts due to meaning flowing in the opposite direction, again via *relation* concept **R**. And the relation itself, concept **R**, becomes individualized by being the relation concept between sense-adjusted concepts **A** and **B**. *Relation* concepts (such as **R** in this example) process meaning received from the *object* concept. They process this meaning and then relay it on to the *subject* concept. And vice versa - it is a two way, two step, settling process. However, in the grand scheme of things one concept survives modified, to engage in a relationship with another survivor concept at a higher level, in the next round of the tournament.

---

4   The convention in this *Essay* is that bolded words designate concepts.

Most relations are non-commutative,[5] so we refer to *first relative* and *second relative*. We also adopt the convention of calling the first relative of the relation the *subject* and the second relative the *object* of the relation. In the chapter *How Language Expressions Work to Build Complex Concepts,* we will see that in parsing an expression, the subject concept is most often the surviving concept. In the sentence chapter, *How Finite Sentences Work to Apply Reality to Concepts*, we will see that in a parsing a finite sentence the *seam* concept that the verb enriches is the surviving concept.

A telling example of *concept adaptation* occurs when we hear or read the zeugma *"he brushed his teeth and hair",* there is a jarring effect on the reader. One immediately feels that something is wrong - the sensory patterns are hard to reconcile. What has happened is that the sense of verb concept **brush** has become so adapted to concept **teeth** that it has become highly incompatible with concept **hair**. Although the generic brush verb action is completely preserved, there is a marked change in the sense of verb concept **brush.** As one goes from **brush**ing teeth to **brush**ing hair to **brush**ing shoes, there are fundamental differences to the experiences in one's mind. Similarly, when one goes form toothbrush to hairbrush to shoebrush, the physical brush also changes radically.

To sum up, when two concepts are put side by side in the mind or in a language expression, they are *related*, they become *relatives*, and what is between them is a *relation*. The two concepts, joined by a single relation, are in a relationship; the set of three is a *relationship.* This schema allows for a formal technical definition, alluded to above, of the terms "relative" "relation" and "relationship". Mnemonics suggests why these words came into usage; relatives are. "relay-it-offs", sending meaning to each other via the relation, i.e. "relay-it-on", that lies between them.

We have developed *flow-of-meaning-trees* and *Mensa tables* of relations to illustrate how, when one concept is related to another, meaning flow from one to the other. *Flow-of-meaning-trees* and *Mensa relation rows* both indicate the direction of flow of meaning into one of the relative concepts, which then becomes the meaning-enriched "survivor" concept of the relationship.

---

5   Vis. "man bites dog"

Fig. 2.1.1 shows the *flow-of-meaning-trees* and the *Mensa* table row for the three brush concepts.

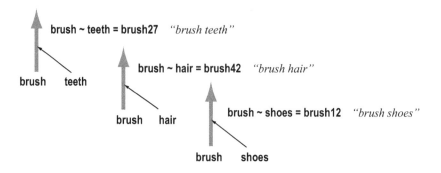

Fig. 2.1.1 Flow-of-Meaning-Trees for three brush relations

The direction of the arrows in the three binary tree graphs above shows the direction of meaning flow from concepts **teeth**, **hair** and **shoe** into verb concept **brush**. In the first example, concept **teeth** is enriching verb concept **brush** with meaning to produce surviving concept **brush27**. The term **brushteeth** might be used instead of **brush27** as a more mnemonic, more human accessible, verb concept symbol. Equally distinct to a computer are **brush42** (*"brush hair"*) and **brush12** (*"brush shoes"*) – different and separate concepts. Our *Mensa* tables, which can precisely define highly complex concepts, are simply tables of such simple binary relations. This **brush** example shows us that in a finite sentence, the syntactical object of the verb has a major "back effect" on the nature of the verb action. The qualitative nature of the brushing is substantially changed by the words "*teeth*", "*hair*" and "*shoes*". But meaning flows forward too, in a similar way to how traditional grammarians talk about "transitive" verbs. In this example, as concept **brush** changes its sense, the **teeth** get **clean**, the **hair** gets **neat** and the **shoes** get **shiny**. A transitive verb is actually a relation concept.

When any two concepts placed in juxtaposition in the mind, they become relatives, they affect each other, Both concepts and the relation itself are modified in the process. Concepts are *polysemous* just like words, assuming different meanings in different contexts. The sense of a concept shifts to fit in its new context. Relations play the huge role that in the construction of complex concepts, where words focus meaning on each other. To quote one of Dwight Bolinger's most apt observations: *"In fevered competition and intervention ... language is at war with itself"*.[6]

It is impossible for computers at present to do the necessary mental calculations to determine the shift in sense that occurs in a concept when related to another concept in the mind and certainly impossible for a computer to appreciate the new sense of the related concepts in some form of machine consciousness. But, fortunately for us, there is an easy way around this difficulty. We markup the symbol of the surviving concept of each matched concept pair to record that it has changed its sense from being in that particular relation. That modified symbol now represents the concept as it is enriched in this context. The same concept modified by a different relation in a different context would have a different sense and be assigned a different symbol. This is an example to the extraordinary power of symbols to *"have an independent existence and an intelligence of their own"*, as Henrich Hertz famously said.

Moreover, in a *Mensa table* each individual concept at every level of complexity is given a carefully composed English text matched to its identifier symbol, sensitive to context. This makes it possible for the computer to parse a complex expression, sentence or paragraph, zero in on its precise concept, and tell you very precisely what that identified enriched concept means, in English, in words you understand. And so furnish you with its precise sense.

BE, DO and HAVE Type Relations

If we accept that meaning flows to and fro between *first relative* and *second relative* via the *relation*, we can further study language and characterize the ways this meaning-flow occurs. We find that there are three ways, denoted in English by use of the auxiliary forms of verbs BE, HAVE and DO. In sentences like *"He is old"*, *"the house has a tin roof"* and *"birds do fly"*, there is a different type of meaning flow between relatives in each case. More than half of all sentences in English express a BE relationship.

In BE type meaning flow, the default relation that is not required to be explicitly specified in language, the first mentioned *subject* relative acquires the sensory pattern of the other *object* relative. In BE relations sensory pattern from the second relative concept blends into the first relative,

---

6   Bolinger D, *Degree Words*, Mouton, The Hague - Paris, 1972, p18

modifying it by adding some or all of its sensory pattern "as is", to it. The most straightforward example of BE type meaning flow from one concept to another is where an adjective contributes its sensory pattern to a noun's sensory pattern or an adverb adds its sensory pattern to a verb's. With the sentence *"the roof is red"* the sensory pattern **red** is fused, *as is*, into the sensory pattern **roof** to create surviving concept **redroof**, which shares both sensory patterns. To describe this mental operation of *concept fusion* we use the auxiliary form of verb *be* as in *"the car is fast"* which is why we call it BE type flow of meaning, a BE relation. We have to say *"The roof is red"*; we can't say *"The roof has red"*; or *"The roof does red"*.

In a BE relation, two concepts are seen together at the same time in the same place and they blend into a single concept. It is easy to see **sky** and **blue** together in the same view merging into a single concept, modified noun concept **sky** being the surviving concept. The popular humorous *"happiness is"* sayings like *"happiness is a warm gun"* illustrate a point about the BE relation.[7] The saying *"happiness is a dry martini"* blends concepts **happiness** and **adrymartini** in we see them together in the same space. We can't resist mentioning here our own, we think, original improvement of Fuzzy Zoeller's famous saying *"Happiness is a long walk with the putter"* to *"Happiness is a long walk without the putter"*.

In HAVE relations two discrete related entity concepts are placed in mental juxtaposition, the two relatives staying distinct yet influencing each other. Each relative induces a change in the other. An example of a HAVE type is expressed by the sentence *"Jim has a hot temper"*, which relates concepts **Jim** and **badtemper**. Jim is characterized by the HAVE relation as hot-tempered. We can't say *"Jim is a bad temper"*; or *"Jim does a bad temper"* because **is** and **does** indicate relationships that are not BE relationships.

The phrase *"container of milk"* is example of entity type concepts in a HAVE relationship; noun concept **container** is related to noun concept **milk**. Although the two sensory patterns are seen together, they remain distinct. Both concepts adapt - the carton will efficiently contain and dispense milk through a port and be labeled to make its contents clear to an observer. The milk inside the carton will take the shape and volume of the carton. Note that this relationship requires explicit relation grammatical **of** to indicate it is a HAVE relationship.

---

7   Google "happiness is" for many examples

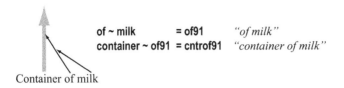

Fig. 2.1.2 FOMT and Mensa table for the relationship "container of milk"

The container itself receives none of the fluid sensory pattern of **milk**. Meaning flow is not an *as is* BE type fusion of the **milk** sensory pattern into the **container sensory pattern. R**ather, concept **milk** *induces* change in concept **container** and vice versa. The modified **container** concept assumes its nature because milk is an essential part of the product. We have to say *"the container has milk (in it)"*; we can't say * *"the container is milk"*; or * *"the container does milk"*.

In another HAVE example, when we say "the car **has** five doors" concept **thecar** develops an SUV sensory pattern and concept **fivedoors** adapts to be the sensory pattern of SUV doors, namely in the fact that the fifth door opens backwards. We can't say *"*the car is five doors"* or *"*the car does five doors"*.

Note that relations expressed by verb *have* are cognate with relations expressed by preposition **of**. The car **has** a fifth door expresses the same relation as *"the fifth door of the car"*. This probably explains why *"I shouldn't of done it"* somehow feels right – while phonetic drift can explain why people say it, there is also an implicit HAVE relation built into this **of** expression. Much more on mnemonic cueing of meaning later.

DO relations lie between a first relative subject entity concept and second relative object verb concept. For example, in the sentence *"Jim does eat broccoli"* **does** relates noun subject concept **Jim** to verb action object concept **eatbroccoli**. The corresponding *Mensa* table allowing a computer to parse this sentence, comprises three constructive relations.

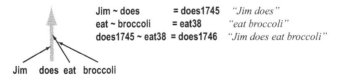

Fig. 2.1.3 FOMT and Mensa table for the relationship "John does eat broccoli"

We have to say *"Jim does/may/will/shall eat broccoli"*; we can't say *"*Jim is eat broccoli"* or *"*Jim has eat broccoli"* because **is** and **has** do not relate a subject to a verb concept. The symbols for modals: *can, could, shall, should, must, might, would, will* and others are variants of **do** and relate a subject concept with a verb phrase concept just like **do** does.[8] The irony here is that a verb concept is an "object" concept in DO sentences.

BE, HAVE and DO relations are employed to mediate *affirmation*, *negation* and *modality* in what we call *subject-seam* sentences, where the subject concept enriches a BE, DO or HAVE auxiliary or modal grammatical. The function of *auxiliaries* and *modals* is to relate its "subject" concept with its "object" concept and to indicate whether this relation applies or not, and the *degree* of its existence, its *modality*.[9] Sentences defining *affirmation, negation* and *modality* are *analytical sentences*, as opposed to *narrative* or *descriptive* sentences that set a scene or move the story on.

To summarize, To *summarize*: BE, HAVE and DO relations all serve to connect relatives by defining the three classes of relations that can occur between them.[10] With BE type relations the object relative "infects" the subject relative with its sensory pattern. With HAVE type relations, the object relative "affects" the other's sensory pattern. DO relations are the third type of relation, between a subject entity and a verb phrase concept.

How Language Manages Relations

Now, let's look at how language orthographs relations, starting with elementary relations and proceeding in order to more complex relations. This section anticipates the next chapter on grammaticals which describes how grammatical symbols, particularly prepositions, stand for and specify relations. In language, the standard representation of a relation between two concepts is made by placing two symbols adjacent to each other, in order, with a relation symbol in between. The result is an *expression*. This is the form of all finite sentences.

---

8   **do** is the auxiliary *does* the verb

9   This "object" is the object of the BE, HAVE and DO relation, not the syntactical object of a transitive verb.

10 As Peggy Lee sings: "Is that all (the relations) there is?" To hear here sing it, Google "Is that all there is Peggy Lee? I'm feeling lucky.

There is progression from simple to complex relations. When a relation is obvious, a *space* is employed to represent the default relation between those two concepts. But, for straightforward simple relations when there may be several common alternatives, a single grammatical relation symbol is inserted between the concepts to define which relation it is in a particular case. More complex relations have to be defined by even long strings of symbols between the relatives.

When there is only one possible relation between two relative concepts, the well known default relation, the second person or addressee will know how the senses of these two particular relatives shift when they are paired. Then a specific relation symbol is redundant. So, a *space* is used as the simplest grammatical relational symbol that can represent a relation between two concepts. When meaning flows between the relatives via a *space* relation the standard shift in the senses of the relatives ensues.

Here are examples of default relations designated by a *space*:

> Big mouse big house old man   blue sky   better understanding
> many possibilities   one thing   a threat   the Internet

To see how relations like these are modeled in the computer by means of *Mensa* tables, consider the following adjective-noun relations:

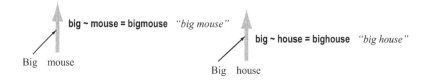

Fig. 2.1.4 FOMT for the relationships "big mouse" and "big house"

Obviously **mouse** and **house** concepts are modified surviving BE type relative concepts, in each case with a changed sense.[11] Concept **house** now has sensory features of both concepts. Perhaps more importantly, one's idea of concept **big** also adapts. Concept **big** in *"big house"* is quite

---

11 This is an exception to the rule that first concept in word order is the surviving concept of a relation. In English adjectives precede nouns; in French, Spanish and Italian they follow. English often complicates the rules both human and software parsers must follow so as to enrich the surviving concept of relations correctly.

different from our idea of **big** in *"big mouse"*. Here **big** is "relative"; context matters. Adjective concepts change their sense just as nouns do when related.

Preposition Grammaticals - The Basic Relations

At the next level, if there is not an obvious standard default relation between two particular relatives – there may be several common relations possible - then, a single relation grammatical symbol like **of** or **to** replacing the space between the relatives suffices to define the relation. For example, when a **lamp** and a **table** are related, the specificity of the relationship is achieved by placing a particular relational grammatical particle, in this case a preposition grammatical, between the pair of concepts since there are many possible relationships between any two given relatives. Concept **lamp** could be said to be **at, on, in, above, below, under, over, with, from, to, beyond, before, or** in a relation defined by some other preposition. So, a need arises to specify precisely which relation applies in any given instance. It is the preposition that is chosen that determines exactly what meaning is transferred between them in a given context.

However, keeping for now to a low level of relation complexity, let's look at some *flow of meaning trees* and *Mensa* tables for relations represented by a single symbol. A single preposition *relation grammatical* placed between the relatives suffices when there is only a need to specify which one of several possible relations between the two relatives applies in a particular instance. Here are some examples, including one that does not make sense:

> glass **of** water   road **to** Boston   learn **from** experience
> *response **with** a crime   (turn) a minor problem **into** a crisis

We illustrated earlier with the dry bones lyric that a series of relations between element concepts can precisely build a complex unitary concept structure. Such a list of elementary relations, which all expressions comprise, is the basis for our *Mensa* table as shown in this table of four relations.

> a ~ lamp   = a47   *"a lamp"*
> a ~ table   = a94   *"a table"*
> on ~ a94   = on52   *"on a table"*
> a47 ~ 0n52   = a48   *"a lamp on a table"*

Here, the concept expressed by the five word phrase *"a lamp on a table"* is constructed by four pairs of relations between element concepts and between sub-complexes. Meaning is transferred from the table to the lamp that is on the table in four steps.

Fig. 2.1.5 shows the *flow-of-meaning-tree* that illustrates the flow of meaning from concept **table** to determiner **a**, and then the further relay of meaning form enriched determiner **a** to preposition grammatical **on**, which now stands for a particular **on** space concept.

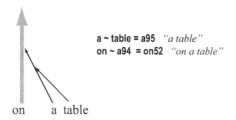

a ~ table = a95 *"a table"*
on ~ a94 = on52 *"on a table"*

Fig. 2.1.5 FOMT and Mensa table for **on** concept "on a table"

The surviving concept is an **on** relation concept, **on52**, an enriched relation that expects to *relay-it-on* to an entity concept like **abook** or a **alamp**. Lets relate it to a lamp with the following *Mensa* row:

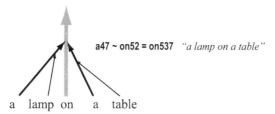

a47 ~ on52 = on537 *"a lamp on a table"*

Fig. 2.1.6 FOMT for the ment "a lamp on a table"

The narrative for the construction of concept **on537** as defined by this *Mensa* table is as follows: determiner grammatical concept **a** is enriched by lexical concept **lamp** to give surviving concept **a47**. Another separate determiner grammatical concept **a** is enriched by lexical concept **table** to give surviving concept **a94**. Meaning is first loaded onto the preposition grammatical particle **on** by the *relative*, **a94** to yield **on52**. This creates an individualized **on** with a special sense - *"on a table"* - carrying a meaning that is perfectly clear to us. We arbitrarily assign symbol **on52** to it to distinguish it from the generic empty **on** concept, and the myriad of other meaning-filled **on** concepts. Finally, surviving concept **on52** is enriched by **a47** to give **it** concept **on537**, which is a *ment* concept, an arrange**ment**.

This expression *"a lamp on a table"* can be parsed another way. It can be talking about a lamp rather than a relationship. In this case the *flow-of-meaning-tree* defined by these four relations is governed by a different last row where the-lamp entity is the surviving *endit* concept rather than the a-lamp-**on**-the-table *ment* relationship. Grammatical **on** accepts a particular meaning from its *object concept* **a94** and relays it back onto *subject concept* **a47**. The meaning transferred to the lamp is a temporary location attribute. The lamp gains an *accidental* property, *location*. Once we know or assume it is a table lamp, concept **table** becomes an *essential* adjective property of the lamp.

This time, the *flow-of-meaning-tree* shows surviving concept **a47** being enriched by **on52** to make **it** into concept **a48**, which is an *endit* concept.

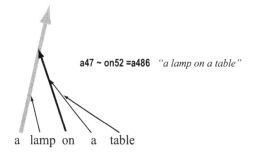

a47 ~ on52 =a486   *"a lamp on a table"*

a lamp on a table

Fig. 2.1.7 FOMT for the endit "a lamp on a table"

Many expressions and sentences have this duality of meaning, being either and *endit* or a *ment*. A diligent reader will parse them both ways, a form of mental play. We will see later that any one of the concepts mentioned in an expression can be made the **it** concept by mental play and this can be forced by an appropriate *Mensa table*. This is the basis of subordinate clause formation where one concept chosen to receive meaning from all the others relays this meaning into a concept in the main clause.

These examples illustrate the idea that the main function of prepositions is to define the structure of relations between concepts. The various preposition and conjunction grammatical particles are the basic relation symbols and they are nothing if not idiosyncratic in their relay functions. Prepositions like **at, on, in** and **with** indicate temporary relationships that change the *accidence* of the surviving concept, for example its location, not its *essence*. On the other hand a surviving concept's *essence* is modified by preposition **of**, for example, the door **of** a car is a different kind of door in its *essence* from a door **of** a house, whereas a door (stored) **in** the garage is just the same door, with new *accidence*. The relative concepts of *prepositional phrase* relations are entity concepts.

The next level of relational complexity needs more than one of the standard set of preposition grammaticals to specify it. For more complex relations something more multifaceted than a single *relational grammatical* or a short *relational phrase* to is needed to specify which relation of the possible relations pertains in a particular instance to model our highly nuanced world, where the number of possible relationships between two concepts becomes enormous and diverse. The short list of preposition grammaticals may not suffice. Fortunately, language is able to define an infinite number of different relations between two relatives with relational expressions that parse to a preposition relation grammatical, which may be considerably enriched by adjacent lexical concepts.

Simple relations can be defined by a short relational phrase. More complex relations have to be defined by placing a longer string of symbols, a *relational expression*, between the two relatives. Although a *relational expression* renders its *flow-of-meaning-tree* very *articulate*, it parses to a single enriched grammatical concept that defines a complex relationship,

Here are some examples of short relational phrases that enrich a relation grammatical to make a relation more complex than a simple preposition can:

well **into** in terms **of** heavier **than** not
enough **to** not coextensive **with** as well **as**

Authors can control the exact meaning of a relation with a carefully composed relation expression and, fortunately, it is very easy to compose a *Mensa* table that defines an *articulate flow-of-meaning-tree* and thereby a *complex relation*. The benefit of *flow-of-meaning-trees* is that they illustrate exactly what authors intend to say with perfect clarity.

Now, let's look at some examples of complex relations and their corresponding complex relational expressions. For example, the relation between concepts **metamaterials** and **superconductivity** in the sentence *"Metamaterials provide a flexible platform for modeling and mimicking superconductivity"* can be expressed as

metamaterials **R** superconductivity

There are many possible relationships between metamaterials and superconductivity. But the one we are interested in communicating can be defined as **R** = *"provide a flexible platform for modeling and mimicking"*.

Fig 2.1.8 shows the relevant *flow-of-meaning-tree* and *Mensa table.*

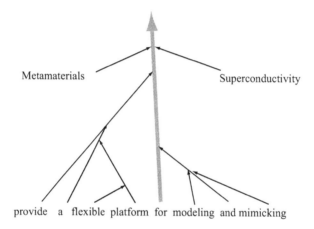

Fig. 2.1.8 FOMT for the complex relation between metamaterials and superconductivity expressed by "provide a flexible platform for modeling and mimicking"

Flexible ~platform	= FP	*"flexible platform"*
a ~ FP	= AFP	*"a flexible platform"*
provide ~ AFP	= PAFP	*"provide a flexible platform"*
and ~ mimicking	= AM	*"and mimicking"*
Modeling ~ AM	= MAM	*"modeling and mimicking"*
for ~ MAM	= for1	*"for modeling and mimicking"*
PAFP ~ For1	= for2641	*"provide a flexible platform for modeling and mimicking"*

This *Mensa table* enables our parser to parse this relation expression to a single symbol that relates metamaterials and superconductivity.

And, here is the flow-*of-meaning-tree* that explicates the dam and chick relation of Locke's cassowaries in St. James Park.

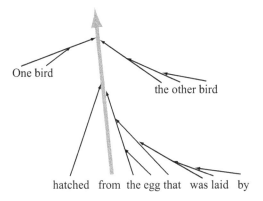

Fig. 2.1.9 FOMT for the complex relation "hatched from the egg that was laid by"

Here is the *flow-of-meaning-tree* and *Mensa* table that defines this relation

hatched ~ from	= HF	*"hatched from"*
the ~ egg	= TE	*"the egg"*
that ~ was	= TW	*"that was"*
laid ~ by	= LB	*"laid by"*
TW ~ LB	= TWLB	*"that was laid by"*
TE ~ TWLB	= TETWLB	*"the egg that was laid by"*
HF~ TETWLB	= from3452	*"hatched from the egg that was laid by"*

The long relation expression *"hatched from the egg that was laid by"* parses to concept **from3452**. And it turns out that should you ask "what is the relation between the two birds?", *"from the egg"* is an appropriate answer as is metonym *"the egg"*.

Relations between Clauses are Relations between Relations

So far we have mainly considered relations between entity relative concepts. What about relations between relation concepts? The most easy to understand grammaticals that mediate relations between relations are the conjunctions **after, although, as, because, before, if, once, since, so, so that, though, till, until, when, where, while,** all of which can relate two clauses to each other. So, we will examine how an entire clause, which is itself a relation, can relay conceptual content onto another clause, another relation. Meaning flows from one clause to the other via the conjunction relational grammatical. This is recursion.

Take the sentence *"As I had no car, I stayed home."* and its variations: *"As/since/because I had no car, I stayed home." "I had no car, so I stayed home."*

The the *flow-of-meaning-tree* for this complex sentence is shown in Fig. 2.1.10.

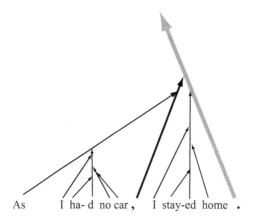

Fig. 2.1.10 FOMT for the Sentence "As I had no car, I stayed home."

Here is the *Mensa* table for this complex sentence.

stay ~ ed	= stayed	*"stayed"*
stayed ~ home	= -ed67	*"stayed home"*
I ~ -ed67	= Ied68	*"I stayed home"*
Ied68 ~ .	= Ied68.	*"I stayed home."*
no ~ car	= no269	*"no car"*
ha ~ -d	= had	*"had"*
I ~ had	= Ihad	*"I had"*
Ihad ~ no269	= Ihad270	*"I had no car"*
as ~ Ihad270	= as270	*"As I had no car"*
as270 ~ ,	= ,as270	*"As I had no car,"*
,as270 ~ Ied68.	= Ied69.	*"As I had no car, I stayed home."*

The observation concept expressed by *"I stayed home"* is packaged in the period concept. The concept expressed by subordinate clause *"I had no car."* is enclaused (sic) in grammatical **as**, which is thereby enriched to

as270 and then enclaused in comma concept **,as270**. This comma concept is then included in the period concept. Substitute **since** or **because** for **as**, and try to sense the effect on the nuance of the main clause. Each conjunction puts its idiosyncratic stamp on the subordinate clause concept that it enclauses (sic) and therefore contributes subtly different nuance to *"staying home"*.

Here, grammatical **as** picks up meaning from the relation in a subordinate clause and, via the comma, uses it to put a special spin on the sense of the relation in the main clause. We will see later that when high level concepts are enclaused in punctuation marks, which are then related with each other to produce a surviving punctuation mark concept we are in the realm of *logic*. Note if I say *"I have no car, so I will stay home."* You might reply *"That's logical."*

In another example of **as** function, compare *"I don't know how I can do that."* and *"I don't know as how I can do that."* Grammatical relation **as** expects a relation object concept. In the first case, **how** concept **howIcandothat** is simply the object of verb concept **know**. In the second case **as** is looking for a relation and so concept **Idontknow** is questioning the **can** relation between concepts **I** and **dothat**.

Metaphors

It turns out that relations between relations are very useful in explaining what we mean. And they are the basis of metaphor. Metaphor is a technique able to enrich one relation by saying it is the same as or close to another relation that the second person already fully understands. Metaphor piggybacks on the reader's grasp of that other relation garnered from experience in another context.

Relation grammatical **as** signifies a relation between two relations, usually employed in a metaphor to explain or enrich the first relation, vis. a multiple choice question like this in a SAT exam:

A is to B
as
C is to D, E, F or G?

This multiple choice question aims to find out whether the testee is able to discern which of the relations CRD, CRE, CRF, or CRG is the same relation as relation ARB. If he didn't get ARB in the first place, it would be helpful to be told ARB was the same as CRF for instance. Then he would probably figure ARB out. This is why metaphors are so useful for explaining subtle meanings.

Colorful and vivid metaphors make a point. For example, a Wall Street Journal editorial on Rupert Murdoch's comeuppance over the News of the World hacking scandal describing comments by rival publications: *"the shadenfreude is so thick you can't cut it with a chainsaw"*. Here a relation is extracted from one context and transferred colorfully to another context with one common concept, *shadenfreude*.

A case can be made that other prepositional relation grammaticals like **for** can expect that their object be a relation concept, e.g. *"It is for Harry to buy the drinks"* or *"He roots for the Mets (to win)"* Sometimes, when **for** is followed by an object concept that may appear at first just to be a relative, we have to treat it as a *metonym* for a relation. When the speaker knows that the addressee knows what the relationship is, the second relative can be omitted. The relation between two sentences normally serviced by a conjunction can be serviced by **of** and an entity subject concept, e.g. *"Because James paid, I still have cash"* can be equally well stated with *"Because of James, I still have cash."* Symbolically, **because ARB, CRD** can be replaced by **because of A, CRD**. This line of thought suggests that James is a metonym for a subordinate clause.

To help understand relations between relations as opposed to relations between relatives, it is helpful to study the distinction between grammaticals like **like** and **as**. Let's analyze the 1950's cigarette TV commercial jingle *"Winston tastes good like a cigarette should"* Prescriptive grammarians scolded the R. J. Reynolds Tobacco Company and their advertising agency for bad grammar, suggesting that relative **as** should have been employed instead of **like** to say *"Winston tastes good as a cigarette should."*[12] In both sentences relation **taste-s** is a relation between concepts **Winston** and **good**. Relation **as** specifies a relation between relation concepts whereas **like** specifies a relation with a single end concept. In the **as** sentence, grammatical concept **as** is a relation between the two observations, enriching the main verb action. In the **like** sentence, grammatical **like** is

---

12   To play this jingle, Google "YouTube Winston tastes good", I'm feeling lucky.

a relation between the second observation and concept **good**, enriching concept **good**. On this basis use of **like** is perfectly legitimate and good grammar and certainly more catchy.

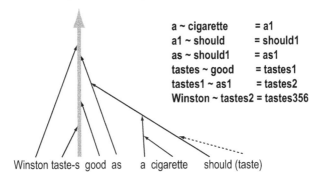

```
a ~ cigarette          = a1
a1 ~ should            = should1
as ~ should1           = as1
tastes ~ good          = tastes1
tastes1 ~ as1          = tastes2
Winston ~ tastes2 = tastes356
```

Winston taste-s good as   a cigarette   should (taste)

Fig. 2.1.11 FOMT for the sentence "Winston tastes good as a cigarette should"

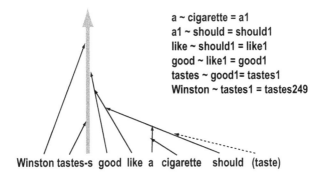

```
a ~ cigarette = a1
a1 ~ should = should1
like ~ should1 = like1
good ~ like1 = good1
tastes ~ good1= tastes1
Winston ~ tastes1 = tastes249
```

Winston tastes-s good like a   cigarette   should (taste)

Fig. 2.1.12 FOMT for the Sentence "Winston tastes good like a cigarette should"

Mensa tables enable our parser to make a sharp and precise distinction between these two very close concepts, parsing one sentence to concept **tastes356** and the other to concept **tastes249**, a subtle distinction that the human mind notices instantly, but which is very difficult for someone to explain without a *flow-of-meaning-tree* and *Mensa* table.

Our theory makes clear the idiosyncratic function of grammatical **like**, which admits adjectival conceptual concept only, with a strong evaluation component by the speaker. The other use of **like** that, for which modern young people are widely scolded as in *"I'm like, how could she say that"* is entirely legitimate and conveys precise subtle meaning, Here, **like** is enriched with adjectival meaning from the whole juxtaposed finite sentence. Then, subject relative **I** in the main clause is enriched by enriched object relative **like**.

Relationships

As an illustration of the power of a series of relations between relatives to organize a large number of concepts into a *relationship*, consider that the Swiss National Tourist Office might want to get a certain complex of concepts into the heads of visitors to Zermatt. Their brochure might say *"The visitor to Zermatt must take the cogwheel railway to the summit of the Gornergrat for magnificent views of 29 alps over 4000 meters and 7 glaciers"*. 2.1.13 shows the *flow-of-meaning-tree* of this long sentence,

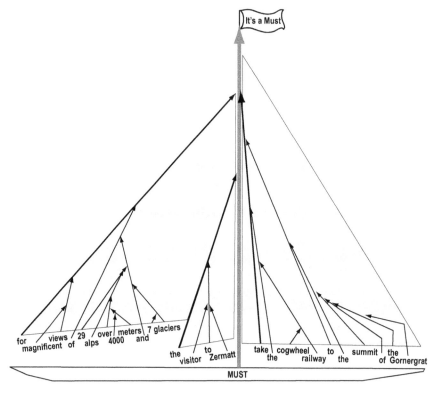

Fig. 2.1.13 FOMT for the relationship expressed by a long sentence

This finite sentence parses to a complex but unitary **must** concept mustering 27 separate mental concepts, showing all binary connections between concepts and the direction of meaning flow. All meaning contributed by each symbol ends up in enriched concept **must**. Any system of interactive symbols relaying meaning back and forth like this is a **relationship**. In this case **it** is a **must**. With access to a *Mensa* table containing these relations, our parser can easily parse this long sentence.

Interestingly, we have observed that the meaning flow arrows of a *flow-of-meaning-tree* cannot cross on the way to the **it** if the expression is to make sense. A telling example of the validity of this idea is suggested when someone says *"Everything's gone haywire."*

The unmistakable pattern above of a sailing ship suggests why a complex tree of n-1 paired relations is called a relation*ship*. The tall **must** concept is a *mast*. Or is it vice versa? This suggests that the unconscious mind literally uses the pattern of a tree figure to muster observed concepts into a gestalt. We realize that this is a claim very likely to evoke "pushback" but we can't avoid the suspicion that the unconscious mind uses a literal tree diagram to manage understanding of what we see in the world.

When an Expression does not Make Sense

What happens in the brain when a language expression or a picture does not make sense has been closely studied by neuroscientists looking at electroencephalographic signals that occur when research subjects read language expressions, with 1000 scientific papers written since the discovery of N400 by Maria Kutas and Steven Hilliard in 1980.[13]. There is the N400 ERP signal when the expression does not make sense and the P600 signal when syntax is violated See the very interesting reviews by Kutas and Federmeier[14] and Hagoort.[15] The brain seems to be busy casting about to see if there is another context where the relationship expressed would make sense.

Whether a language expression "makes sense" is determined by whether the relationship it expresses occurs in the world or not. For example, to

---

13   Google "n400 ERP" I'm feeling lucky
14   Kutras M, and Federmeier K D, *Thirty Years and Counting: Finding Meaning in the N400 Component of the Event-Related Brain Potential (ERP)*, Annu Rev Psychol 62, 14.1-14.27, 2011
15   Hagoort P, The fractionation of spoken language understanding by measuring electrical and magnetic brain signals, Philos Trans R Soc Lond B Biol Sci. 2008 March 12; 363(1493): 1055–1069.

say that the lamp is *"of the table"* does not make sense. This suggests that phrase *"make sense"* means that the concepts match up in a way that we may well see out in the real world, and "not make sense" means that we never see it that way out in the world. Which expressed relations do make sense has to be based on our knowledge of the world. Judging this is difficult for a computer because it cannot avail itself of consciousness, which is why *Mensa* tables have to be composed by a human curator at present. As discussed in the previous chapter, to see if an expression makes sense, the parser has to judge whether the language expression gets through to a neuron involved with the conscious experience of the relevant concepts.

The relation between the two concepts that correspond to those two things, the relation between the symbols that correspond to the two real things, and the relation between the two real things, is exactly the same relation. And a relation between the real thing and the concept or symbol that corresponds to the second real thing is also exactly the same relation. The mind appears to mix and match real things, concepts and symbols unreservedly in mental structures. The mind's picture of the world is a free mixture of real things and associated mental concepts.

There is another way to look at relations. One can think of the object relative of a relation grammatical like **in** defining a particular type of mental space that concepts, named by the subject relative, can be contained in. To pass muster so as to be fit (**of-it**) to be in such a space concepts have to adapt appropriately. This idea, which is in effect is the same as having one concept relay meaning into its neighbor, will become useful in our discussions of preposition relation grammaticals **for** and **to** for their roles in defining the mind's *command and control (comcon)* system and for parsing **how** and **why** questions.

And one can look at relations another way: the object concept of a relation governs a space that the mentioned subject concept is shaped in. More on this view in the discussion of how preposition relation concepts **to** and **for** work in Book III, Chapter III.

BOOK II
CHAPTER II

Grammaticals and Lexicals

Language consists of two subsystems of symbols, lexical words and grammaticals. Lexical words are the content words: nouns, verbs, adjectives and adverbs. Grammaticals are the structure words comprising free particles: pronouns, determiners, prepositions, auxiliary verbs and conjunctions, also bound grammatical affixes and inflections of lexical words. Notably, we include punctuation marks among the grammaticals. Children obtain a full command of grammatical functions before the age of five; achieving this skill is tantamount to learning the ropes of the English language. Natural language understanding systems that ignore grammaticals and punctuation marks will never be adequate to recover the full meaning of language.

E volution of the human brain endowed us with the ability to create and employ a symbol such as a sound or ordered string of sounds, a graphic shape or a hand, head or eye gesture to represent a mental concept, and often something in the real world or in an imaginary world as well. Language is often said to consist of two subsystems of symbols: *lexical* words and *grammatical* words. Lexicals are the content words, nouns, adjectives verbs and adverbs. Grammaticals are the free grammatical function words of language as well as bound affixes of lexicals. Grammaticals are a framework upon which the lexical concepts are hung. Lexicals can be considered to stand for the conceptual content that grammaticals hold and relay. The metaphor of the stark branches of the "bare ruined choirs" of Shakespere's Sonnet 73 which become verdant (word-ant) with leaves (leaficals - lexicals) again in spring is apt. We will argue that punctuation marks are also fully fledged grammaticals.

Leonard Talmy has provided the best approach to this dichotomy and his analysis is key to identifying which elements of language are which and to understanding their roles.

To quote Talmy: [12]

> "A fundamental design feature of language is that it has two subsystems,
> which can be designated as the grammatical and the lexical .... The
> grammatical elements .... determine the majority of the structure ....
> while the lexical elements provide the majority of its content"
>
> Leonard Talmy
>
> "this set of grammatically specified notions collectively constitutes the
> fundamental conceptual structuring system of language"
>
> Leonard Talmy

Let's deal with grammaticals first. Grammaticals are perfectly clear concepts in their own right. People often say something is a **must**. Salespeople are advised to welcome a **yes**, push for a **no**, and avoid **maybes**. And want no **ands, ifs** or **buts**. David Hume appears to have realized that grammaticals are concepts in their own right when he famously said *"you can't get an* **is** *from an* **ought***"*. Just as algebraic unknowns like **x** and **y** can hold any one of millions of values, an empty grammatical like **yes, no,** or **that** can

---

1   *Leonard Talmy, Towards a Cognitive Semantics, Vol.1, MIT Press, Cambridge, 2003,*
     pp. 21-37

2   Leonard Talmy, *Towards a Cognitive Semantics, Vol.1*, MIT Press, Cambridge, 2003,
     p. 1

be filled with any one of multi-millions of different meanings of the kind expressed by a finite sentence, depending on which sentence relays its meaning into it. Similarly, personal pronouns like **he**, **you** or **me** can stand for any one of billions of people. On the other hand it is rare to hear of a **the** or an **in** or a **from** or a **to**.

There are several hundred English grammatical particles, determiners, pronouns, relative pronouns, reflexive pronouns, conjunctions, prepositions, affirmatives, negatives, modals, lexical word affixes, punctuation marks, etc., each one idiosyncratic and very specialized in its function. Talmy claims they are a closed system, No new ones have been introduced into English in the last two hundred years but you will see we have a quibble about this statement.

Grammaticals are just as important to meaning as lexical words. Natural language processing systems that ignore grammaticals and punctuation marks will never be adequate to recover the full meaning of language. Our *Mensa* tables take into account the meaning contributed by every single grammatical in an expression, including word inflections and punctuation marks. Throughout this essay much will be said about grammaticals and how our system can garner their sum total of meaning.

Grammatical particles and word inflections become fully fledged concepts when filled with meaning in context. Like algebraic variable symbols, grammatical concepts have to be thought of as variable symbols that receive their meaning content via a flow of meaning from related symbols. Grammaticals divide into two types: *relative* or *entity grammaticals* that are containers of meaning, and *relation grammaticals* that relate concepts and control meaning flow between them.

Relative grammaticals hold meaning and put their idiosyncratic stamp on it. A *relative grammatical* symbol is like the milk carton described earlier. It has to be thought of as an empty container of specific shape that can receive a certain kind of content that it measures and shapes. Another analogy is an algebraic variable: in the formula to calculate **g**, the acceleration of gravity at any point on the surface of the earth, $\mathbf{g} = \mathbf{Gm}_1/\mathbf{r}^2$, symbol **G** can only contain one content, the gravitational constant, **m1** only the mass of the earth and **r** only its radius or rather the distance from the center of the earth at that point.

Relation grammaticals lie between two relative concepts, taking input and giving output. *Relation grammaticals* are selective as to what kind of meaning they will receive from one relative concept and selective of what meaning they will relay on to the other relative. A *relation grammatical* symbol is like a screwdriver which transmits turn motion from the hand to the screw.

Determiner Grammaticals

Determiners like indefinite article symbol **a** or **an** and definite article **the** are archetypical *entity grammaticals*. They provide a good opportunity to demonstrate how *entity grammaticals* can be filled with meaning from the words that follow them. They then shape this conceptual content.

Indefinite article symbol **a**, when filled with meaning from the count noun phrase that follows it, represents a singular count entity, not yet identified, not yet declared to exist in the present world of the observer or in an imaginary or memory (past) world. For example, in the noun phrases *"a treaty"* and *"a party"*, determiner grammatical **a** is enriched by flow of meaning from the lexical noun following it to represent a specific but not yet instantiated something. Many linguists consider the noun to be the head word of a noun phrase but in fact the determiner is the head.

Definite article determiner symbol **the**, when filled with meaning from the noun phrase that follows it, represents something, singular or plural, known to speaker and assumed to be the only one to exist in the universe of the addressee.

Determiner **that**, filled with meaning from various sources, represents one concept that exists, and is identifiable when there is more than one concept in consideration.

Now, let's reintroduce *flow-of-meaning-trees (FOMTs)* and *Mensa tables* with which we model mental concepts.

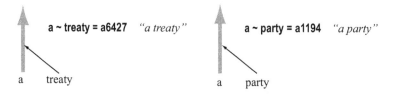

Fig. 2.2.1 FOMT and Mensa table rows for phrases "a treaty" and "a party"

Fig 2.2.1 shows flow-of-meaning-trees and *Mensa* rows that illustrate concepts *"a treaty" "a party"* being formed by meaning flowing into singular indefinite and definite article grammaticals from a following noun concept.

Figs 2.2.2 and 2.2.3 show *Mensa* tables and a *flow-of-meaning-trees* using symbols to explicate how the concepts expressed by *"the Internet"* and *"the earthquakes"* are formed by flow of meaning into the definite article grammatical.

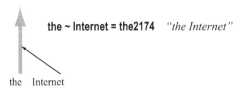

the ~ Internet = the2174   *"the Internet"*

the   Internet

Fig. 2.2.2 FOMT and Mensa table row for noun phrase "the Internet"

The **-s** grammatical suffix of plural nouns as in *"earthquakes"* is another determiner; it functions as an indefinite article, but a plurality article. And, and just like **a** and **an**, when filled with meaning from its noun's stem, represents an unidentified group or plurality that does not currently exist in the world.

Fig. 2.2.3 shows *flow-of-meaning-trees* and *Mensa* rows illustrating how concept **earthquakes** and **the1435** are formed by meaning flowing into the **-s** suffix of a plural noun and then on into determiner concept **the**.

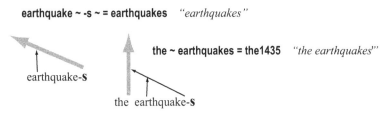

earthquake ~ -s ~ = earthquakes   *"earthquakes"*

earthquake-**s**

the ~ earthquakes = the1435   *"the earthquakes'"*

the earthquake-**s**

Fig. 2.2.3 Flow-of-meaning-trees and Mensa table rows for plural indefinite noun phrase "earthquakes" and plural definite noun phrase "the earthquakes"

In addition, the apostrophe s (**-'s**) of a possessive functions as a determiner grammatical. It is filled with meaning from both the relative noun before and the relative noun following. Possessive phrases are an example of meaning flow from symbols before and after the apostrophe **'s**. Take the example *"Coogan's Bluff"*. Here, HAVE type meaning flows from proper noun concept **Coogan** into the **'s** grammatical, and BE type meaning flows into it from concept **Bluff**. Unless the preceding noun is a proper noun, a **the** determiner is required for the concept to represent something that exists in the world.

Fig. 2.2.4 shows the flow-of-meaning-tree and *Mensa* table defining the meaning flow into determiner **'s** from both sides:

Fig. 2.2.4 FOMT and Mensa table for possessive noun phrase "Coogan's Bluff"

In this case, *"Coogan"* is a capitalized proper noun. Capitalization functions as determiner **the** incorporated in the proper noun, indicating an instantiated and identified thing, making the surviving concept equivalent to *"the Bluff"*, something that exists in the world and is identifiable by the second person. No need for a **the** determiner.

Pronouns

Another important class of entity grammaticals are the pronouns: personal pronouns and relative/interrogative pronouns. Personal pronouns and relative pronouns receive meaning from concepts defined in other nearby sentences and clauses, by remote meaning transfer. Pronouns are conventionally thought to refer out to concepts not expressed in the present expression, so called pronoun reference. We prefer to think of pronouns being filled with meaning flowing in from a concept defined in another expression or from more remote concepts.

The first way pronouns receive their meaning is from a concept taking part in appositional phrase(s) or subordinate clause(s) in the same expression or sentence. Another way is to bring in meaning by way of its participation in neighboring sentences, in separate paragraphs of different chapters, or by allusion from what Stanislas Dehaene calls the "mental lexicon". [34]

Such teletransfers of meaning between concepts are mediated between sentences by personal pronouns. The chapter on subordinate clauses discusses concepts in a main clause receiving meaning relayed via relative pronouns from remote concepts enriched in subordinate clauses. Meaning can also transfer between sentences in paragraphs and poems without the intercession of relative pronouns. Language (and *Mensa*) can detail this extended meaning accrual process precisely.

Personal Pronouns

Personal pronouns well illustrate how grammaticals can contain only certain meanings and put their individual stamp on them. They can receive gender, number, person, identity etc. from a remote concept. Personal pronoun symbols **he** and **him** can only contain the sensory pattern of a singular male human (or male anthropomorphic personality). Thus, they can contain the concept of any one of the billions of individuals on earth or in the literature. Like determiner concepts **the**, **this** and **that**, personal pronouns also indicate that the person is readily identifiable to the addressee. Usually, in a particular instance **he** or **him** will contain the single male human mentioned anaphorically nearby in the text. In a particular context "he" could stand in for *"Fiorello La Guardia, the former mayor of New York"* or *"James Bond, 007"*.

The relative concept words that contribute meaning to **he** are not usually next to *"he"* in the text, but occur in the same context in another part of the expression or in another nearby expression. Meaning has to jump across a space. In the case of divine **He**, content does not come from a neighbor concept but from the mental lexicon.

Personal pronouns are a good example of the use of bare grammaticals to contain complex concepts, serving the purpose of data compression to

---

3   Stanislas Dehaene, *Reading in the Brain, Viking, New York, 2009*, p.41

4   When the relative concept receiving meaning is widely separate from the sending concept, it "t-lay-s" rather than re-lays the meaning, illuminating the meaning of prefix **tele-** as in telegram, telescope, television, telepathy etc., Such remote *tele*-relay of meaning from another expression, where the message is transmitted over a distance, can make pronoun reference, so called anaphor and cataphor resolution, difficult for parsers. However, Mensa tables allow precise management of pronoun reference.

ease the low bandwidth speech channel. The addressee has to cast about to figure out which meaning to fill the grammatical with. We are good at it but it is difficult for a computer to figure it out. However, the problem is easily solved with a *Mensa* table.

Personal pronouns don't normally need to be enriched locally as their referents are obvious from context, (pronouns are **it** already). However, we do say things like *"we democrats" "us guys"*, and there is one famous instance of personal pronoun enrichment: *"She who must be obeyed"*. This literal expression defines a certain kind of woman. But in this case, who the woman is has to come from somewhere else by allusion.

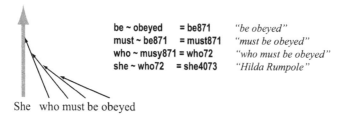

```
be ~ obeyed     = be871       "be obeyed"
must ~ be871    = must871      "must be obeyed"
who ~ musy871 = who72          "who must be obeyed"
she ~ who72     = she4073      "Hilda Rumpole"
```

She   who must be obeyed

Fig. 2.2.5 FOMT and Mensa table showing rare enrichment of grammatical **she**.

These examples of meaning flowing into personal pronouns from contextual concepts spotlight the general function of all grammaticals as receivers, squeezers and shapers, and relayors of meaning. Personal and relative pronouns are further discussed in the chapters on subordinate clauses and the chapter on pronouns and poetry which deal with *teletransfer* of meaning from non-adjacent concepts.

Concept order in a sentence determines the role of a concept to be the *subject* of the sentence, or the *object of the verb*. In English concepts have place value and take on these roles by virtue of their order in the sentence. In Latin these roles are formally indicated by the cases of nouns. English personal pronouns do retain case markings; concepts **I, thou, he, she, we** and **they** can only be subject concepts; **me, thee, him, her, us** and **them** can only be verb object concepts.

Parsing a finite sentence, personal pronouns **I, he, she, they** are subject concept grammaticals that get a bye to the final top level concept matchup of the parsing tournament. Analogous to the incumbent world boxing champion who gets a bye all the way to the championship match while his competitors fight it out to become the challenger.

Pronoun Reference

Mensa tables are structured so as to enable our parser to work in local sections of the *Mensa* database where a pronoun has clear-cut reference. The following *Mensa* table shows how our parser is able to obtain the same meaning from these sentences: *"The Duke of York did arrive late"* and *"He did arrive late"*. With this *Mensa* table, whether the speaker uses either the full subject entity phrase or the subject personal pronoun **He**, both sentences will mean the same and our parser will arrive at the same concept.

of ~ York	**= of356**	*"of York"*
Duke ~ of356	**= of357**	*"Duke of York"*
The ~ of357	**= the357**	*"The Duke of York"*
The357 ~ did	**= did2396**	*"The Duke of York did"*
He ~ did	**= did2396**	*"The Duke of York did"*
arrive ~ late	**= arrive86**	*"arrive late"*
did2396 ~ arrive86	**= did2397**	*"The Duke of York did arrive late"*

The flow-of-meaning-trees for the two sentences are as follows:

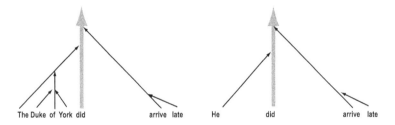

Fig. 2.2.6 FOMT and Mensa table showing pronoun reference for **he**.

Concept Duke of York has a built in covert **he** grammatical inside it.

Reflexive Pronouns

Language tells us something about the mind-body problem. It distinguishes between the mind and the body. Concepts **I** and **me** refer to my mind, my personal-ity, **myself** to my body, my person. The common greeting heard in Ireland *"How are you yourself"* focuses concern on your physical self. The mind and language see the world as a *command and control (comcon)* system. **Myself** is thought of an *agent* or *relation* that mediates between **I** and the outside world. **I** am in command, **myself** is in control. Only **I** can deal with **myself**; others have to deal with **me**.

Language reflects how entities are made up of two parts, the physical and the conceptual, the real and what exists only in our minds. Reflexive pronouns like **myself, yourself, himself, ourselves, yourselves, themselves** are used to refer to the physical parts of an entity. *"The White House endorses debt reduction at last"* is not referring to the physical building, the White House itself.

The modeling system of the mind also treats reflexive pronouns as physical relations. Physical **myself**, the agent between my consciousness and volition and the outside world is the *relation* between a *subject* and an *object* relative just like all other relations. The subject deals with **myself** and **myself** the physical relation deals with the object. Third persons have to deal with **me**. Reflexive pronouns refer to this interface. And the boundary of **myself**, is movable out to the extremities of my body. We can think of our volition dealing with our hands or our voice, **myself**, and then **myself** is my agent, dealing with the world.

As discussed in Book III Chapter IV language seems to view this as a *command and control* (comcon) system. Sometimes I may feel **myself** extending out past my hands into my personal space, *myspace*, out to the business ends of my knife and fork. And in an automobile *myspace* may extend out to the limits of my car. Our neural console interfaces with the rest of our body, **ourself**, which in turn interacts with the outside world, allowing us to live effectively and safely.

Relative/Interrogative Pronouns

The next pronouns to consider that receive and shape remote meaning are the relative/interrogative pronouns, As explained in Book II Ch. VI on subordinate clauses, relative pronouns mediate interflow of meaning from a party concept in one clause to a party concept in another clauses of the same complex sentence, but not from separate sentences or paragraphs. Once fulfilled with meaning, and brought to the front of a subordinate clause, they take part in the main clause, influencing other party concepts there. Each relative pronoun has its idiosyncratic function of admitting just its own kind of conceptual content, whether it be *time, place, reason, manner, a person, a thing* or *a choice*. The relative/interrogative pronouns,

who, which, what, when, where, how, and **why**, are the six honest serving men of Kipling's poem.[5]

A nice example of the virtuosity of the relative pronouns to move meaning back and forth is illustrated with the sentence *"Djokovic, who won the Australian Open, wins Indian Wells"*. Here relative pronoun **who** is not identifying Djokovic but saying something new about him. At other times **who** can service identity just like **that**.

Fig. 2.2.7 shows the *flow-of-meaning-tree* for this complex sentence drawn with vertical text, which is more convenient when text is too long to fit across the page and allows trees to be drawn for very long texts, even paragraphs.

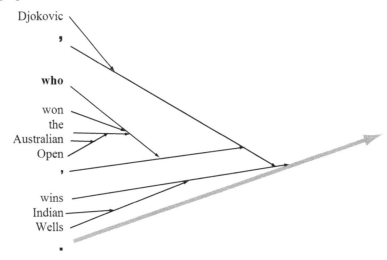

Fig. 2.2.7 FOMT and Mensa table for sentence *"Djokovic, who won the Australian Open, wins Indian Wells"* showing pronoun reference for relative pronoun **who**.

---

5   Rudyard Kipling   *The Elephant's Child*

I keep six honest serving-men
(They taught me all I knew);
Their names are **What** and **Why** and **When**
And **How** and **Where** and **Who**.
I send them over land and sea,
I send them east and west;
But after they have worked for me,
I give them all a rest

Table. 2.2.1 shows the *Mensa* table with the pairings required to parse this sentence.

Djokovic ~ ,	= ND	*"Djokovic,"*
Australian ~ open	= AO	*"Australian open"*
the ~ AO	= theAO	*"the Australian open"*
won ~ theAO	= WtheAO	*"won the Australian open"*
who ~ WtheAO	= who284	*"who won the Australian open"*
who284 ~ ,	= ,who284	*"who won the Australian open,"*
ND ~ ,who284	= ND284	*"Djokovic, who won the Australian open"*
Indian ~ Wells	= IW	*"Indian Wells"*
wins ~ IW	= WIW	*"wins Indian Wells"*
ND284 ~ WIW	= ND284WIW	*"Djokovic, who won the Australian open wins Indian Wells"*
ND284WIW ~ .	= ND284WIW.	*"Djokovic, who won the Australian open wins Indian Wells."*

Table. 2.2.1 Mensa table for sentence "Djokovic, who won the Australian Open, wins Indian Wells"

Here, relative pronoun **who** receives conceptual content anaphorically from *"Djokovic"*. It is thus enriched with meaning to establish Djokovic as the subject concept of the subordinate clause, acquire meaning there and then transfer its enriched meaning back to Djokovic in the main clause.

Narrative of this sentence: concept **Djokovic** is first bundled in the comma to form concept **,Djokovic**. Relative pronoun concept **who** is enriched by predicate concept **wontheAustralianOpen** and bundled in the comma, relays meaning back to enrich concept **,Djokovic**, which now is the enriched subject concept to predicate concept **winsIndianWells**, forming the main clause *"Djokovic (enriched) wins Indian Wells."* Finally, this *main clause* is packaged in the end period to become an *observation concept* that could be included in a paragraph describing what he did. This sentence helps us consider how a *Mensa* table manages the problem of pronoun reference.

To enable pronoun reference in this case we would put three *Mensa* rows in local context, i.e. year 2011 of the *Mensa* tennis database, as follows:

he ~wontheaustralianopen	= djokovicwontheaustralianopen
	"Djokovic won the Australian Open"
who~wontheaustralianopen	= djokovicwontheaustralianopen
	"Djokovic won the Australian Open"
djokovic ~wontheaustralianopen	= djokovicwontheaustralianopen
	"Djokovic won the Australian Open"

Then, whether the input text used *"He"*, *"who"* or *"Djokovic"* as subject, the parser operating locally in year 2011 context of the database will arrive at the concept row in the *Mensa* database with the text: *"Djokovic won the Australian Open"*. If the parser had been operating in a different context area of the tennis database, perhaps dealing with year 2010, the same input would be parsed to at a different concept row, say the one with text *"Federer won the Australian Open"*.

THAT

One of the pleasures of our project has been to take a common expression like *'that's it'* that you know the meaning of perfectly yet it is very obscure how it got that meaning, and puzzle over it until an explanation emerges, usually with some worthwhile insights into the function of grammaticals. So, let's tackle the difficult question of distinguishing exactly how grammatical **that** functions, since **that** is very a useful grammatical. *Flow-of-meaning-trees* and *Mensa tables* can help explain how expressions that we know the meaning of but do not see how the expression get their meaning.

Here is Dwight Bolinger dealing with **that** and giving the problem some flavor:

> *"So far as I know, there has never been any doubt in any grammarian's mind about the absolute equivalence of sentences having and sentences omitting the relative word that. ... The question is, does a sentence such as I noticed you were there mean the same as one such as I noticed that you were there? For traditionalists and transformationalists alike, they have been regarded as being in free variation."*

Bolinger goes on to argue they are not the same. [6] In the first sentence the clause *"you were there"* is singular new information. It is saying something was noticed. However, when grammatical **that** is filled up with the meaning in *"that you were there"* it makes it into a already established fact, and the affirmative one of two possibilities, **yes** or **no**..

How does **that** differ from the relative pronouns? Relative pronouns pick up only their own type of meaning; **where** picks up location, **when** time, **how** manner or way, **why** reason or cause, **who** a human or humans, **what** a thing and **which** a choice. **That** does behave like a relative pronoun in that it can pick up meaning from a concept mentioned in another clause

---

6   Dwight Bolinger, Meaning and Form, Trans. NYAS, 1974, pp.218-134

and insert the meaning into the present expression but **that** it is much more versatile than any relative pronoun in that **that** can carry the meaning of any one of concept types carried by the relative pronouns. **That** can also pick up meaning type of *noun, verb, adjective* and *adverb* type concepts, as well as meaning from whole expressions sentences and paragraphs. Moreover **that** can play the role of any part of speech depending on it's place value in a sentence.

The essential thing about grammatical **that** is that it differs from the relative pronouns in that it refers back anaphorically to and identifies one of several concepts that is already in the record, whether explicitly mentioned previously or not.

That picks up its meaning from outside the present view, from knowledge that is not new information, and that is accepted to already exist by first and second person. **That** can't be used to introduce a new concept, whereas the relative pronouns can. And, even if a concept has not been mentioned in previous text it can still be loaded into **that** which has the effect of inserting it into the record as something that is already known. In contrast, relative pronouns are used in an expression to add new meaning to the concept they refer to. For example the time concept *"when I get home"* can be a novel concept newly introduced in the present sentence.[7]

In the sentence *"the issue that won the election for Obama was hope"*, just like a relative pronoun **that** picks up identity as subject of this subordinate clause. It then supplies that meaning to a concept in another expression, i.e. the issue hope, by BE type meaning transfer. Here the purpose of **that** is to identify which issue it is by extracting meaning from known information. So, in the sentence *"the issue, which won the election for Obama, was hope"*, new information is being supplied about the issue and concept **which** is functioning as a relative pronoun subject of the subordinate clause picking up its identity anaphorically from the subject concept of the main clause to say something new about it. In the sentence *"Bill's not that*

---

7   Anyone who looks up the definitions of exaphora, cataphora, anaphora, deixis, indexicality, demonstrative, pronoun, and relative pronoun in Wikipedia will see that these processes are well understood by linguists. It is not the purpose of this monograph to teach them, but to make the point that linguistic processes can be precisely represented by flow of meaning trees and Mensa tables in a form that is fully manageable by computer programs.

stupid", **that** implies that a statement has been made describing the degree of Bill's stupidity. Use of **that** here implies a previous judgment of Bill's intelligence, explicit in previous text or to be imagined.

One can talk about a **that** concept. One can deny the concept by saying *"that's not true"* but one cannot erase it from the record. It's as if **that** concepts are part of an established existence regardless of whether anyone, speaker or listener, knows of it. One can say *"I didn't know that."*

So, based upon the above thinking we can tackle the problem of understanding why the phrase *"that wife of Harry's"* gets its special meaning. First **that** in determiner position usually reaches back anaphorically to a finite observation to obtain meaning. This implies that **she** is involved in statements of some interest, implying *"thereby hangs a tale"*. Then, we don't say *"that wife **of** Harry"* because the phrase *"that wife **of** Harry's"* is short for *"that wife **of** Harry's wife"*. She is already identified; Harry is being excluded from interest. In any case that **that** is easily managed in *Mensa* tables.

Trying to figure out just what kind of conceptual content grammatical **so** will accept and what kind of stamp it will impose on it is another exemplary exercise in getting to understand the grammaticals. Grammatical **so**, in contrast to **that**, receives concepts that are known because they have been seen recently, and are somewhat esoteric.

Prepositions and Conjunctions

At the core of every relation concept there is an explicit or implicit relation grammatical. Relation grammaticals are discussed in the previous Book II Chapter I on relations, in Book II Chapter VI on subordinate clauses again at some length in Book III Chapter III where the functions of preposition grammaticals **by**, **for** and **to** are analyzed with regard to their role in defining the *command and control* system that is the basis of the life of the mind.

Bare Grammaticals

A study of grammatical **to** will bring out many of the properties of relational grammaticals. Relation grammatical **to**'s object concept is the intended fixed endpoint of a process or a path. It may be a real end point, but one that has not been reached yet, so **to** is a concept that is held in the mind, a very useful grammatical that can help us say what we mean in several ways. In an infinitive the verb following **to** names the end of a process. The concepts preceding **to** are the process required to get there.

But in some contexts the addressee can readily figure out **to**'s object concept so it does not have to be explicitly specified. For example, *"pull the door to"* which means pull the door to the end of its closing travel but don't latch it. The verb action of *pull* does not include latching. With *"When he comes to"* specification of the contents of **to** is unnecessary because an addressee aware of the context would be able to "figure out" what concepts to bundle into **to** in this case, i.e. he comes (back) **to** the present, to consciousness". "Figuring out" is literal in a *flow-of-meaning-tree*.

Grammaticals can contain very complex concepts. This function is practical. Once a complex concept has been precisely expressed by a long expression, using a short proxy symbol instead of repetition in a slow speech channel is practical. It is usually the core grammatical of the expression. Grammatical "do" is exemplary:

> *"Do you, Jane, take Harry, to be your husband, to have and to hold, for better or for worse, for richer, for poorer, in sickness and in health, but not for lunch, to love and to cherish; from this day forward until death do you part?"*
>
> *"I do"*
>
> *"Put your left hand on the bible and raise your right hand. Repeat after me. 'Do you swear to tell the truth the whole truth and nothing but the truth so help you God?'"*
>
> *"I do"*

In the first example, it is clear that in the sentence *"I do"* grammatical *"I"* contains concept Harry, the bridegroom and *"do"* contains the meaning of the complex of verb phrase action expressed by: *"take Jane, to be my wife, to have and to hold, for better or for worse, for richer, for poorer, in sickness and in health, but not for lunch, to love and to cherish; from this day forward until death do you part"*. And, in the next example the meaning in *"do"* is expressed by *"swear to tell the truth the whole truth and nothing but the truth so help me God"*. But, the next time *"do"* is used it will mean something totally different in that context. These are examples of grammaticals serving data compression needs of discourse by replacing long text strings.

The Value of Grammaticals for a Human-Machine Interface

For a human-machine interface to be effective it is necessary to be able to both give very clear instructions and for the machine to be able to understand them perfectly. It is not possible to give a specific order of any complexity without using grammaticals. Key words cannot attain the necessary sensitivity and specificity essential to prevent mistakes. However, by parsing grammaticals for the meaning they contribute, one can give a precise instruction, an order to do something or not to do something, or never to do something, or to do it in a certain way at a certain time. Grammaticals provide flexibility to issue orders in your own words with only a responsibility to be clear and precise.

Lexical Words

If, as Talmy teaches, grammaticals are a closed class admitting no new members, lexicals are an open class with new words being dreamed up every day. The 2006 Official Scrabble Players Dictionary (OSPD) contains 178,691 words. Lexicals are classified according to which part of speech (POS) noun they belong, *noun, adjective, verb* or *adverb*. Lexicals are symbols that stand for known sensory patterns, which when heard or read will evoke the same mental concept as will the sensing of the real thing or of a graphic rendering of it.

However, most if not all lexical words have a grammatical within them, Modern English words of all parts of speech (POS) end in a systemic set of suffixes like –ly, -al, -ity, -ment, etc. The affixes of nouns and inflections of verbs are bound grammaticals. Meaning flows intraword from the lexical root into the grammatical suffix, the surviving concept. Thus, All lexical words are grammatacized, prefilled with lexical content. Because the suffix grammatical puts its well known stamp on a word's concept, this allows us to instantly add ten or more new lexical words to our vocabulary for every lexical root we learn. Here is our quibble with Talmy. He does not articulate that all lexical words are in fact grammaticals comprising an incorporated grammatical prefilled with meaning from its lexical root.

A word is an ordered series of symbols, letters. The simplest representation of flow of meaning within a word is between the morphemes. It appears that every lexical word has a surviving grammatical in it, receiving conceptual content from all of the other morphemes. The ordered series of morphemes constitute an intraword expression defining a binary tree;

language uses the same system from the most primitive concepts to the most complex.

Stanislas Dehaene in his book *Reading in the Brain,* realizes that the visual system treats lexical words as trees using the word *"unbuttoning"* as his example when he says *"The final point in visual processing leaves the word parsed out into a hierarchical structure, a tree made up of branches of increasing sizes whose leaves are the letters".*[8]

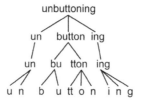

Fig. 2.2.8 Stanislas Dehaene's tree diagram for word "unbuttoning"

We can also model single lexical word concepts with *flow-of-meaning-trees* and *Mensa* tables. Fig. 2.2.9 shows *"unbuttoning"* modeled as a flow-of-meaning-tree and a *Mensa* table:

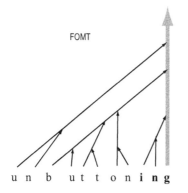

Mensa Table	
u ~ n	= un
b ~ u	= bu
t ~ t	= tt
bu ~ tt	= butt
o ~ n	= on
butt ~ on	= button
i ~ n	= in
in ~ g	= ing
button ~ ing	= buttoning
un ~ buttoning	= unbuttoning

Fig. 2.2.9 FOMT and Mensa table for word "unbuttoning"

Because the letters are ordered, adjacent letters fall into natural pairs that can be viewed as relations. Such a series of relations can organize a set of symbols into a congruent complex tree structure best modeled as a directed

---

8   Dehaene S. Reading in the Brain, VIKING, Penguin Group, New York, 2009, p.25

binary tree graph. Inside a word the morpheme relative symbols touch each other; there is no space between relative symbols; there is a default relation and so no relation symbol is necessary. Words can be thought of as "prepaired" concepts.

Within multisyllablic words meaning flows from left to right from the lexical syllable symbol into the grammatical suffix symbol concept. For example, within the word *"baker"* there is a relation between root concept *bake* and bound suffix grammatical concept *–er*. Lexical root **bake** and suffix **–er** are relatives in juxtaposition within the word with no space between them. Meaning flows from concept **bake** into concept **–er**. The **–er** grammatical is the surviving concept and puts its stamp on the word as a doer. The verb root **bake** indicates what is done. The sensory pattern of a lexical word root flows into its suffix or inflection, and the suffix in turn has an effect on the sense of the lexical root. When meaning flows between intraword relatives with no space between them, there is no need for explicit definition of the relation because it is the known default relation.

We will treat many other instances of meaning flow to grammatical suffixes within lexical words. Adverbs are generally marked with an **–ly** suffix bound grammatical that marks it as an adverb. Such adverbs are concept enriched grammaticals. The same applies to the following words:

Odd-**ity** amuse-**ment** red-**ness** deriva-**tive** petr-**ify** relat-**ion** fluoresc-**ent**

In terms of *flow-of-meaning-trees* and *M5 tables* one has to consider the suffix or inflection grammatical of lexical words to be the surviving symbol, enriched by the meaning of its root morpheme(s). Here **amuse** flows into **–ing**, **relative** flows into **–ity**. Intraword flow of meaning into a surviving grammatical is illustrated by the following *flow-of-meaning-trees* and *Mensa* row relations:

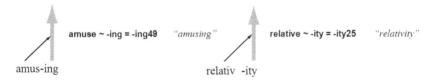

Fig. 2.2.10 FOMT and Mensa table for words "amusing " and "relativity"

Within a lexical word there is a relation between the root conceptual content and the bound grammatical suffix. Meaning flows into the suffix and vice versa. There is no space inside the word between the two relative symbols; the morpheme relatives touch each other. The default flow of meaning between root and suffix and therefore the relation between them is well known to the addressee and does not have to be specified with a intraword relational symbol.

If the suffix grammatical of lexical words is the surviving symbol receiving and shaping the flow of meaning from the lexical root, then the prefix grammatical of lexical words appears to control whether the flow of meaning occurs. For example, the **un** prefix of *"unamusing"* prevents **amuse** flowing into **–ing**. The prefix grammatical **un-** seems to be a control symbol that determines whether this meaning flow within the word occurs or not. In this case the **un-** grammatical at the beginning of the lexical word indicates that the verb action stops or flows backwards.

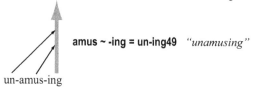

amus ~ -ing = un-ing49   *"unamusing"*

un-amus-ing

Fig. 2.2.11 FOMT and Mensa table for word "unamusing"

Affixes **un- in-** on lexical verbs reminds one of the transistor where a signal on the base terminal controls the flow of current from emitter to collector.

Nouns and Verbs

Except for adverbs, which are marked with an **-ly** suffix, all lexical words have unmarked grammaticals within them indicating which part of speech (POS) they are, noun, adjective or verb. Personal first names like *John* and *Julia* incorporate a gender grammatical. Some English nouns, and all French nouns carry gender not indicated with an explicit grammatical suffix, e.g. *man, girl, ship.* Count nouns like *house* and *tree* have an unmarked grammatical within them indicating they are bounded units. Mass nouns like *milk* and *water* also have an included unmarked *mass* grammatical that makes them unbounded. There are other lexical words where a covert plurality grammatical is incorporated, for example, *people* and *sheep.*

Another more subtle example of lexical nouns holding unmarked grammaticals occurs when they find themselves in subject position in a sentence. Third person subject noun phrases by virtue of their location in a finite sentence have an unmarked **he**, **she**, **it** or **they** grammatical within them and verb object noun phrases an unmarked **him**, **her**, **it**, or **them** within them.

Most verbal lexicals comprise lexical verb roots that enrich verb inflection grammaticals, **-es, -ed, -ing, -en, -ion, -ation, -ment.** Older English irregular strong verbs like, *steal/stole, stand/stood, take/took* lack a past tense **-ed** inflection, their tense being indicated by a contained hidden grammatical.

Here we get a glimpse of the distinction between verbs and nouns that allows us to understand exactly what confers nounhood or verbhood on a lexical word, Nouns enrich standard noun suffixes, verbs enrich standard verb inflections. A lexical word in *noun-subject* or *verb-object* position is a noun. The existential difference, however, is that a noun sensory pattern can be recognized in a photograph; recognizing a verb sensory pattern requires the passage of time, as in a video or moving picture.

BOOK II
CHAPTER III

Algebraic and Language Expressions

In this chapter, noting the power of symbols to model reality, we explore the close parallel between algebraic and language expressions. Lexical words, phrases, clauses, sentences and paragraphs can be mapped onto a directed binary tree structure. Algebraic expressions and equations also encode directed binary trees in a similar manner. We make clear exactly how our parser program works. And we demonstrate the ability of the same softwareparsertoparsebothalanguageandalgebraicexpression.

A lgebra operates effectively on symbols to model real world systems without having to consider what the symbols mean. Follow the formula mindlessly and get the right answer. We will show that language also operates on symbols in a very similar manner.

Frank Wilczek in his book *The Lightness of Being* quotes Heinrich Hertz, who uncovered the radio waves that Maxwell's equations had predicted:

> *"One cannot escape the feeling that these mathematical formulae have an independent existence and an intelligence of their own, that they are wiser than we are, wiser even than their discoverers"*

Wilczek also quotes Paul Dirac, whose equations predicted the existence of antimatter, when asked how he discovered new laws of nature:

> *"I play with equations"*

Paul Dirac liked to point out that he and his fellow discoverers of quantum mechanics did not comprehend why their equations worked. Leibniz called it "blind reasoning." Isaac Newton noted how powerful algebra was operating on symbols.

Harvard biologist Jeremy Gunawardena explains how the behavior of biological networks can be inferred mathematically from their architecture:

> *"Mathematical models are fashionable in systems biology, but there is a world of difference between a model and a theorem. When researchers build models, they make assumptions about a specific experimental setting and have to choose values for rate constants and other parameters. A theorem, by contrast, can apply to a setting of arbitrary molecular complexity, such as a biochemical network with many components."*
> Gunawardena, J, Biological Systems Theory, Science, 328, 581 – 582, 2010

Symbols have long been used in algebraic expressions and equations by scientists and engineers to create mathematical models with extraordinary explanatory and predictive power in many fields. Equations, by operating on symbols, can completely describe "the way it is" without ever having to assign absolute values to the symbols. Equations say a lot about a system before any value is put in any variable. The history of physics illustrates how powerfully equations model the world. Newton's equation: f=ma, Ohm's Law: V=IR, Einstein's equation: e=mc^2 are able to explain how the universe works with amazing fidelity. Simultaneous equations force variables to take absolute values. Equations are by far the most compact and powerful way to model the behavior of a system. Once we have the right equation we observe that the world has to obey it.

Algebraic expressions delineate an ordered series of binary mathematical operations to be performed in strict order of precedence. Language expressions delineate an ordered series of binary mental operations required to be performed in strict order of precedence. They assemble mentioned concepts into a unitary complex and define its structure in exact detail. If each symbol in an expression stands for a concept, then an expression is first of all simply an ordered list of the members of an associated group of concepts. The order of symbols in an algebraic expression has the effect of positioning symbols into adjacent pairs, which then interact with each other. Each interaction is a mathematical or mental operation that results in one symbol of the pair surviving, but transformed by the other. And the order of the symbols in the expression and the rules of syntax control the precedence of the operations, which is critical for its correct evaluation.

The power of identifying concepts with unique concept symbols and then modeling relations between complex concepts by relating the symbols is the strength of algebra. Simple symbols can stand for enormously complex concepts. Isaac Newton came to realize that manipulating symbols was a very powerful technique. A good example is how the law of gravity, which controls planetary systems, solar physics and vast galaxies, can be expressed by exploiting a very simple formula, $F = m_1 m_2 / d^2$, It is not surprising that evolution adopted the use of symbols to advance the functions of the human mind.

Algebraic Expressions Have a Tree Structure

Niklaus Wirth in his book *Algorithms + Data Structures = Programs*, in his chapter on tree variables, has some highly relevant things to say about algebraic expressions. We thank Wirth for pointing out to us that algebraic expressions have a tree structure.[1] Also Wirth explains how *"an arithmetic expression with dyadic operators"* functions *"with each operator denoting a branch node with its operands as subtrees".*[2] We highly recommend reading Wirth's chapter on tree variables.

---

1   Niklaus Wirth, *Algorithms + Data Structures = Programs*, Prentice Hall 1976 pp. 193-194

2   Niklaus Wirth, *Algorithms + Data Structures = Programs*, p.193

Wirth uses the algebraic expression **(a +)/c*(d - c*f)** as an example to show how an expression can be represented by a tree. Fig. 2.3.1 shows Wirth's diagram of the *tree*, of a component node *element*, and of the *array* implementing his tree variable for this expression:

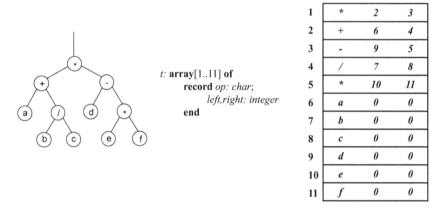

1	*	2	3
2	+	6	4
3	-	9	5
4	/	7	8
5	*	10	11
6	a	0	0
7	b	0	0
8	c	0	0
9	d	0	0
10	e	0	0
11	f	0	0

t: **array**[1..11] **of**
  record *op: char;*
    left,right: integer
  end

Fig. 2.3.1 Niklaus Wirth's diagrams of a tree representing an algebraic expression, a node of this tree and the array that represents this tree

His array lists the six leaf nodes and the five operations mentioned in the expression. One can see that each row of his array defines a node element and that his array as a whole defines the primary tree structure precisely.

Let's redraw Wirth's tree diagram to show his method of numbering nodes in binary trees so we can understand his table.

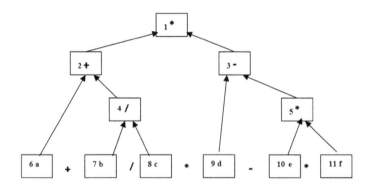

Fig. 2.3.2 Niklaus Wirth's tree diagram redrawn to show his method of numbering nodes

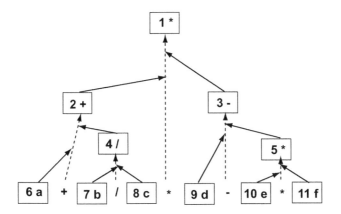

Fig. 2.3.3 Niklaus Wirth's tree diagram redrawn to show precedence of operations

Figs.2.3.3 and 2.3.4 show Wirth's tree morphing into the *flow-of-meaning-tree* of our system keeping its meaning identical.

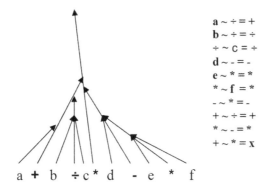

Fig. 2.3.4 Niklaus Wirth's tree diagram redrawn in our flow-of-meaning-tree format, with Mensa table

Higher level programming languages have elegant methods to implement trees. One standard way to represent trees they use is an array. Each row of a binary tree array specifies an *element* [3] consisting of a *root* and two

---

3   We will see that all words ending with suffix −**ment** represent tree concepts. The simplest **ment** (our neologism) tree consisting of just one root and two branch nodes is an ele-**ment**.

branch *nodes*. Each row of a *Mensa* table models a Wirth tree element, and even the final row where each of its two elements represents a complex sub-expressions. When a tournament reaches its final match, it becomes a single element with two branches, as Holmes would say, *"It's elementary, my dear Watson."*

Each element is assigned an index to identify it, which can be a integer or other unique symbol. And each element can carry information or "cargo" to organize items of information. Tree variables are widely used for sorting, modeling and indexing among other uses. They are dynamic, they can grow larger or smaller as programs that process them run. Our interest is in using trees for modeling declarative knowledge.

Parsing as a Tennis Tournament

We thank Wirth for pointing out that an algebraic expression defines a tree and that the history of a tennis tournament, *"with each game being denoted by its winner and the two previous games of its combatants as its descendants"*, is an excellent metaphor for helping understanding of how parsers process an expression to compute its meaning with successive rounds of concept matches. We will make use of the metaphor of the history of a tennis tournament throughout this essay, to explain how parsers work to parse language phrases, expressions sentences and paragraphs. A March Madness bracket is another well understood example of a binary tree.

Language concepts at all levels of complexity are structured as binary trees. The history of a tennis tournament, which is usually represented as a binary tree, is a very good analogy for a language expression. In a tennis tournament any one of the players can become the winner. In an expression any one of the symbols can become the **it** concept.

If we let Wirth's algebraic expression be equal to **x** as shown in the equation

$$x = a + b \div c * d - e * f$$

This equation can be represented perfectly by our *flow-of-meaning-tree* and orthographed as the above *Mensa* table. If expression **a + b ÷ c * d - e * f** is entered into our standard language parsing program accessing this *Mensa* table it will be parsed correctly to **x**.

In a *Mensa* table, algebraic operations are executed in two steps. We treat operators and operands as equal terms in the expression. We do this to make these operations binary and so much easier for our software to manage. First we enrich the relation, the algebraic operator, with the first relative, an operand, and then we further enrich it with the second relative, the other operand. As the surviving term product of the junction it recursively becomes a relative/operand in a higher order relation.

We feel that it is no coincidence that Wirth's tree diagram, node diagram and array representing an algebraic expression is precisely the same in structure as our *flow-of-meaning-tree*, *Mensa* table row and *Mensa* table array structure. Trees are well understood, both in terms of Graph Theory[4] and programming languages.[5]

Parsing Algebraic and Language Expressions

We will now demonstrate that algebraic and language expressions can be parsed in the same manner by showing that the exact same parser (askme. exe) that can evaluate an arithmetic expression can also parse a language expression. The same parser program, by doing lookup of a single *M5* database table, can a evaluate an algebraic expression and also parse a language expression that has the same tree structure. This demonstration will show how our parser program works and the principles behind our *Mensa* tables and *flow-of-meaning-trees*.

The *Mensa* table in Fig. 2.3.6 shows the seven term expression **304 * (637 + 214) ÷19**, specifying six arithmetical operations that result in a single surviving but enriched term. This table of such operations shows how each pair of adjacent symbols mentioned in the expression interact to produce a single surviving symbol that replaces the pair. Then, pairs of higher level surviving symbols interact in later rounds of the tournament to give surviving symbols until there is only one left, which represents the value or meaning of the whole expression.[6] This table format of six mathematical

---

4   Google "Graph Theory"

5   Niklaus Wirth, *Algorithms + Data Structures = Programs*, Prentice Hall 1976 pp. 189-242

6   Relating the symbols in pairs, "putting two and two together". This is maybe why the word *parsing*, (pairsing), has stuck to name the process; much more on pairing elsewhere

operations, *Mensa*, the *Fifth Medium* or *M5*, is exactly equivalent in every way to the expression itself.

Fig. 2.3.5 shows a run of the parser program on expression "304 * (637 + 214) ÷ 19 " directed by the *Mensa* table.

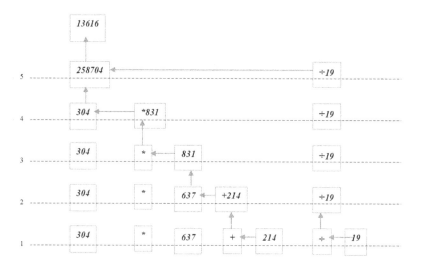

Fig 2.3.5 A run of the parser program on expression "304 * (637 + 214) ÷ 19 " directed by the Mensa table.

Here is narrative for the full series of operations specified by expression 304 * (637 + 214) ÷ 19. In the first round (of the tournament) as specified by the first two rows of the *Mensa* table, the **+** symbol, the generic multiply operator, is enriched by **214** to form special addition operator **+214**, i.e. *add* 214, that will add 214 to what it operates on; the **÷** symbol, the generic divide operator, is enriched by **19** to make it a special divide operator, **÷19**, i.e. *divide by 19*, that will divide what it operates on by 19. In the second round **+214** operates on **637** to put **831** into the third round where it enriches * to send special operator ***831** into the fourth round. In the forth round ***831** operates on **304** to place **258704** in the final round. In the final round **÷19** operates on **258704** to give **13616**, the value of he whole expression.

Now to explain this typical parser operation: the parser program has access to the table above which might be embedded in a large M5 database. *Mensa* table controls precedence of operations essential to evaluating an expression correctly. When this expression in input into our parser program, it will evaluate the expression by performing the operations in he correct order of precedence.

This is the same simple loop algorithm involving about five lines of code employed in Reverse Polish hand calculators. The results of operations are precalculated in an M5 table in the same way that operations are in a 1-12 multiplication table, so there is no need for the parser program to perform the calculations. The expression can be input into the parser without parentheses as precedence of operations is controlled by the *Mensa* table.

In Fig 2.3.6 see the tree graph made of arrows showing direction of flow of value (or meaning) from symbol to symbol until all the value (or meaning) rests in a single surviving symbol. It also shows the precedence of operations for operand **304** to be serially enriched from **304** to **13616** by inflows of value from two subtrees.

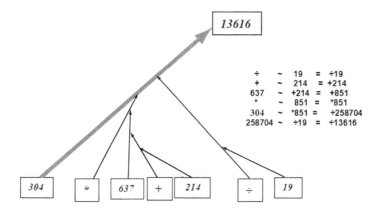

Fig 2.3.6 Flow of Meaning Tree and M5 Table of Operations essential to evaluating Expression 304 * (637 + 214)÷19

The narrative is the same for tree graph and the *M5 table* of operations of expression *"304 * (637 + 214) ÷ 19 "*: symbol *214* enriches symbol + and retires. Enriched symbol +*214* in turn enriches symbol **637**, which in turn enriches symbol *, which in turn enriches symbol **304**. Separately symbol **19** enriches symbol ÷ which further enriches enriched symbol **304**. It shows **304** being serially enriched from **304** to **13616**, an enriched version of **304**, by inflows of meaning from two subtrees.

Now we will show that a language expression and an algebraic expression both have the same underlying structure. Both are ordered lists of symbols that code for a binary tree structure, and both can be parsed for their meaning by a parser using equivalent rules of syntax. Our *flow-of-meaning tree* and *Mensa table* can represent a language expression just as well as it can represent an algebraic expression.

Another way to see an expression system like this is as a mathematical or software *function* with *arguments*.[7] Pick the first symbol of the function expression, the function name, as the **it** symbol. It operates on arguments in order, each time to map on to an enriched function, until the final result is returned into the function name variable. Such a function expression defines an ordered binary tree with much much simpler rules of syntax than apply in a regular function with many lines of code. In function theory this is called *currying*. [8]

In our system, we treat all three of the elements of language expression, lexical words, grammaticals and punctuation marks as symbols that stand for mental concepts. See in Fig. 2.3.7 that the *flow-of-meaning-tree* for the language expression *"Paris the city of light in Europe"* has an identical tree structure and *Mensa* table structure to the algebraic expression above but with algebraic symbols being replaced by language element symbols.

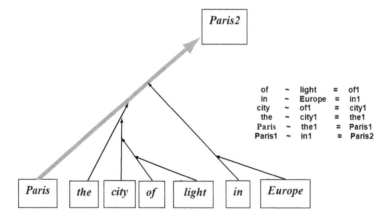

Fig 2.3.7 Flow of Meaning Tree for Expression "Paris the city of light in Europe"

---

7   Google "wiki mathematical function" I'm feeling lucky
8   Google "currying"

Here is a run of the parser program as it parses this language expression:

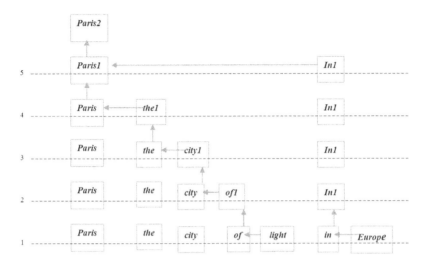

Fig 2.3.8 A Run of the Parser Program on Expression "Paris the city of light in Europe"

Here is narrative for the tree graph and the *M5* table of operations of expression *"Paris the city of light in Europe"*: symbol *light* enriches symbol *of* and retires. Symbol *of* in turn enriches symbol **city**, which in turn enriches symbol **the,** which in turn enriches symbol **Paris** to symbol **Paris1**. Separately symbol **Europe** enriches symbol **in** which further enriches symbol **Paris1**. It shows **Paris** being serially enriched from **Paris** to **Paris2**, a meaning enriched version of **Paris**, by inflows of meaning from two subtrees. Note that lexicals function as operands and grammaticals function as algebraic operators.

Notice that new symbols not present in the original expression have been created to stand for surviving higher level concepts formed as the original symbols of the expression are enriched. Just as the mind assigns a specific higher level cortical neuron to each more complex concept,[9] we assign a row in a database, a physical address in computer memory analogous to a neuron's location in the cortex.

Once it becomes clear that language expressions, like algebraic expressions, force their terms into pairs that match up and produce a survivor, thus

9   Stanislas Dehaene, *Thinking in the Mind,* pp. 131-140.

defining a binary tree, it is possible to see many aspects of linguistics and cognition in a different light. Language is a precise notation for the symbolic system the unconscious mind uses. Very compact language symbols, in the form of a string of words and punctuation marks, can evoke very rich non-graphic conceptual structures in the mind. The only sensory patterns used then are the very compact auditory or pictographic sensory patterns of the words themselves. Processing texts while reading or listening is largely automatic with little conscious appreciation of the sights or sounds of the actual symbols. It looks as if both natural language and algebra have succeeded to an ultimate degree in reducing complexity to a form that can "produce a detailed, accurate model of the natural world."

The Power of Expressions to Compress Knowledge

Because algebraic expressions are an ordered series of symbols which specify connections between adjacent symbols in order, they are an economic one dimensional way to specify the list of connections able to define a directed binary tree. Because the symbols are ordered, adjacent symbols fall into natural pairs that can be viewed as relations. Such a series of relations can organize the whole set of symbols into a congruent complex structure. And this structure is best modeled as a graph, as a directed binary tree. The lexicals of the expression are the leaves of the tree and the grammaticals are the articles, nodes that match up in later rounds of the tournament. Faithful to the theorems of Graph Theory both algebraic expressions and language expressions powerfully direct the construction of complex mathematical constructs.[10]

Following the rules of English syntax, which operate just like the rules of a tennis tournament, expressions mention the **it** symbol first. The flow of meaning is generally from right to left through the ordered symbols, words and punctuation marks, of an expression into the first symbol. There are important exceptions to this left to right syntax rule which will be discussed fully. A language expression, with its strict order of symbols, specifies precedence of "relay of meaning operations", and thus specifies precisely just how meaning flows to the end **it** symbol. The end symbol, the **it** symbol, the **it** of *"that's it"*, becomes a unitary symbol that can, once having received meaning from all the other symbols in the expression, serve to represent the meaning of the whole expression. An end **it** symbol thus

---

10 Google "Graph Theory" I'm feeling lucky

represents an "ent-**it**-y" concept. Thus, symbol order in the expression is critical for directing meaning into the **it** symbol, linearly, from right to left, from each and every other word or punctuation symbol of the expression.

With access to a *Mensa* table our parser program can put "two and two together", i.e. sort concept symbols into pairs. Each pairing of concepts is a relation. It can *parse* an expression to one surviving unitary concept enriched with meaning from all the other concepts **ment**ioned in the expression, and control the precedence of mental operations preventing premature relations. The table also ensures that they will occur at the right level, i.e. in the right round of the tennis tournament, only when subconcepts are sufficiently assembled to be joined together. If there are **n** terms in an expression there are a minimum of **n-1** matches. More if there is a need to accommodate synonyms and paraphrases that people might use yet preserve the same meaning. The importance of the *Mensa* table lies in the fact that it enables the exact same parser program that can evaluate an arithmetic expression to parse a language expression and identify precisely which unified concept it means. The structure and function of *Mensa* tables and their interaction with our software based parser are at the heart of our system of natural language processing and modeling of human thought. *Mensa* tables raise the hope that an uncomprehending computer can be programmed to mimic human thought by manipulating symbols according to the methods of algebra.

BOOK II
CHAPTER IV

How Language Expressions Work
to Build Complex Relationship

A well constructed language expression that makes sense addresses a very particular complex concept. And expressions mention enough of the key concepts taking part in the complex to allow construction of a full mental picture in our minds. Their symbols (words and punctuation marks) are in an order that allows adjacent symbols to fall naturally into pairs. Meaning flows from symbol to adjacent symbol of each pair in both directions and then is relayed on to other symbols so that each symbol in an expression receives meaning from every other symbol directly or indirectly. All concepts adjust their sense to fit in. This many-to-many meaning flow is captured by picking one concept to be the **it** *concept and designing the expression that directs all meaning flow to that one* **it** *concept, which now represents the whole relationship of concepts.* **It** *binds all the concepts together so that meaning from every mentioned concept is entailed. If desired, the addressee can calculate not only the sense of* **it** *but also the importance and meaning of each mentioned concept, and also of other concepts implied but not mentioned. This clever method of tournament and path was invented in lockstep with language by the intelligent designer, evolution, 200,000 years ago. With Mensa tables we can readily biomimic this technique in the computer to obtain the same power in building and managing relationships between symbols representing mental concepts.*

T he purpose of this chapter is to show the power of an expression to gather and organize a roster of concepts. A well constructed language expression that makes sense puts all its mentioned concepts in their correct place in relation to each other, thereby defining the structure that makes them a single coherent system, a cohesive unit of thought into which all of the concepts mentioned have contributed meaning. We will call this unitary mental concept the **it** concept, the **it** of *"that's it"* and *"he doesn't get it"*. The **it** grammatical symbol is the survivor symbol that, when an expression is parsed, will have received meaning from all the other concepts mentioned. How concept **it** is arrived at, the path to **it** defined by an expression, can be illustrated with a *flow-of-meaning-tree* and defined precisely with a *Mensa table*.

Each symbol receives meaning directly from a flanking symbol but indirectly from each and every one of the other symbols by relay. Every symbol contributes meaning to every other symbol. Meaning flow is many-to-many. Change one symbol in the system, add or remove one, and all the others change reciprocally. First, each party concept is put in correct relation with all the others. And, then, each concept, once in the group, adapts in a special way to fit in with the others in the group. Change trembles back and forth the through the system until it settles down in equilibrium. This is very analogous to a spreadsheet where values in cells related by algebraic formulae settle down to a new equilibrium after the value in any one is changed.

Meaning from each symbol does not flow directly to the **it** symbol. It is relayed, modified and filtered through intermediary relaying symbols. Each relay step is a mental operation and the order of precedence of these operations is critical. In language, only one pathway of meaning flow out of many, may be intended by the author, but once this one pathway is defined by a sensible expression, all of the other possible pathways of meaning flow are implicit and can be derived. And the marvelous part is that a single expression of ordered symbols can fully entail the overall many-to-many meaning flow of the complex system and fix the precise adjusted sense of each of the party concepts. In every expression that makes sense, when a single default relay path is defined, the meaning flow to each of the other symbols is implicit. There is no need for explication of these other paths since the reader is free to explore them mentally.

It would seem like a very difficult task to model the omnidirectional meaning flow that occurs in a system like this, and the extremely complex set of relations between all the concepts. However, both language (and algebraic) expressions have found a binary way to greatly simplify the orthography. In a coherent system of symbols denoted by an expression that makes sense, one master final receiver symbol, the **it** symbol, is chosen to receive meaning from all the other symbols. Since every symbol in a related system of symbols receives meaning directly and indirectly from each of the other symbols, the choice of the **it** symbol is arbitrary. Because any expression comprises a string of symbols, an author can reorder an expression to make any one of them enrich to the intended surviving **it** concept. And which concept is intended by the author to become the **it** must be settled on by the second person. The literary context often determines which meaning an author intends.

Language Expressions Are Trees

Concepts at all levels of complexity can be precisely named by a language expression which defines the structure of a particular binary tree. The history of a tennis tournament, which is usually represented on the scoreboard as a binary tree, is a very good analogy for a language expression at work. Before a tennis tournament any one of the players can theoretically become the winner. Analagously, any one to the symbols in an expression can end up as the **it** concept. One can view an expression as picking the winning symbol and tilting the playing field to such an extreme as to force that symbol's path to **it** through several rounds of a tournament. However, the chosen symbol when **it** reaches the final is very different from what **it** was in the first round, greatly modified by **its** interactions with other symbols on **its** way to the top. **It** has assumed a particular one of billions of possible configurations governed by the order of the symbols in the expression.

A Word is an Expression

A word, an ordered string of phonemes, is a language expression How many concepts can be addressed by a single word expression? With 42 phonemes available in English to be paired up, each word of two phonemes can specify any one of 42^2 or 1744 pathways for its survivor to go. If a word comprises **n** phonemes, and they are randomly matched into pairs of adjacent phonemes, with survivors being matched again in subsequent rounds of the tournament, the number of possible tournament structures can be calculated to be about 1744^{2n-1}. This number is much limited by the rules of phonology which forbid many matches, but for all practical purposes the number of words that an ordered string of phonemes can define is infinite. Less than a million of these possibilities are words in actual use. Then, how many concepts can be addressed by a language expression? An expression of just several words can address can address a space of an infinite number of concept.

Expressions that Don't Make Sense

The meaning of an expression is contributed to critically by the order of its words. Change the order of even one word and an expression will often no longer make sense. If it does by coincidence it may mean something else in a different context. It is necessary for a parser to be able to determine when an expression does not make sense. The test is whether all of the party concepts represented by bye ordered symbols in the expression list can be incorporated in the *flow-of-meaning-tree* with no loose ends.

For example, the expression *"the truth about American manufacturing"* makes sense. It precisely describes a clear concept. Fig. 2.4.1 shows the *flow-of-meaning-tree* diagramming the parsing for this expression:

the truth about American manufacturing

Fig. 2.4.1 Flow-of-meaning-tree for the expression "the truth about American manufacturing".

Here is the valid *Mensa* table for this expression:

the ~ truth	**= the345**	*"the truth"*
American~manufacturing	**= manufacturing01**	*"American manufacturing"*
About~manufacturing01	**= about438**	*"about American manufacturing"*
the345~ about438	**= the34538**	*"the truth about American manufacturing*

With access to this *Mensa* table our software parser can determine that the expression means a very specific concept, i.e. concept **the34538**. All of the party concepts are joined in appropriately. And, with access to this table our parser can determine that any one of the other 119 order variant expressions (factorial 5 minus 1) using the very same words in different order do not parse to make sense.

Fig. 2.4.2 shows *flow-of-meaning-trees* for two order variants of the above expression: *"truth the about American manufacturing"* and *"the manufacturing about American truth"*, that have just one word moved.

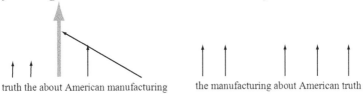

truth the about American manufacturing   the manufacturing about American truth

Fig. 2.4.2   "Pointless" *flow-of-meaning-trees* show failure of concepts to connect up".

The *FOMTs* for this expression with a word moved no longer connect all the concepts, do not make an **it**, do not make sense. Although, with a stretch, in another context, an FOMT for variant *"*the manufacturing about American truth"* could be contrived that would allow this expression to make some sense.

Our parser program determines that an expression does not make sense or is bad grammar when it cannot parse the expression down to one single **it** concept, taking into account all of the words and punctuation marks. There are connections missing in the *flow of meaning tree*, which in this case literally shows that the expression "does not make a point".[1]

Now, here are two exemplar expressions showing exactly how an author can intend two very similar phrases to parse into two different type **it** symbols. The phrases *"changing times"* and *"changing tires"* differ in only one letter and appear to have the same grammatical structure. Fig. 2,4,3 shows their *FOMTs* and *Mensa tables*. Our *FOMT* and *Mensa* tools show precisely how the human mind parses one to a noun concept and the other to a verb action concept and a *Mensa table* provides a computer with

---

1   Using "pointless" *flow of meaning trees* in conjunction with N-400 experiments might provide extra insights.

the means to do the same. It's up to the addressee to figure out the author's intention, to identify the **it** concept at the start and enrich it serially by meaning flow from peer concepts.

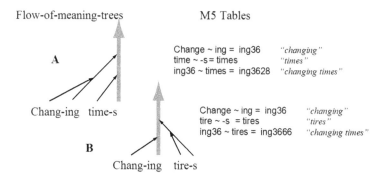

Fig. 2.4.3 FOMT distinguishing between expressions "changing tires" and "changing times".

Both expressions parse to an **it**. However, parse A parses its expression to what we call an *endit*, end **it** or entity noun concept, and parse B parses its expression to a mean**it**. or *ment*, which is in essence an enriched relation concept. Parsers of expressions must be able to determine for any expression which of these two ways a parse will go. This is a truly global problem that entails some new rules of syntax, a more inclusive English grammar. We deal with it more fully in our discussion of subordinate clauses and finite sentences.

Next, *"The benefits of a lowfat diet"* is an *endit* expression where relational grammatical concept **of** relays a determiner **a** concept into a determiner **the** concept.

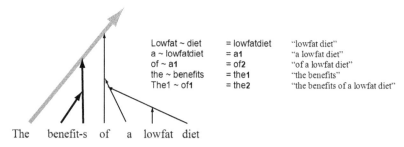

Fig. 2.4.4 FOMT and Mensa table for the expression "the benefits of a lowfat diet".

Narrative: **lowfat** enriches **diet** which then relays meaning to article **a** which in turn adds meaning to **of**. Determiner concept **the** is enriched to **the2**, first by **benefits** and then from meaning relayed via **of**, to produce a highly differentiated **the** concept. One can see from the meaning-flow-tree and the M5 table in Fig.2.4.4 how meaning from all the terms flows into single surviving grammatical **the**, making an *endit*.

Fig 2.4.5 shows a flow-of-meaning-tree and *Mensa* table for the phrase *"up with which I will not put"* famously attributed to Winston Churchill.[2] They show how the expression parses simply and correctly to an enriched **up** grammatical.

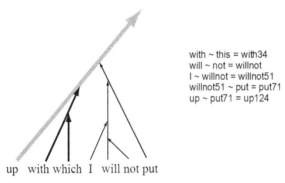

with ~ this = with34
will ~ not = willnot
I ~ willnot = willnot51
willnot51 ~ put = put71
up ~ put71 = up124

up with which I will not put

Fig. 2.4.5 FOMT and Mensa table for the expression "up with which I will not put".

With access to a table it is trivial for our parser to parse this intricate **up** concept expression, which even demands a degree of parsing dexterity from a human mind. *Flow-of-meaning-trees* and *Mensa* tables can show graphically the order of precedence of serial relay of meaning from each and all of the symbols of a long sentence into a surviving grammatical to make a complex enriched **it** concept.

Group Expressions

This is a good point to discuss how the mind models group concepts, groups of things, groups of concepts, pluralities, using grammaticals **and** and **or**. Expressions defining **and** and **or** groups are ubiquitous in language texts and, like all expressions, parse to a single unitary concept that represents the whole group.

---

2   Google "up with which I will not put"

Consider the group concepts s expressed by *"mother and father"* and *"horse and carriage"*.

Fig. 2.4.6 shows the flow-of-meaning-trees and   for this group expression.

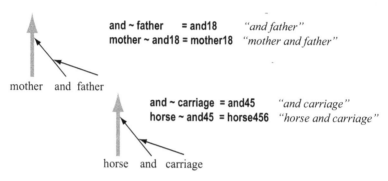

Fig. 2.4.6   FOMT for two group expressions.

Here, **mother, father**, **horse** and **carriage**, are relative entity concepts and concept **and** is a relation concept. Meaning flows from the second entity into concept **and**, which then becomes an "and" concept in the sense of *"no ifs ands or buts"*. Then, **and** relays its meaning back into the first entity to morph the single concept into a plurality concept, from a *mother* into *parents*, from a *horse* into a *transport vehicle*.

For another example take the expression *"Tom, Dick and Harry"*, which expresses a group of three concept. Fig. 2.4.7 shows the *flow-of-meaning-tree* and *Mensa table* for this group expression.

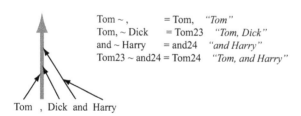

Fig. 2.4.7 Flow-of-meaning-trees and Mensa rows showing construction of group expression "Tom Dick and Harry".

Here concept **Tom** at first represents a single person, a group of one, and is bundled into a comma to make **Tom,** comma concept. **Dick** is added in to make **Tom23,** concept, a group of two. **Harry** is bundled into **and** concept to make **andHarry.** Then concept **andHarry** is added to **Tom23** to make **Tom 24**, a group of three. An *"or"* in the expression would make the whole group a singleton **or** group.

The way that groups are modeled in language in the mind is informative about meaning flow in expressions allowing some remarkable effects to be achieved. One curious function of an **and** group is that it shifts its relatives into a certain class set by the first mentioned member. When a concept is put into an **and** group expression like *"knaves, thieves and Republicans"*, Republicans are forced into a class in a way that may not be flattering. Another example: - there is a lot going on in this expression - *"A bar frequented by whores, smugglers, policemen and lawyers"* - the order of terms matters. The author's intent here is to set the tone by starting the with a lowlife kind of person, *whores*, reinforce criminality with *smugglers*, endow these characteristics on *policemen* establishing the idea that mainstays of the law can be corrupt, and then add *lawyers*, who are supposed to be the height of probity, to this camp, calling to mind the old hate-lawyers saw, deriving intended humor from the contrast between the two views of lawyers. To use *as well as* after *smugglers* instead of *and* would redeem *policemen* and *lawyers* by allowing them to be a respectible subgroup of frequenters of the bar. Group concepts do illustrate the truly awe-inspiring power of expressions to manipulate the sense of party concepts. Another example of expressions being as economical as possible in expressing subtle meaning and subtext.

The Tree is Universal in Nature

Expressions define trees to organize complex concepts. But this is in line with nature in general. A word is a tree. All plants and the roots of plants are "trees". The animal body can be modeled as a tree as can the solar system. The placenta is an actual tree. The Bible, book, chapter and verse, is a tree. Trees appear to be the general construction system of life, and language.

A good example of the power of compact expressions to define trees that model things in the world is to use a tree defining expression to model the arrangement of atoms in two molecules with the same atomic elements.

Take the formula for the ethanol molecule: C_2H_5OH

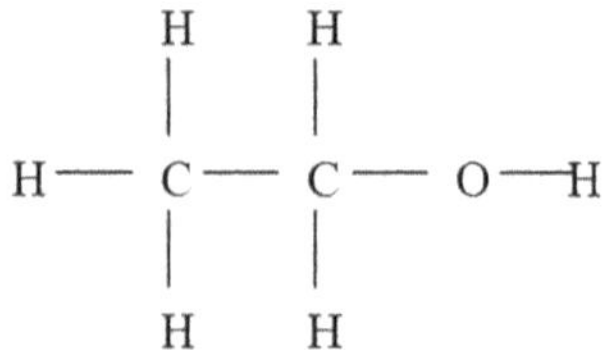

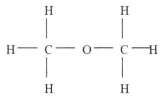

Fig. 2.4.8 Chemical structure of the ethanol molecule: CH_3OCH_3

Dimethyl ether comprises the same elements in a different structure: CH_3OCH_3

Fig. 2.4.9 Chemical structure of the dimethyl ether molecule

The ethanol molecule can be represented by the following one dimensional string of atomic symbols: H H H C C H H O H. And, when this spaced string of symbols is input into our parser program, it gets parsed and the output is *"ethanol"*.

Here is the ethanol molecule modeled with a flow-of-meaning-tree (FOMT):

C_2H_5OH

H H H C C H H O H

Fig. 2.4.10 FOMT for the ethanol molecule

The dimethyl molecule can be modeled with the same set of symbols in a different order, encoding a different *FOMT* structure.

CH_3OCH_3

H H H C O C H H H

Fig. 2.4.11 FOMT for the dimethyl ether molecule

This molecule can be represented by the expression: H H H C O C H H H, for which, upon input into our parser, the output is *"dimethyl ether"*.

Here is the combined 11 row *Mensa* table that enables parsing expressions defining either molecule:

H ~HHC	= HHHC	*"methyl"*
C ~ H	= CH	" ... "
CH ~ H	= CHH	" ... "
HHHC ~ CHH	= HHHCCHH	" ... "
O ~H	= OH	*"hydroxy"*
HHHCCHH ~ OH	= HHHCCHHOH	*"ethanol"*
C ~ H	= CH	" ... "
CH ~ H	= CHH	" ... "
CHH~H	= CHHH	*"methyl"*
HHHC ~ O	= HHHCO	" ... "
HHHCO ~ CHHH	= HHHCOCHHH	*"dimethyl ether"*

The important point to be made here and in the chapters on paths, tournaments, and algebra is that language expressions are not unstructured information as it is usually characterized. Expressions are exquisitely highly structured for a parser who/that respects the order of symbols and knows the applicable rules of syntax. Mensa tables bypass this requirement completely, with human preparsing of language into a format that renders the information accessible to a simple and mindless parser program that knows nothing.

BOOK II
CHAPTER V

How Finite Sentences Work to Apply Reality to Concepts

The main function of a finite sentence is for an observer to describe an act of observation, by mentioning all the concepts observed and by defining the structure of the relationship that exists between them. This observed relationship of concepts models the way it is in the world. Finite sentences, as opposed to non-finite expressions, parse to enrich a very special type of relational grammatical, a seam concept, to become an observation concept. Finite sentences are bimodal, subject-seam sentences with the seam in the subject, and predicate sentences, where the seam is on the verb. The seam is the main central grammatical of a sentence accruing conceptual content from all the other concepts mentioned. It stamps its accrued content as comprising what is being seen in the mind of the author of the sentence, which content mirrors what exists in the present real world or in an imaginary world. Thus, the seam grammatical of a sentence is key to how language confers existence, non-existence or modality upon concepts mentioned in the sentence and upon the relations observed between them. A second person, hearing or reading the sentence, can rerun the observation in his mind and make a copy of the observation concept in his long term memory. Thus, a finite sentence can communicate a statement, a state of affairs, an event, an action, a custom, a habit, a rule, a process or a project.

A finite sentence is a language expression that expresses in symbols what is seen when its narrator makes an observation on the real world or on a world in his memory. All finite sentences involve both consciousness and attention and contain a *seam symbol*. What is a *seam symbol*? To understand how a sentence works we had to notice that at the core of every sentence there is an explicit or implicit *seam grammatical*, a special kind of grammatical that turns an expression into a finite sentence. Finite sentences fall into two types: *subject-seam sentences* where the seam is found in the subject phrase, attached to an auxiliary verb or modal, and *predicate sentences*, where the seam is the **-s** or **-d** verb inflection of the lexical verb.[1]

A well constructed finite sentence mentions all the concepts in a local world system that are sensed and defines how they are related to each other. Therefore, the common purpose of all finite sentences is for an observer to use an ordered string of symbols to define a *relationship-of-concepts*. And then to indicate whether he does or does not see this *relationship-of-concepts*, which means that that *relationship-of-concepts* does or does not exist in the world he is observing. The seam grammatical endows the *relationship-of-concepts* with reality, or not. Or, by using a seam modal, it can state the likelihood that it does or does not exist.

Observers record their observations with finite sentences, an order of words and punctuation marks that expresses what is observed. The symbols reflect concepts aroused in the observer's consciousness, their arrangement mirroring what he sees or saw out there in the physical world, or retrieves from a memory world. The thought, the way it is in the world, and the ordered symbols of a sentence are all equivalent. Importantly, the observer notices and records what is missing there as well. He compares what he sees with his *idea* of what he should see. He might say *"This is not my idea of a good steak"*.

A finite sentence can communicate its contained knowledge to a second person. As an observer utters and second person hears a sentence they monitor the mental operations evoked in consciousness to see if they make sense. Sentences can tell the second person stuff he does not know or remind him of something he does. A finite sentence can communicate a

---

1   This leads to the idea of a subject-seam as a linguistic entity on the same rank in grammar as a predicate.

statement, a state of affairs, an event, an action, a custom, a habit, a rule, a process or a project.

All finite sentences and mental observations involve both consciousness and attention. Both understanding and uttering a sentence is a mental operation integral with an active conscious thought, mustering concepts into a structured whole. The neurons corresponding to observed features of the world fire for hundreds of milliseconds. And, if what is observed is important enough, a trace of the firing will be stored immediately by Long Term Potentiation (LTP), and much more permanently in long term memory in both cortices as an *observation concept* that can be reenacted in consciousness at will.[2] The mind's eye can make an equivalent observation in an imaginary world that exists only in the mind. An observation concept, although inert in stored memory, can, like a software program, be rerun to cause a mental thought and or an utterance. Of course such a recall may closely parallel what went on out in a world that the observer is not presently observing. An observer can have a silent thought where there is no utterance, or the thought can be voiced via Broca's area in the lower left prefrontal cortex.

Whenever an observer senses the world he experiences a conscious experience of what he senses in his mind. The limbic system of the brain is activated: thalamus, hippocampus, amygdala, et al.[3] And, if the observation involves graphic sensory patterns, it may be a very rich conscious experience. If it involves emotions he may experience strong conscious feelings. Individual observations activate conscious concepts for 750 milliseconds but their information is held in *short term memory* and or *working memory* for up to thirty seconds so they can interact with the next and previous observations.

The Seam Grammatical

Finite sentences contain a *seam grammatical*, non-finite expressions do not. The presence of a *seam* in an expression makes an expression into a sentence. But wait, o'boy, o'boy, hey, the seam differs but good from the other grammaticals!![4] The seam is the one grammatical that indicates that

---

2   Google "LTP" 'long term memory" "short term memory"
3   Google "limbic system"
4   Wake up!

the concepts mentioned in the language of the sentence are being sensed live by the speaker and therefore have existence in the world observed.

One can look at this way: as a sentence is parsed the *seam concept* receives meaning from all the other concepts **ment**ioned in the sentence. Seam symbols are serially enriched to become, just like other grammaticals, a container of conceptual content relayed from all the other symbols of a finite sentence. Thereby, the seam concept of a sentence becomes the final survivor of the parser tournament, a *ment* concept.

Just like every other grammatical, a *seam grammatical* puts its own special stamp or mold on the conceptual content that it obtains. Thereby, by virtue of its idiosyncratic stamp the *seam* the sentence declares that its concepts exist or don't exist in the real world or in an imaginary world; thereby recording reality as the *observer* is seeing **it**. A seam containing this congruent complex of observed and implied concepts comprises a unitary **it** concept, an *observation concept*. And, because the **it** of an observation stands for what is seen and what is not seen, finite sentences are the way an observer bestows existence and reality, or not, on the whole assembly of related concepts that are mentioned in or implied by the sentence. The seam grammatical is a truly critical idea in the conceptual framework we describe in this essay.

When a sentence is parsed so that the surviving concept is the *seam* enriched with meaning from all the other concepts, we call it a *ment* concept. Parsing the string of symbols **ment**ioned in a sentence for understanding is a **ment**al process. Lexical words enriching a –**ment** suffix grammatical, like state-**ment** instru-**ment** resent-**ment** argu-**ment** docu-**ment**, all stand for *ment* concepts, the root node of a sentence parse tree.

The most used seam is grammatical **is**, which basically means *"I see"*. The meaning of the statement *"the folder is on the desk"* which expresses a particular reality is the same as *"I see the folder ... on the desk"*. The seam's contents comprise what the observer first sees or saw. The order during parsing in which concepts are enclosed into the seam or the point where the seam confers reality on already parsed concepts is important. In this *subect-seam* sentence, concept **thefolder** is realized first. I see the folder first, establishing its presence in my view and thereby its reality. Then concept **onthedesk** is folded into the seam, further enriching the seam, thus establishing this **on** relation and making the desk real.

Or one can look at it another way: when the seam grammatical is reached in parsing it confers reality on the concepts parsed up to that point. Now, under this idea, that parsed concept, not the *seam* will be the surviving **it** concept but now denoted as real. The reality rule is: once something has been **is** (i.e. seen), it is ex-**is**, it exists, and concepts related to a concept that exists also exist. These alternatives result in two different *flow-of-meaning-tree* structures. However both work equally well to serve our software parser, and we will use the more convenient one in any one instance.

Finite sentences are constructed in the same way as any other complex expression except that they declare that the concepts mentioned and their organization exist. Whereas non-finite language expressions may describe a complex concept minutely and refer to real things that can exist in the world, they do not confer existence on what is described. On the other hand, by virtue of their seam concept finite sentences do describe what does exist in the real world or in imaginary worlds. They also can indicate what does not exist or what might or might not exist under certain conditions. Non-existence or conditional existence usually has just as strong implications for the world as existence does. Finite sentences say something about whether things exist and how things are and confer reality on the concepts mentioned.

A parallel is relevant, the parallel of language to algebra. We argue elsewhere that a language expression is an algebraic *expression*; that a finite sentence is an algebraic *equation*. An algebraic expression is in essence an ordered listing of terms and the mathematical operations required to be performed on them in order of precedence to calculate a value for that expression; it defines an algebraic entity with structure. Algebraic expressions, although essential components of equations do not by themselves say anything. On the other hand, an algebraic equation says something: it states that expressions on two sides of an *equals sign* are equivalent, i.e. that both have equal values on some scale, normally on a numeric scale. It rules that a change in a value on one side of an equation forces a change in a value on the other side, thus tightly controlling how **it** has to be. It takes an equation to say something about how things are.

If a finite sentence is an equation, where is its equals sign? Think of it like this: the *seam concept* of a finite sentence is its *equals sign*. It equates the conceptual structure built from the language symbols of the finite sentence and the conceptual structure in the mind of the observer. If the observer believes what he is saying, a *seam concept* also equates the concepts in an observer's mind with the reality out in the world that the sentence describes. There is a one-to-one relation between the conceptual structure expressed by the language of the sentence, between the conceptual structure of what is in the mind of the observer, and the reality of what the observer sees in his present world.

World

Every finite sentence has a bimodal property which we will call *world*, which divides the set of all finite sentences into two non-intersecting sets, telling us which *world* the described *relationship-of-concepts* is in. *World* may be the present real world of the speaker, or the *world* where, in Martin Joos' words, *"the referent is absent from that part of the real world where the verb is being spoken"*. Joos, in his discussion of English *tense* uses the terms *actual tense* and *remote tense*.[5] There is an absolute dichotomy between sentences that talk about **how it is** both in the mind of the observer and in the present real world of the observer, and sentences talk about **how it is** just in the mind or memory of the observer and no longer or not yet in the real world. This dichotomy is exactly the dichotomy between present and past tense or between indicative and subjunctive moods. World is determined by strictly bimodal seam concepts.

We will argue that it the *seam grammatical* that determines which world a sentence describes. The two non-intersecting sets of *seam* concept grammaticals that declare *world* are:

> 1. in *subject-seam sentences* the seam carriers, **is does has**, and the "present tense" seam carrying modals **will shall may can**, and in *predicate sentences* the seam symbol **-s** inflection of lexical verbs, all indicate that the sentence is describing the present real world of the observer

> 2. in *subject-seam sentences* the seam carriers **was were did had**, and the "past tense" seam carrying modals **would should might could**, and in *predicate sentences* the seam symbol **-d** inflection of lexical verbs, which do double duty, seam and

---

5   Martin Joos, *The English Verb*, The University of Wisconsin Press, Madison, Milwaukee and London, 1968, pp.120-126.

world to indicate that the sentence is describing an imaginary
or remembered past world.

Thus, every sentences deals with and settles which world the observer
is observing, the present world of the observer or a world that no longer
corresponds to the present real world, which may be the real past world or
it may be an imaginary world existing only in the mind. However, lessons
learned from doing "thought experiments" which involve real things but in
an imaginary world can be very valuable and apply to real strategies.

Seam Placement Manages Sentence Nuance

Sentence nuance can be fine tuned by where the seam concept is placed in
a sentence. We will now examine the several sentence seam placements
in order and note the effects obtained. When the sentence is parsed to
make the seam the main survivor concept of the observation it makes a
statement. Other mentioned concepts serially enrich the seam in strict
order of precedence as determined by word order and rules of syntax. On
the other hand, when the sentence is parsed mentally to make the subject
the **it** concept of the sentence, the seam's role is to confer reality on the
subject concept and its relations to other concepts mentioned.

Seams in First, Second and Third Person Sentences

We will first look for the seam in sentences where singular first person
pronoun **I** is the subject. Here the seam is covert inside subject pronoun
I, which becomes a *subject-seam*. How does first person subject pronoun
I by itself have an internalized seam function that confers reality on the
relation of the sentence between I and its following object concept? Well,
first person observer **I** (eye) does not have to "see" himself to know he
exists - *"Cogito ergo sum"*. **I** "knows" whether what's in his own mind
exists.[6] Then, if **I** exists, concepts related to **I** in the sentence exist without
the need for another seam grammatical to realize them, following the
rule that concepts related to an concept that exists also exist. Anyhow,
grammatical **I** is a natural place to hold a covert seam function; the eye (**I**)
is clearly the equals sign between concepts in the brain and their correlates
in the outside world. For this reason, no overt seam like **-s** inflection on the

---

6   One gets into very interesting aspects of linguistics and metaphysics when
     the observer or his addressee is the subject of a sentence. We leave existential
     philosophers more expert than us to sort all this out.

verb is required in first person present tense sentences when **I** is followed by a *have*, or *do* auxiliary or any other lexical verb.

In the sentence *"I bake a good pie"* the seam concept is covert in subject concept **I** and concept **bakeagoodpie** is the "seamless" verb phrase object of the subject relative. Because it is "seamless" it does not contribute to the statement's reality. This renders its object relative as a verb phrase with a bare uninflected verb. We consider that such a verb phrase is not a *predicate*.

On the other hand **I** past tense sentences depicting a relation in a memory world require a overt **-ed** seam to indicate *world*, e.g. *"I walk-ed down the street" "You ask-ed for it" "I bak-ed a good pie"* Here we argue that the seam is covert in the **I**, that the first person pronoun establishes reality, and the only function of **–ed** is *world*.

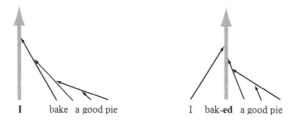

Fig. 2.5.1 Flow-of-meaning-trees illustrating presently real and not presently real first person observations.

Singular first person present tense verb *be* sentences with subject **I** always use seamlike symbol *am* and start with *"I am ... "* as in *"I am a dilettante"*.[7] One can debate whether the seam of the sentence is carried in seamlike symbol **am** rather than in **I**. Or **am** just reinforces first person. It doesn't matter. Either way there is finitude.

The same lack of an overt seam applies with second person addressee pronoun **you**. Present tense sentences with subject **you** do not require an overt seam either, e.g. as in *"You tell a good story."* How can second

---

7   Why this exception? A sentences like "I be confused" should be grammatical if the seem is covert in subject **I**, Although it is clearly a finite assertion, doesn't feel grammatical. Seam *am* may be residual from olden times when English strictly demanded agreement of person between subject and relation in a sentence.

person subject pronoun **you** carry a seam, confer reality? Well, the first person knows the second person exists and therefore does not have to "see" **you** to "realize" **you**. Just as **I** know **I** exist **I** know **you**, as my addressee, exist. So, following the rule that once concepts are related to an existing concept they too exist, any concepts related to second person **you** in a sentence exist without the need for another seam grammatical.

You   tell a good story

Fig. 2.5.2 Flow-of-meaning-tree illustrating hidden seam in 2nd person pronoun You.

So, concept **tellagoodstory** and the relation between it and **you** are realized. As with first person sentences, second person sentences require an inflected verb to indicate unreal or past *world*. Third person pronoun subject singular sentences require an overt seam symbol, because the observer looks out to see a relation a third person is party to.

Seams in Plural Subject Sentences

The next example of seam concepts being associated with the subject concept first occurs in present tense sentences with plural subjects, e.g. as in *"Australian-s travel"*. Now, the pluralizing **-s** suffix of the subject noun has become the seam symbol of the sentence, literally jumping off the main lexical verb onto the subject. In plural subject clauses, grammatical suffix **-s** does double duty, indicating *plurality* and being the *seam*. Again the verb phrase is seamless, is not a *predicate*, and does not participate in contributing reality to the expression.

The seam reality function also moves from the main verb to be covert inside a plural subject noun like *"people"* or *"children"* as in *"people elect their leaders"* or *"children play games"*. And, there is a mental leap required to appreciate that a seam function can be covert within plural personal subject pronouns *we, you, they* as in *"They make news"*.

Flow-of-meaning-tree figures in Fig. 2.5.3 show the similar figure of plurality concept *flow-of-meaning-trees* and finite sentence *flow-of-*

meaning-trees. That both look like a *ment* tree could suggest to why plural subjects can carry a seam.

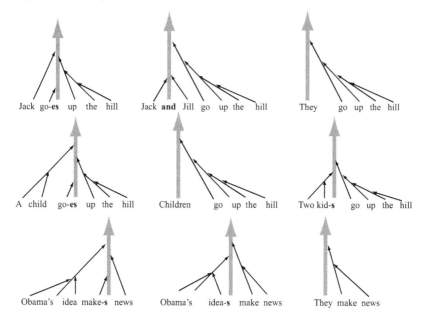

Fig. 2.5.3 Flow-of-meaning-trees of plural entities have *ment* figures very like observation flow-of-meaning-trees.

Note that the figure of the *flow-of-meaning-tree* of subject possessive phrase *Obama's idea*, is the same as that of a plural subject. However, we automatically recognize that this possessive subject does not carry a seam because there is already another seam. There can be can be only one seam in a clause. The apostrophe **'s** simply functions as an enriched subject determiner.

Subject-Seam Sentences

The first kind of *be* sentence occurs when a **s***eam* is intimately attached to a personal pronoun subject concept as a singular apostrophe**'s** as in *"It's a party"* or *"He's foolish"*. Parsing this *be* sentence type, the seam will be enriched first by the subject concept to form a *subject-seam*, which is then enriched by the object concept, which in this case is a BE type property. The order of enrichment of the seam particle here is first by the subject concept then by second relative concept.

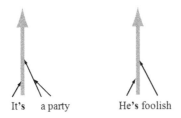

Fig. 2.5.4 Flow-of-meaning-trees for apostrophe –s be sentences.

Although these sentences make a state**ment**, it is obvious that an enriched subject is the product and perhaps their main purpose. This *subject-seam* union is the mirror image of a *predicate*, discussed below, where a seam is intimately embedded in the verb-object phrase to confer reality on the verb action before the subject concept is annexed. The purpose of *subject-seam* sentences is primarily to enrich the reality status of the subject. There is no English word equivalent to *predicate* for this *subject-seam* unit, perhaps because its very useful role in realizing subject entities first has not been recognized by linguists, until now. A *predicate* is like glue being spread on the wallpaper before it is applied to the wall; a *subject-seam* is like glue being spread on the wall before wallpaper is applied.

Next are *be* sentences where the seam is on free grammatical particles *am, art, is, are, was, were.*

Fig. 2.5.5 Flow-of-meaning-trees for be sentences

Be sentences express a relation between the subject and a complement second relative that may be an adjunct property/characteristic, an activity or a role. A closed set of verbs: *become-s seem-s* and the five sense verbs *look-s sound-s feel-s taste-s smell-s* are enriched -s seams that like **is** can blend many adjunct concepts into a subject in *be* fashion, e.g. *"It looks/tastes/smells good."* In a special subset of *be* sentences where the complement

is a present participle, the object of the *be-seam* relation is a property
that blends into the subject when the subject is performing a verb action.

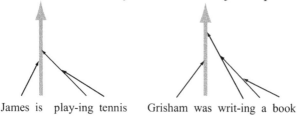

James is   play-ing tennis   Grisham was writ-ing a book

Fig. 2.5.6 Flow-of-meaning-trees for be sentences where the complement is a present
participle.

In sentences like this the *be-seam* relation and its first relative subject are
joined first. This is shown by the fact that they stay together in questions
which are formed by the subject "coming about", i.e. swinging to the other
side of the seam.

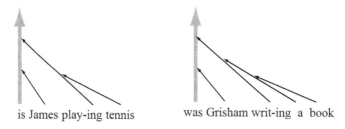

is James play-ing tennis   was Grisham writ-ing a book

Fig. 2.5.7 Flow-of-meaning-trees illustrating seam associated with subject rather than
verb or modal in plural observations.

Although such sentences make a statement, at the same time they can be
construed to be about the first mentioned concept, the subject concept.
In some sentences it is clear that the author's main intention is to inform
us about changes to the subject entity. Sentences are constructed so that
the first concept mentioned, the *subject concept*, gets favored enrichment.
Sentences are designed to ferry meaning into their subject more so than
into any of the other party concepts. This has the effect of keeping the
rules of syntax more transparent, first concept mentioned is the surviving
concept. The subject concept is expressed by that part of the sentence
coming before an enriched seam grammatical. It is appropriate for a parser
to parse the subject expression to a single concept before dealing with its

enrichment by the seam concept's transfer of its collected meaning on to the subject.

Let's parse another finite sentence to show how *Mensa* tables direct our parser to see seam concepts serially enriched by the other concepts expressed in that sentence, to become an observation concept. Take the sentence *"Henry is going to give the money to John"*. Here is the meaning flow tree of the observation concept expressed by the finite sentence *"Henry is going to give the money to John."*

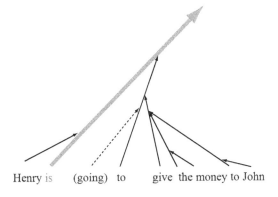

Henry is   (going)   to   give the money to John

Fig. 2.5.8 Flow-of-meaning-tree and flow diagram for sentence *"Henry is going to give the money to John".*

The M5 table of mental operations specified in this sentence is as follows:

Henry ~ is	= is1	*"Henry is"*
going ~ to	= to1	*"going to"*
the ~ money	= the1	*"the money"*
to ~ John	=to2	*"to John"*
give ~ the1	= give1	*"give the money"*
gjve1 ~ to1	= give2	*"give the money to John"*
to1 ~ give2	= to2	*"going to give the money to John"*
is1 ~ to2 =	= is2	*"Henry is going to give the money to John"*

The meaning flow narrative is as follows: in the first round seam **is** is enriched by **Henry** from its left to make **is1**; first concept **to** is enriched by **going** to **to1**; concept **the** is enriched by concept **money** to **the1**, and second concept **to** is enriched by concept **John** to concept **to2**. In the second round concept **give** is enriched by **the1** to **give1**. In the third round concept **give1** is enriched by concept **to2** to make **give2**. In the fourth round concept **to1** is enriched by **give2** to **to2**. Now, in the grand final round, **is1** is enriched by **to2** on its right to become **is2**, the observation concept expressed by the finite sentence "*Henry is going to give the money to John*". This explains how a *Mensa* table enables a software parser to parse a sentence, detect the seam and enrich it in the correct precedence. Alternate *Mensa* tables can be composed to allow invariance, so that a different symbol string that means the same will parse to that same concept.

Here, concept **is**, which is basically an **-s** inflection enriched by covert verb *be*, carries the seam symbol that receives meaning from all the other symbols in the sentence to make **it** a state**ment**. Enriched inflection **–s** ends up containing meaning from all the concepts that the observer sees, which mirror what is going on in the world.

If the observer had said "*Henry was going to give the money to John*". Here, concept **was** is basically covert verb *be* with an included covert **–d** inflection. Once enriched by all the other concepts mentioned, this covert inflection **–d** seam can be mentally parsed to contain all the concepts that the observer saw, which mirror what was going on in a not-present world that exists only in his memory or in his imagination.[8]

Passive Voice Sentences

Passive voice sentences are the other case where the focus lies heavily on what change occurs in the object of a verb. The concept that would normally be considered the object concept of the verb is made the subject concept of a passive voice sentence. Passive voice is only properly employed to focus attention on a concept that is significantly changed by taking part in a relationship. Dwight Bolinger brings out this point especially elegantly with his examples:

> *The army was deserted by a private.
> The army was deserted by all its generals.
> *The lake was camped beside by my sister.
> The old bridge has been walked under by generations of lovers.

There is a requirement than only verb objects that are changed by the verb action of a transitive verb can be the subject of passive voice sentences. For the last example Bolinger notes that the bridge may be deemed to have

---

8   Phonetic reversal cueing at work again: "It is" means "I see **it**", "it was" "I saw **it**"; once seen "**it** is ex-**is**", "it exists".

become romantic as a result of the verb action of being walked under by generations of lovers.[9]

Passive voice is used in sentences where the observer wants to make absolutely certain that the object concept of a transitive verb is the first concept to enrich the seam grammatical, the first concept to be *realized*. With the passive voice a speaker moves the *home* point of view of the sentence from agent concept to patient concept. The focus of passive voice sentences on the patient concept allows roles of actor or agent to be downgraded, famously by Ronald Reagan with his *"Mistakes were made"*.

As noted earlier, verb *is* of the passive voice has the same meaning as *I see*, *was* the same meaning as *I saw*, as in *"Federer was beat-en at Wimbledon"* *"I saw Federer beat-en at Wimbledon"*. In passive voice sentences the **-ed** inflection that the lexical verb enriches is not the seam of the sentence. This distinction was more explicit in olden days when the lexical verb inflection used to be **-en**.

Auxiliary Verb Sentences

Auxiliary verbs *am, art, is, was, were, has, had, does, did* are formed when *be*, *have* or *do* enrich a seam.

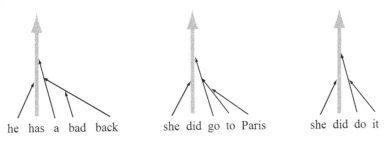

he has a bad back   she did go to Paris   she did do it

Fig. 2.5.9 Flow-of-meaning-trees illustrating that auxiliary verb seams are associated with subject rather than verb or modal.

In a sentence like *"she did do it"* **did** is the auxiliary and **do** the lexical verb. That these auxiliary verbs are linked to the subject and not to the object is shown in that subject and auxiliary reverse order to form questions. No lexical verbs can reverse order with the subject to form a question.

---

9   Dwight Bolinger, Meaning and Form, Trans. NYAS, 1974, p.223.

Modality - Seams in Modal Sentences

All sentences tell which *relationship-of-concepts* is being observed, or not observed. And they answer one or more of the following *context* questions: does the *relationship-of-concepts* exist in reality? Or not? Ever? Never? And when we do not observe it directly, is the relationship possible? Is it inevitable? Is it likely? Does it have the observer's permission to exist? Will he make sure it will exist? Answering these questions is what finite sentences do. By answering one or more of these questions, a finite sentence confers modality, an appropriate degree of reality on the concepts that have been observed.

So, the next sentence subtype comprises the modal group of sentences with the following free standing already enriched seam grammaticals as their seams: *do, can, could, will, would, may, might, shall, should, must, ought* and *dare*. Their second or object relative is always a "seamless" verb phrase concept. They enable language to assign truth, existence, reality, certainty, probability, possibility, necessity or legality of existence of a relationship-of-concepts defined by a finite sentence being held in he observer's mind. [10]

Modals incorporate seam and world as well as modality. Fig. 2.5.10 shows *flow-of-meaning-trees* for modal sentences:

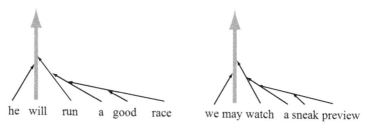

Fig. 2.5.10 Flow-of-meaning-trees illustrating modal seam associated with subject rather than verb in plural observations.

Seam-subject sentences are the only type of sentence used for *affirmation*, *negation* and *modality*. and for questions. They are negated by putting negator grammatical *not* immediately after the seam or *never* before or

---

10 There is no overlap of this group of grammatical words with the lexical elements of language except for will and can, which are also lexicals. For this reason they are excellent markers of the end of the subject phrase for parsers

after the seam, which indicate the observer does not see the relation.

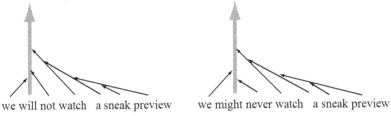

we will not watch   a sneak preview   we might never watch   a sneak preview

Fig. 2.5.11 Flow-of-meaning-trees illustrating showing negator symbols not and never associating with subject-seam.

There is only one default relation between subject and modals like **do will** or **may**. Again, it is never explicit and it can be enriched only by a limited number of grammaticals that modify *seams*, like *always, often, sometimes, rarely, almost, nearly, hardly* etc. Only these words can appear in this position in a sentence as in *"He often will (will often) visit New York."* They contribute to the Cartesian Product of a sentence to specify an infinite number of meanings. A good rule of thumb test for a grammatical particle to qualify as a member of this modal group is whether it can be the first word of a yes/no question, appearing before the subject. When word order is reversed in this manner it has the special and crucial function of turning a finite sentence into a question. This is evidence that they are associated with the subject concept first rather than the verb phrase concept.

Verb-Seam Predicate Sentences

The next group of sentences is where the seam is found as the inflection grammatical of the main lexical verb and thus located between the verb and its object. This is classical SVO word order, which occurs in only a minority of English sentences. Here, seam concepts are the bound **–s** or **–d** inflection grammaticals seen inflecting tens of thousands of lexical verbs in finite sentences and finite clauses. Examples of such verb enriched seams are verbs like promise-**s** and walk-**ed**.

Fig 2.5.12 shows *flow-of-meaning-trees* for two typical sentences: *"The theater critic review-s many plays"*, *"The chess player steadi-ed his nerves."* Here the observer first sees the relations, symbolized by grammatical seam **-es** between verb concept **review** and object concept **manyplays** and by grammatical seam **–ed** between concept **steady** and object concept **hisnerves**.

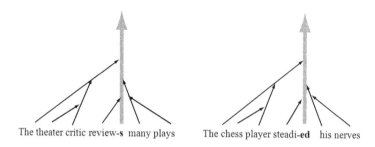

The theater critic review-**s** many plays   The chess player steadi-**ed** his nerves

Fig. 2.5.12 Flow-of-meaning-trees for sentences with the seam placed between verb and object forming a *predicate.*

For another example, lets consider *flow-of-meaning-trees* for two finite sentences *"he watch-es a sneak preview"* and *"he watch-ed a sneak preview"*. The seam concepts of these sentences that indicate *world* are the **–es** and **–ed** inflections of verb *watch* . They distinguish present *world* from not-present *world*.

Fig 2.5.13 shows two *flow-of-meaning-trees* that show the order of precedence of enrichment of the surviving seam concepts that determine *world*.

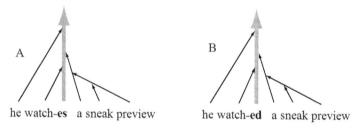

he watch-**es** a sneak preview   he watch-**ed** a sneak preview

Fig. 2.5.13 Flow-of-meaning-trees illustrating presently real and not presently real observations.

Seam grammaticals **–es** and **–ed** are serially enriched by concepts **watch, asneakpreview** and then **he** in order of precedence. Sentence A where the verb has an **–es** inflection is a record of an observation in the present world of the observer equivalent to "I *see* him watch a sneak preview." The verb inflection is the surviving concept and the lexical verb merely enriches it. Sentence B where the verb has an **–ed** inflection is a record of an observation in a memory world equivalent to *"I saw him watch a sneak* *preview. "* [11] These sentences have the same meaning as – *"I see him watch a sneak preview"* and *"I saw him watch a sneak preview".*[12]

The effect of *predicate sentences* is to focus attention first on the verb action concept and second on change in the object concept and often some meaning will rub off on the subject. Because grammatical **do** is the only possible relation between subject and verb phrase concepts, it can be omitted. Any change caused in the subject is secondary and comes from being party to an observation, which may range from almost nothing to very significant, The verb action, not the subject, is made real first in a predicate sentence. The bound inflection grammaticals of a verb, **–es** or **–ed**, not its lexical verb stems, are the surviving concept of that matching. In some sentences the seam concept is not explicit but is covert in strong past tense verbs like "came" or "broke" but is still the surviving grammatical. This kind of sentence where the seam is in the predicate are *descriptive* sentence or *narrative* sentences that move a story on. They are always affirmative and cannot be used for negation or for questions.

A subtle point again here: there is an invisible default relation, **to**, between a transitive lexical verb and its object. Because this relation between verb and its object is a default relation, **to** can be omitted. This covert **to** relation is enriched by the verb's object and then it enriches the seam concept already enriched by the verb to form a *predicate* concept.

Although, like all sentences, *predicate sentences* are state**ment**s; they have the effect of enriching the syntactical object of the verb concept much more than they enrich the subject concept. This verb phrase concept is thus realized and set as a *predicate* before the subject further enriches it.[13]

Phrasal Verb Sentences

The next *predicate sentence* subtype comprises sentences with a phrasal verb, like *"look up"* and *"take out"*. Phrasal verbs are a compound of

---

11 Incidentally, this is why verbs in headlines and stage instructions are in the present tense. They are describing the present text content or stage instruction not the actual event being reported.

12 It is no coincidence that "see" and "is", and "saw" and "was", are phonetic reverses.

13 We would argue that a seam enriched first by the subject is not a predicate. In such sentences the verb phrase is just that, a verb phrase.

a lexical verb and a grammatical particle.[14] They have lexical meaning flowing from a following free grammatical particle into a lexical verb. Phrasal verbs are needed when the relation between verb action and syntactical object is not the default obvious one and so has to be made explicit.

In the phrase *"turn off the cell phone"* the nature of the action, i.e. *"offing"* the cell phone, is determined by grammatical concept **off**. The phone is "offed" not turned. Enrichment of lexical verb concept *turn* by **off** indicates how the *"offing"* was done. The sense of the *"offing"* is further enriched by its object, in that it is being done to a cell phone. Phrasal lexical verbs can adopt a very different meaning, often metaphorical, like *"ripped off"*. Consideration of phrasal verb sentences gives further insight into the function of lexical verbs as enrichers of their inflections rather than the other way around.

As an example the FOMT and *Mensa* table for the sentence *"He turn-s off his cell phone"* are shown in Fig. 2.5.14

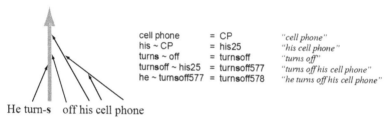

cell phone	= CP	*"cell phone"*
his ~ CP	= his25	*"his cell phone"*
turns ~ off	= turnsoff	*"turns off"*
turnsoff ~ his25	= turnsoff577	*"turns off his cell phone"*
he ~ turnsoff577	= turnsoff578	*"he turns off his cell phone"*

He turn-s   off his cell phone

Fig. 2.5.14 Flow-of-meaning-tree and Mensa table for a phrasal verb with **-s** seam placed between verb and phrasal particle.

In this sentence grammatical seam **-s** is the surviving concept, enriched first by *turn* and then by **off**. The purpose of phrasal verb sentences is to realize the completion of the verb action first by placing the *seam* between the verb and its completing phrasal particle. Phrasal verbs often denote verb processes that go to conclusion; the particles are said to be completitive.

Seam outside Sentence

There is a small closed subset of only eleven English verbs that move the reality function out of the clause itself. These are the very special verbs, *see watch look at hear feel let make help require that* and

---

14 Google "wiki phrasal verbs" I'm feeling lucky

have. For example, *"I heard him make the speech."* means *"he made the speech."* And *"I saw John get the firewood"* means *"John got the firewood".* They are mostly sense verbs that indicate that the relation in the sentence between subject and second relative object has been observed and therefore is real. And the relation and all the concepts mentioned in the sentence are realized. These verbs perform the same reality function that a *seam* does within a sentence.

Parsing Sentences Mentally

One can take the sentence *"Tom assigned the job to Jim"* and mentally parse it in various ways other than the default parsing. Fig. 2.5.15 shows how working with the same reality the sentence may be parsed mentally.

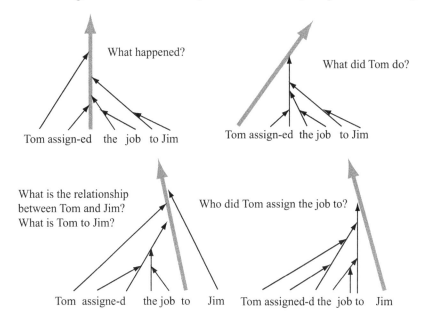

Fig 2.5.15 Flow-of-meaning-trees showing alternate mental parsings of an expression

These *flow-of-meaning-trees* are meant to show how a sentence describing an action might be parsed in the mind of an addressee to focus meaning on which of the party concepts is the appropriate answer to each question. To force our computer parser to direct all meaning to a particular symbol would require replacing it with a relative pronoun grammatical and reordering the expression.

Parsing Sentences Actually

When we read or hear a language expression how do we know immediately whether it is a *finite sentence* and not just a *non-finite expression* that may well describe an equally complex thing?[15] To develop a computer parser we have to be clear about what makes a sentence *finite*? What confers *finitivity* on a sentence? What is special about a finite sentence as compared to a *non-finite* language expression? What differentiates its syntax from that of a non-finite expression? How do we figure out which is which? Humans do this easily and automatically. But, how does a human parser detect that a seam is present in an expression to make it a finite sentence, and thereby recognize that a given language expression is a sentence? It's easy for us, but how will a software parser program identify which is the seam symbol in a sentence and where it is?

So much for theory. Let's get practical. Parsing any utterance, the first task is to look for a seam symbol carried on or in one of the words to see whether it is a finite sentence or just an expression. By the time we first perceive a seam, it is always already incorporated in a lexical word or a grammatical particle. Finding the seam concept in a sentence is automatic for a literate human but not that easy for a computer parser program.

The anatomy of every observation comprises a first relative, the *subject concept*, a second relative, the *object concept*, and a BE, HAVE or DO relation concept between them.[16] A finite sentence thus gathers its string of symbols in order into three discrete complexes of symbols, a *subject complex*, an *object complex*, with a *relation complex* in between. Every observation expressed by a finite sentence is thus a relationship observed between two often complex mental concepts.

The first steps in parsing a finite sentence are to pre-build the *subject concept* and the BE, HAVE or DO relation concept, and the *object*

---

15 Here's are some finite sentences without a verb in them. There is no verb in finite sentences like "Yes." "No." "Never" "Alright." "OK." "Indeed." "Bummer." "The more the merrier." or a headline like "Obama in Hawaii for Xmas", all of which are affirmations of the existence of a relationship of interest. Verbs are often left out completely from headlines without loss of reality, in the interests of conserving type space.

16 Note that here the *object* is the *object* relative of the *subject* relative, not the syntactic object of a lexical verb as is usual in grammar.

concept. Then, other metaconcepts like time, place, reason, and manner which will serially flow meaning directly and indirectly into the enriched seam are added to complete the observation. Each step of this process is the same as construction of an expression concept around its **it** concept but an observation is a *ment* concept built around a central seam concept that indicates its equivalence with what is in the observers mind

In the *predicate sentence "FedEx delivered the package to Harry's office"*, the seam symbol is the **-ed** inflection enriched by verb *deliver* and is incorporated in the predicate.

The *flow-of-meaning-tree* diagram in Fig. 2.5.16 illustrates the *observer* "overseeing" the relay of meaning into the *seam symbol*, which in this *flow-of-meaning-tree* is the remote world **-D** inflection on verb *"deliver"*.

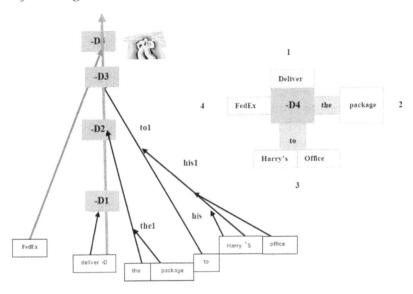

Fig. 2.5.16 Flow-of-meaning-tree and flow diagram for sentence *"FedEx delivered the package to Harry's office"*

Verb inflections are seam grammaticals and the embedded **-D** symbol in this past tense verb is the seam symbol standing for the seam concept that turns this expression into a finite sentence. The **-D** inflection on the verb indicates the verb action is not in the present world. This seam grammatical will be enriched directly and indirectly with meaning from all to the other concepts in the finite sentence to become the observation concept.

The concept block diagram shows the meaning gathered in -**D4** from four component concepts. They become real as they are included in order into the -**D** seam grammatical.

The M5 table below lists the eight mental operations on symbols that document this meaning flow:

Harry ~ -s	= his	*"Harry's"*
his ~ office	= his1	*"Harry's office"*
to ~ his1	= to1	*"to Harry's office"*
the ~ package	= the1	*"the package"*
deliver ~ D	= D1	*"delivered"*
D1 ~the1	= D2	*"delivered the package"*
D2 ~ t01	= D3	*"delivered the package to Harry's office"*
Fedex ~D3	= D4	*"Fedex delivered the package to Harry's office"*

The meaning relay narrative of this sentence is as follows: In the first round possessive symbol **-s** is enriched by **Harry** to give **his**. Symbol **the** is enriched by **package** to give **the1** and the **–D** seam symbol is enriched by **deliver** to give intermediary concept **D1**. In the second round **his** is enriched by **office** to give **his1** and **D1** is enriched by **the1** to give **D2**. In the third round **to** is enriched by **his1** to give **to1** and **D2** is enriched by **to1** to give **D3**. Finally, **D3** having gathered meaning from all the symbols following it receives meaning from subject **FedEx** to become *ment* **D4**. Here the sentence is being parsed to a statement rather than to an enriched subject concept.

It is worthwhile making a somewhat subtle point again here about covert relations. We have remarked before that when a relation is a well known default relation, the explicit grammatical symbol for it is omitted. This is one of the reasons language has been so hard to computerize. Relation grammatical **do** is the default relation between subject and verb concepts in a sentence. So, **do** can be left out as in predicate sentences like the above. And, relation grammatical **to** is the default relation between a transitive verb and its object concept in a sentence. So, **to** can be left out as in *predicate sentences* like the above. There is only one default relation between verb concepts and their syntactical object concepts, **to**. However, both **do** and **to** are needed in the question *"What did she do to her hair?"*, where the verb is not yet explicit. And **do** is required when affirmation or negation is being stated or questioned. Just because default relations are not represented by a grammatical in language, it does not mean they are not there. They still are. For example, when omitted BE relation symbol is enriched with seam -s, all we see is verb *"is"*. It is convenient to refer to the seam enriched relation as the seam concept itself because it makes *flow-of-meaning-trees* and *Mensa* tables more accessible. We adopt this convention.

Deixis

The word *deixis* means that context is required to know what words are referring to. Every sentence has a *deictic center* or *origo* which is its home. The origo is mostly where the subject is but sentence may have a point of view which is the home of another concept. And the *origo* can be transferred from the mind of the narrator here and now to another person, time, place or social position. Language sentences can also indicate what is going on in the mind of a person other that the narrator, for example, *"I am coming to New York to see you"* and be sensitive to the other person's home status as if were our own resulting in feelings of empathy and sympathy. Deixis is well understood by linguists.[17]

Communication by Sentence

The mental process of performing an *observation* creates in the observer's mind a structured *relationship-of-concepts* that reflects in depth what is going on in the world observed. It involves consciousness and attention. When the observer actively reruns an observation in his mind it is a *thought*. Thus a *thought* is mentally observing a relation between observed concepts. Sentence texts are like program code that when run can result in reactivation of the memory of the observation as a conscious thought and support an utterance. This illustrates another distinction between finite sentences and non-finite expressions: sentences are programs that operate on data to form new data, expressions are data. This whole process of observation and recall is completely analogous to making a live video recording and playing it back later.

Again the famous triangle of Richards and Ogden is applicable to the processes of employing a finite sentence to communicate a message. Knowledge goes from real world to first person directly, from mind to mind indirectly via text, which is the medium. With language, the first

---

17 Google "Deixis" and jump to "Deictic Center"

person generates text; text is fixed, and like letters carved in a tablet can't be changed; the second person reads the text and gets the message.

Let's redraw the triangle of Ogden and Richards letting S be the symbol for the conceptual content of the message and letter T stand for the fixed text. The phonemes, *say* (words), *see* (world) and *sci* [18] (knowledge), cue the three corners of the O&R triangle.

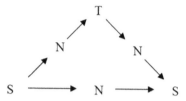

Fig. 2.5.17 Direct flow of meaning from world to mind versus flow via text.

The word *"sense"* is a phonetic palindrome, S-N-S. These symbol can be taken to mean knowledge going directly from world to mind directly; S-N-S is a phonetic palindrome that suggests the origin of the word *"sentence"*. A sentence *makes sense* indirectly via text S-N-T-N-S is a phonetic palindrome that suggests the origin of the word *"sentence"*. So when a judge pronounces a sentence, the text is set in stone, that's **it**. That phonemes are mnemonic cues to meaning is a constant theme of this monograph.

And a sentence is a medium of communication. Sentences are instructions to a second person to build more complex concepts from already known concepts. And, the symbols used can communicate the *relationship of concepts* to another mind. A sentence is the choreography of a thought, a program that allows a second mind to think the same thought and make its own memory trace, which again can be reactivated at will. A first person generates and utters a sentence to communicate with a second person so as to enable the second person to build the same conceptual structure in his mind and thereby learn something about the real or imaginary world that is known to the first person. So, by uttering a sentence with a seam concept, an author speaking his mind, assigning symbols to all the concepts in his mind and relating them to each other, declares that the concepts and their organization that his words describe do exist or do not exist in his

---

18 From Latin verb *scio*, to know, understand

mind, and by inference exist or not exist out in the real world or only in a memory world. Fortunately, all of this can be managed deftly with *flow-of-meaning-trees* and *Mensa tables*.

The mission of our project has been to develop practical methods that enable a computer to model language and human thought. And computers love symbols. It turns out that *flow-of-meaning-trees* and *Mensa tables* can model all the functions of a sentence perfectly.

BOOK II
CHAPTER VI

How Subordinate Clauses and Questions Work

Subordinate clauses take advantage of the fact that when an expression musters a series of concepts into a congruent relationship, each party concept adapts its sense and status to fit into context. Each concept embedded in an expression takes on a very subtle and nuanced sense. Authors use this exquisite molding of sense to formulate very special versions of a concept by placing it in a particular expression. Then they extract this meaning by packaging it in a relative pronoun grammatical. By the time we see it, the party concept has been transformed, embedded in a grammatical, the grammatical has been moved to the front of the subordinate clause leaving its original position empty in the subordinate clause, its "trace". We can record this process precisely by rearranging a flow-of-meaning-tree and Mensa table so as to flow all meaning into the initial relative pronoun grammatical. Then, the relative pronoun then contributes its special meaning into a target concept in the main clause. Questions are framed by a similar process. We show that flow-of-meaning-trees and corresponding Mensa tables are an orthography that can precisely document such steps of mental play so that a computer program can mimic them.

In this chapter on subordinate clauses and questions we will show that conceptual content induced in a party concept of a subordinate clause is relayed to a party concept of the main clause to enrich that party concept. In those cases, inter-clause transfer of meaning between party concepts was the reason for putting main and subordinate clauses in juxtaposition. Questions are framed by a similar process whereby relative pronouns become interrogative pronouns.

Subordinate clauses take advantage of the fact that when an expression musters a series of concepts into a congruent relationship, all the concepts mentioned in an expression receive meaning directly and indirectly from their peer concepts and adapt in very subtle ways by way of being party to that expression. Concepts in the middle of an expression with many relatives contributing meaning to them can adopt very nuanced shades of meaning. They are squeezed into shape and come out with exquisite molding. The interflow of meaning between the concepts mentioned in an expression is omnidirectional. Each party of an expression or sentence concept adapts its sense and status to fit into context, taking on a special meaning suitable to the context it finds itself in, receiving meaning flowing from each and every one of the other concepts.

A good reader is free to parse an expression mentally in many ways, in ways that direct this flow of meaning into any one of the party concepts, making it the **it** concept of the expression. So, a reader or listener, the second person, who has performed such alternate parsings of an expression in his mind, can go on to calculate mentally how each and every one of the mentioned concepts is affected by being involved. This mental play often requires the second person to come up with ideas, concepts not mentioned, reach for allusions, to enable parsing that lets us determine exactly what the author intended. *Flow-of-meaning-trees* and corresponding *Mensa tables* are an orthography that can precisely document such steps of mental play so that a computer program can mimic them. First, lets see how a subordinate clause is constructed.

Authors use this exquisite molding of sense to formulate very special versions of a concept when they place it in a particular expression. Then they extract this meaning by packaging it in a relative pronoun grammatical. By the time we see it, the party concept has been transformed, embedded in a grammatical, the grammatical has been moved to the front of the subordinate clause leaving its original position empty in the subordinate clause, its "trace". We can record this process precisely by constructing a *flow-of-meaning-tree* and *Mensa table* that flows all meaning into the relative pronoun grammatical at the front of the expression. The relative pronoun then contributes its special meaning into a target concept in the main clause. This is the basis of the method for the construction and function of subordinate clauses.

Like any player in a tennis tournament can be the winner, any one party concept in an expression or finite sentence can be the surviving **it** concept. And, an author, by changing the order of the symbols in the expression and if necessary inserting grammaticals appositely, can force parsing that makes any one of the concepts mentioned in the new expression the **it** concept. The strong method for doing this in English is to mention the **it** symbol at the beginning of the expression where a *flow-of-meaning-tree* would show meaning being directed into it.

Writers make use of grammaticals to harvest the meaning a concept may acquire in one expression and use it to enrich the same or another concept in another expression. They use one of the relative pronoun entity grammaticals **what, which, who, when, where, how** and **why**,[1] and anaphoric grammatical **that** as well as using conjunction grammaticals like **as, so, since** and **because** to harvest the meaning that a concept may acquire as a party concept in a subordinate clause. Then transfer this acquired meaning to just one of the concepts in the main or higher level clause that the author wants to enrich. In that way they can shape the sense of the receiving concept exactly the way they want.

There is a vast linguistic literature dealing with subordinate clauses and questions under the rubric of transformational grammar, context free grammar, and parse trees such with nodes labelled NP for noun phrase

---

1   Rudyard Kipling   The Elephant's Child
     I keep six honest serving-men
     (They taught me all I knew)
     Their names are What and Why and When
     And How and Where and Who.
     I send them over land and sea,
      I send them east and west;
     But after they have worked for me,
      I give them all a rest

and VP for verb phrase. Rules to process such parse trees using so called context free grammar have been developed that rely largely on parts of speech (POS) of words and rules for moving them into different positions in the sentence. Although these trees have much the same figure as our *flow-of-meaning-trees*, the difference is that our scheme emphasizes concepts, not words and our trees are always context specific Our scheme parses the expression for a survivor **it** concept along the lines of a *single elimination tournament*. And the ability to precisely define the structure of context specific concept trees with an array makes computer processing very straightforward.

Constructing Relative Pronoun Subordinate Clauses

Let's start with the finite sentence expression *"margin lending can be highly profitable"*, and make a relative clause from it. This sentence mentions two concepts, and here is a *Mensa table* that can force our parser to make one of the concepts be the surviving concept, Here, the *flow-of-meaning-tree* drawn with text vertical in the manner that is more convenient for long sentences:

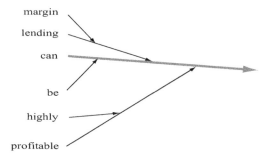

Fig 2.6.1   Flow-of-meaning-tree for sentence "margin lending can be highly profitable"

Here is its *Mensa table*:

margin ~ lending	= ML	*"margin lending"*
can ~ be	= canbe	*"can be"*
ML~ canbe	= MLcanbe	*"margin lending can be"*
highly ~profitable	= HP	*"highly profitable"*
MLcanbe ~ HP	= MLcanbeHP	*"margin lending can be highly profitable"*

Now we can make it into a relative clause by replacing *"margin lending"* with *"what"* to get *"what can be highly profitable"*.

Here is its *flow-of-meaning-tree*

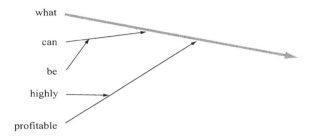

Fig 2.6.2 Flow-of-meaning-tree for subordinate clause "what can be highly profitable"

Here is its *Mensa table*:

can ~ be	= canbe	*"can be"*
what~ canbe	= WCb	*"what can be"*
highly ~profitable	= HP	*"highly profitable"*
WCb ~ HP	= WCbeHP	*"what can be highly profitable"*

Now, we can, using this relative clause, construct a whole new sentence, saying something else: *"margin lending is what can be highly profitable"*, without changing the underlying world situation. The new sentence picks subject-seam concept *"margin lending is"* as the **it** concept and enriches it with the **what** concept that has absorbed meaning from all the other terms of the reordered **what** subordinate clause expression.

Here is the *flow-of-meaning-tree* of the whole sentence:

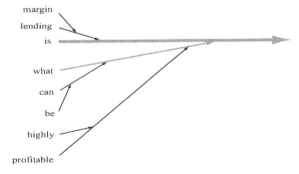

Fig 2.6.3 Flow-of-meaning-tree for sentence "margin lending is what can be highly profitable

Here is the *Mensa table* for the whole sentence::

margin ~ lending	= ML	*"margin lending"*
ML ~ is	= MLis	*"margin lending is"*
can ~ be	= canbe	*"can be"*
what~ canbe	= WCb	*"what can be"*
highly ~profitable	= HP	*"highly ~profitable"*
WCb ~ HP	= WCbeHP	*"what can be highly profitable"*
MLis ~ WCbeHP	= MLisWCbeHP	*"margin lending is what can be highly profitable"*

If you study the *flow-of-meaning-tree and Mensa table* you will see that, in a **what** as subject relative clause, meaning from the relative clause flows into first mentioned subject concept **what** rather than into seam **can**. Rule of syntax: relative pronouns trump seams. Then the meaning contained in this relative pronoun grammatical is relayed on into *subject-seam concept "margin lending is"*, enriching that concept.

In other cases the relative pronoun may not be the subject of the relative clause. Nevertheless, it still receives meaning from the other concepts mentioned and is brought to the front of the relative clause. From there it relays meaning on into a concept in the main clause that it is now in juxtaposition with. And, by reordering the words in a sentence, one can, without changing the reality, rewrite the expression above to make any concept the surviving concept by bringing it to the front.

So, *"highly profitable"* will be made the concept of interest with the sentence *"highly profitable is what margin lending can be"*. Here is the *flow-of-meaning-tree* directed by this reordered sentence expression:

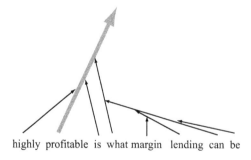

highly profitable is what margin lending can be

Fig 2.6.4 Flow-of-meaning-tree showing alternate mental parsing to a complement concept.

Here is the M5 table that would force our parser to parse it this way:

highly ~profitable	= HP	*"highly profitable"*
HP ~ is	= HPis	*"highly profitable is"*
margin ~ lending	= ML	*"margin lending"*
can ~ be	= canbe	*"can be"*
ML ~ canbe	= MLCb	*"margin lending can"*
what ~ MLCb	= WMLCb	*"what margin lending can be"*
HPis ~ WMLCb	= HPisWMLCb	*" highly profitable is what margin lending can be"*

Figs. 2.6.4 and 2.6.5 shows relative pronoun **what** receiving meaning from being the object relative concept of the subordinate clause. Now, let it "come about" to subject position in the sentence, there becoming simultaneously the object relative concept of the main clause. From there, **what** relays its received meaning to concept **HPis**, *"highly profitable is"*, the *subject-seam* of the main clause.

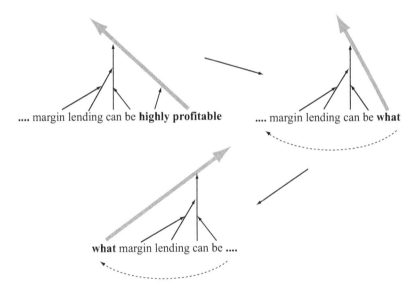

Fig 2.6.5 Flow-of-meaning-trees showing mental parsing of an expression to focus meaning on a relative pronoun

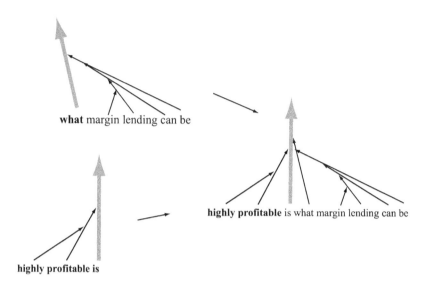

Fig 2.6.6   Flow-of-meaning-trees showing integration of a subordinate clause

Notice that, to write an expression that explicitly makes concept **HP** the concept of interest one had to reorder the symbols and insert grammaticals **is** and **what** appositely. Seam concept **is** combines with concept **HP** to make *subject-seam* concept *"highly profitable is"*, which is then enriched by the **what** concept.

Parse process: bundle the concept in the subordinate clause into a relative pronoun grammatical, which receives the meaning normally delivered to that slot in the clause. Move this enriched relative pronoun grammatical to the front of the subordinate clause leaving an empty trace where it was. Then make it a party to the main clause to contribute its received meaning to a concept there. Subordinate clauses work by substituting a relative pronoun grammatical for the concept of interest, bringing it to the front of the expression, thus having it relay its meaning on to another concept to enrich that concept in a highly nuanced manner.

Constructing an if Subordinate Clause

Conjunction grammatical **if** provides another good exercise in the theory of subordinate clauses. Grammatical **if** can receive and relay only a Boolean value; that's what **if** does, a nice example of how grammaticals have idiosyncratic functions. For example consider the sentence *"If a bird had your brain, it would fly backwards"*.

Figure 2.6.7 shows the flow of meaning occurring in this sentence.

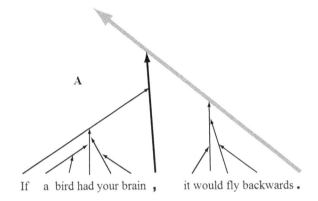

If   a bird had your brain ,   it would fly backwards .

Fig 2.6.7   If subordinate clause supplying Boolean affirmation or negation

Here is the *Mensa* table:

a ~ bird	= a452	*"a bird"*
your ~ brain	= your238	*"your brain"*
a452 ~ had	= had452	*"a bird had"*
a452 ~ your238	= had453	*"a bird had your brain"*
if ~ had453	= if453	*"if a bird had your brain"*
if453 ~ ,	= ,if453	*"if a bird had your brain,"*
it ~ would	= itwould	*"it would"*
fly ~ backwards	= fly26	*"fly backwards"*
itwould ~ fly26	= itwdfly26	*"it would fly backwards"*
itwdfly26 ~ .	= .itwdfly26	*"it would fly backwards."*
,if453 ~ .itwdfly26 = .if45326		*"if a bird had your brain, it would fly backwards."*

Parse narrative: Parsing the subordinate clause *"If a bird had your brain,"* concepts **a** and **bird**, and **your** and **brain**, match up in the first round to form concepts **a452** and **your238**. In the next round **a452** and **had** match to form concept **had453**. In the next round **a453** and **your238** match up to form **had453**. Next round **if** is enriched by **had453** to get **if453**, which in the next round is enclaused (sic) in a comma to form **,if453**.

Parsing the main clause *"It would fly backwards"* concepts **it** and **would**, and **fly** and **backwards** match up in the first round to form concepts **itwould** and **fly26**. Concepts **itwould** and **fly26** match in the second round to form **itwouldfly26**, and **itwouldfly26** and **.** in the third round to enclause this main clause in a period.

Finally the two enriched punctuation mark concepts interact to determine the truth value of the main clause. First, the subordinate clause packages its truth value first in grammatical **if** and then it is enclaused in the following grammatical comma. The enriched comma feeds its affirmation or negation value into the Boolean value of the main clause enclaused in its period grammatical. This determines the truth value of the main clause. In this case one might say *"it's a big if"* or *"it's very iffy"*. This a perfect example of punctuation marks doing logic.

Constructing Questions

This is a good point to show how a statement can be turned into a question by reordering the symbols of an expression in the same manner used to form subordinate clauses. This next example also shows how changing **subject-seam** order in a statement to **seam-subject** order can convert a statement into a question.

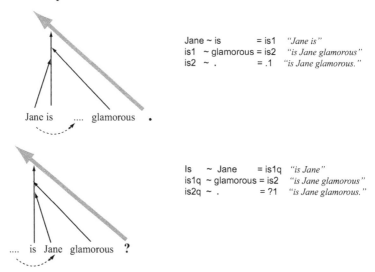

Fig 2.6.8   Flow-of-meaning-trees showing conversion of statement to a question

Questions are formed by swinging the subject symbol expression to the left side of the seam symbol. This indicates that information will flow in the opposite direction, from second person to first person, from you to me.

In the next example, if one asks *"Did the Duke of York arrive late?"* or *"Did he arrive late?"*, our parser with access to the *Mensa* table below would arrive at same row, **did1**, in either case and give the answer *"Yes, the Duke of York did arrive late"*.

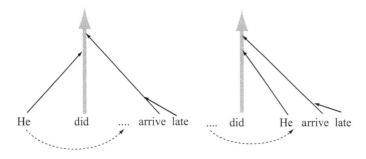

Fig 2.6.9 Flow-of-meaning-trees showing conversion of statement to a question and the method of ensuring pronoun reference

This *Mensa* table demonstrates how correct pronoun reference by a personal pronoun is achieved:

of ~York	**= of1**	*"of York"*
Duke ~ of1	**= Duke1**	*"Duke of York"*
the ~ Duke1	**= the1**	*"the Duke of York"*
the1 ~ did	**= did1**	*"the Duke of York did"*
he ~ did	**= did1**	*"the Duke of York did"*
arrive ~ late	**= arrive1**	*"arrive late"*
did1 ~ arrive1	**= did2**	*"Yes, the Duke of York did arrive late*

In this case the seam is included within the **did** grammatical which is enriched with subject *"The Duke of York"* or *"He"*. The order of **did** and **he** in the expression indicates whether it is a question or a statement. A statement is turned into a question by having the subject symbol come about the seam leaving the seam at the front of the expression. Fig. 2.6.9 shows the subject literally coming about the **did** seam.

The sentence *"Henry is going to give the money to John."* is another example of turning a statement into a question by having the subject "come about" the *seam*. Fig 2.6.10 shows the *flow-of-meaning-trees* that illustrate this transformation.

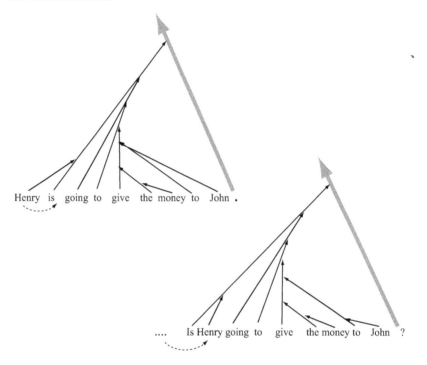

Fig 2.6.10 Flow-of-meaning-trees showing conversion of a statement to a question

This sentence can be turned into a question by reversing the order of subject and seam and replacing the period with a question mark.

Three more rows must be added to the sentence *Mensa* table to enable the parser to parse the question as well:

is ~ Henry	=	isq1	*"is Henry"*
isq1 ~ going1	=	isq2	*"is Henry going to give the money to John*
isq2 ~ ?	=	?33	*"is Henry going to give the money to John?"*

Reversing the order of subject and seam creates an interrogative *subject-seam*. It stamps the meaning contained in it as a question. Kipling's six honest serving men are *relative pronouns* if the speaker knows their content, *interrogative pronouns* if the speaker does not know their content.

Syntax indicates in whose mind the speaker believes the knowledge to be, his or the second person's. If I can indicate I do not know what the contents are, any courteous interlocutor will tell it to me, i.e. fill the seam grammatical with affirmation, negation or modality.

When someone makes a statement about something, one might ask *"How did this come about?"* These *flow-of-meaning-trees* appear to show that the process of having the subject symbol "come about" the seam to turn a statement into a question and vice versa is very like the sail movement as a sailboat changes tack from starboard to port. Our *flow-of-meaning-tree* diagrams literally depict the crossing over of the sail when a sailboat changes tack described by the nautical term "come about". Is this coincidence? Harry Bosch says there are no coincidences.[2] Or does the mind picture literal diagrams like this to manage thought?

Now let's see how to formulate **when where how why who** and **what** questions. Once a yes/no question has been framed in an expression and in a *Mensa* table, its concept can be used to enrich an interrogative pronoun, say **why**, to indicate which **why** question is being asked. Just put **why** up front in the expression.

Fig. 2.6.11 shows the *flow-of-meaning-tree* that diagrams this question.

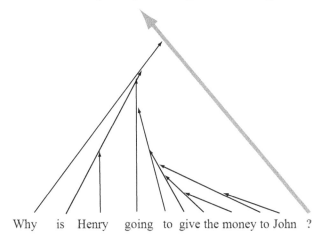

Why   is   Henry   going   to give the money to John   ?

Fig 2.6.11 Flow-of-meaning-tree showing construction of a **why** question

2   3 Michael Connelly, The Black Echo, Warner Books, New York, 2002, p.26

Two more *Mensa* table rows are required to enable the parser to turn it into a why question:

Interrogative grammatical concepts like **why** above say that the meaning they contain is in question. If I can indicate I do not know what the contents of an interrogative grammatical are, my interlocutor will tell me out of courtesy, i.e. fill the grammatical with the desired information. This is one of many occasions when an addressee has to cast about to determine what meaning a particular grammatical is to be filled with. Kipling's six honest serving men are *relative pronouns* if the speaker knows their content, *interrogative pronouns* if the speaker does not know their content. Syntax indicates in whose mind the speaker believes the knowledge to be, his or the second person's.

When someone makes a statement about something, one might ask *"How did this come about?"* These *flow-of-meaning-trees* illustrate the subject symbol "coming about" the seam to turn a statement into a question and vice versa. Our *flow-of-meaning-tree* diagrams literally depict the crossing over of the sail when a sailboat changes tack from starboard to port as described by the nautical term "come about". Does the unconscious mind picture literal diagrams like this to manage thought? Is this coincidence? Harry Bosch says there are no coincidences.

BOOK II
CHAPTER VII

Punctuation

Punctuation marks are symbols for concepts just like lexicals and grammaticals and can be treated as grammaticals. They typically contain more complex concepts like those meant by expressions, clauses, sentences and paragraphs and take part in relations at higher levels of the flow-of-meaning-tree. Relations between punctuation mark concepts are in the realm of logic

Yes, punctuation marks are valid symbols for concepts and henceforth will be included under the term grammatical just like the other grammaticals. Punctuation marks are expressed in spoken language as a silent interval or a dropped beat marking an empty space separating expressions of complex concepts. A longer interval to mark the end of a sentence is a *full stop*. Recently, CA1 neurons, dubbed "time cells", have been found in the hippocampus that fire to record empty intervals between episodes of activity.[1] So, it looks like punctuation marks have their own assigned neurons just like lexical words and grammaticals.

Here we recommend you pick up and read Lynn Truss's wonderful book *"Eat Shoot and Leaves"* which will immerse you most entertainingly in the history, theory and practice of punctuation.[2] Its main thrust is to show that punctuation marks are very useful in making clear what is being said and that punctuation marks can radically change meaning. Inappropriate placement of commas, for example, can introduce and unintended and often very funny double meaning. On testing our *flow-of-meaning-trees* and *Mensa* tables against many ambiguous examples in *"Eat Shoot and Leaves"* they resolved the double meaning in every case.

Punctuation mark symbols function to tell the reader not to go on parsing until the previous text has been parsed to a single concept. However, once a preceding text is parsed to a single concept, where are we to put its meaning? We argue, in the punctuation mark. Punctuation marks are attached to the whole preceding phrase or sentence, not the last word. As Lynn Truss reminds us: the comma used to refer to the whole phrase not just the punctuation mark and the Greek word "comma" means a "cut off piece".[3] Then hold this higher level punctuation concept in short term memory so as to be able to pair it later with another higher level concept, again contained in a punctuation mark, in a later round of the tournament.

We pursued the idea of treating punctuation marks as grammaticals able to hold such parsed concepts. This turned out to be very practical in terms of parser software issues. Under this scheme each punctuation mark or *point*

1   MacDonald CJ, Lepage KQ, Eden UT, Eichenbaum H, Hippocampal "Time Cells" Bridge the Gap in Memory for Discontiguous Events, Neuron, 71, 2011, pp 737-749.
2   Lynn Truss, Eats, *Shoots & Leaves*, Gotham Books, 2004,
3   Ibid. p. 72.

becomes a container of the meaning that flows from a preceding contiguous phrase, expression or finite sentence. Just like the other grammaticals, punctuation marks put their stamp on what kind of concept **it** is. Two good examples: when an expression concept is followed by a question mark, it becomes a question; when an expression is followed by an exclamation mark it becomes emphatic or loud. Punctuation marks contain complex concepts; the irony is that the more compact the symbol the more complex the concept it contains.

How punctuation marks function is best understood by perusing some *flow-of-meaning-trees* and *Mensa* tables for expressions that include punctuation marks. So, now, let's deal first with the comma.

The Comma

Take the sentence *"In a surprise move, Spirit Airlines will charge $45 for carry-ons"*, The prepositional phrase *"In a surprise move, ... "* expresses a mental **in** concept whose meaning ends up embedded in a comma symbol. Here is the meaning flow diagram for this comma phrase:

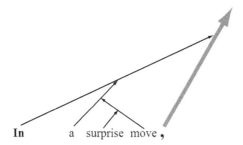

Fig. 2.7.1 Flow-of-meaning-tree for an **in** prepositional phrase concept packaged in a comma.

Here is the corresponding *Mensa* table for this **in** prepositional phrase concept enriching a comma.

surprise ~ move	= surprisemove	*"surprise move"*
a ~ surprisemove	= a1	*"a surprise move"*
in ~ a1	= in1	*"in a surprise move"*
in1 ~ ,	= ,1472	*"in a surprise move,"*

Meaning flow narrative: Concept **move** is enriched by adjective concept **surprise** to yield concept **surprisemove**. Indefinite article concept **a** is enriched by **surprisemove** to yield enriched determiner concept **a1**, which enriches concept **in** to yield **in1**. Concept **in1** relays its meaning in turn into the comma to yield enriched comma concept **,1472**, which now contains the whole **in** concept. This comma symbol packaging a single **in** concept stands ready to relay meaning to the period concept of the main clause. In the next section we will mate this prepositional phrase comma concept with a finite sentence period concept. Now, let's consider the location if the comma in an old AI chestnut comprising the two sentences: *"I saw the Statue of Liberty, flying in from Boston last evening."* and *"I saw the Statue of Liberty flying in from Boston, last evening."* Placement of the comma in the second sentence forces a completely different meaning, one that is highly unlikely.

Figure 2.7.2 shows the *flow-of-meaning-tree* for the first sentence with meaning from *flying in* flowing into **I** rather than into the Statue of Liberty.

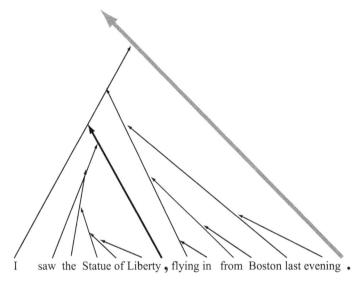

I   saw the Statue of Liberty **,** flying in   from Boston last evening **.**

Fig. 2.7.2   First FOMT for the sentence "I saw the Statue of Liberty, flying in from Boston last evening."

Figure 2.7.3 shows the *flow-of-meaning-tree* for the second sentence with the meaning of *flying in* flowing into the Statue of Liberty:

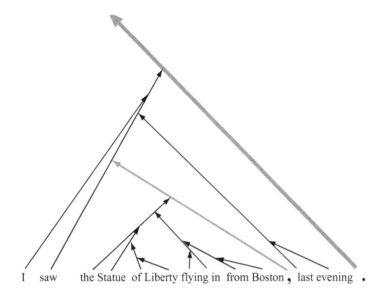

I   saw   the Statue of Liberty flying in from Boston **,** last evening **.**

Fig. 2.7.3 Second FOMT for the sentence "I saw the Statue of Liberty flying in from Boston, last evening."

Placement of the comma makes all the difference!

The Period

The period, obligatory after each finite sentence in a paragraph, is a container symbol that accepts and packages all the meaning from its preceding sentence. Paragraph sentence periods literally "make a point".

The Spirit Airlines sentence analyzed above was contained in the following four sentence paragraph:

> *"There was an announcement from Spirit Airlines last week. In a surprise move, Spirit Airlines will charge $45 for carry-ons. No doubt travelers will resent this. But Spirit Airlines CEO said the charge will improve on-time departures."*

It is easy to see that these sentences relate to each other logically. The point of enclosing the meaning of each finite sentence of a paragraph in its period grammatical is so that the point made by each sentence can be matched with points made by other sentences in a paragraph to form a higher level expression that parses to a much more complex unified *paragraph concept.*

Finite sentence *"In a surprise move, Spirit Airlines will charge $45 for carry-ons."* is the main point of this paragraph. Its main clause, *"Spirit Airlines will charge $45 for carry-ons"* parses to a unitary **will** *ment* concept.

Fig. 2.7.4 shows the *flow-of-meaning-tree* of this main clause:

Spirit Airlines **will** charge $45 for carry-ons

Fig. 2.7.4   Flow-of-meaning-tree and Mensa table for a finite sentence ment concept without a period.

Here is its *Mensa* table:

Spirit ~Airlines	**= SpritAirlines**	*"Spirit Airlines"*
SpiritAirlines ~ will	**= will1**	*"Spirit Airlines will"*
charge ~ 45$	**= charge1**	*"charge 45$"*
for ~ carry-ons	**= for1**	*"for carry-ons"*
charge1 ~ for1	**= charge2**	*"charge 45$ for carry-ons"*
will1 ~ charge2	**= will2**	*"Spirit Airlines will charge 45$ for carry-ons"*

This *Mensa* table shows modal grammatical *will* being enriched twice, first by preceding subject concept **SpiritAirlines** to form a *seam-subject* concept and then by following verb phrase concept **charge2** resulting in parse seam grammatical *will* becoming enriched to an **it** that is a *ment* concept.

It is a rule of syntax that once a punctuation mark concept is filled with meaning there has to be a matching punctuation mark for it to mate with later in the expression, just like parentheses. This explains why the comma phrase *"In a surprise move,"* by itself feels incomplete. We will see the comma of this prepositional phrase matched up with the period of the main clause to form a complete sentence where the period grammatical is the survivor concept. Periods trump commas..

Fig.2.7.5 shows this **will** observation *ment* concept being enclosed in a period, which converts the whole sentence to an *endit* concept.

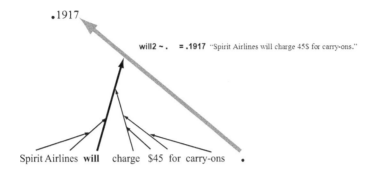

Fig. 2.7.5 Flow-of-meaning-tree for a finite sentence with a period.

The *flow-of-meaning-tree* in Fig. 2.7.6 shows the enriched **will** observation concept and the enriched **in** comma concept both enriching the period concept.

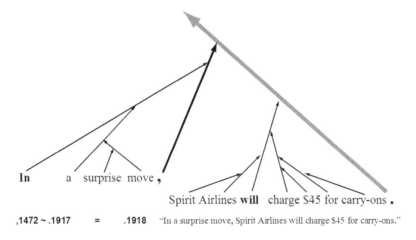

Fig. 2.7.6 Flow-of-meaning-tree for a comma concept enriching a main clause concept..

This *flow-of-meaning-tree* shows the enriched **will** observation concept and the enriched **in** comma concept both enriching the period concept. The *Mensa* table row in the figure shows main clause **.1917** concept being further enriched by prepositional phrase comma concept **,1472** to give **.1918** representing the meaning of the whole sentence.

This complete observation concept is now packaged in a period grammatical. And its sense will be modified by meaning flowing in from the content containing period grammaticals of the other sentences. As explained in Book II Chapter VIII on paragraphs, once the meaning of each sentence in a paragraph is packaged in a period, these period concepts can be combined into a unitary paragraph concept. Meaning flows between them so that the nuance of each sentence adapts, And, it is possible to choreograph subtle logic operations.

Figure 2.7.7 show a string of four periods of the paragraph above forming an expression which parses to a paragraph concept holding the meaning of the whole paragraph and organizing all the concepts of each sentence into an overall relationship. With access to an appropriate *Mensa* table our current parser program can parse this entire paragraph correctly to a single paragraph concept symbol and score the meaning of each sentence and total a score for the whole paragraph.

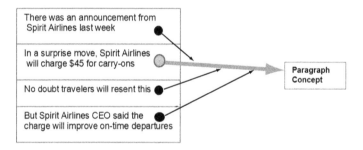

Fig. 2.7.7   Flow-of-meaning-tree for a paragraph concept.

Usually one to the sentences, often the first, will be the main point of the paragraph in which case it is common to say *"the point is ..."*, *"the thing (of it) is ..."*. Here, the second sentence appears to be the main point of the paragraph. It is underscored by the following two sentences.

Notice that when a finite sentence is employed as a newspaper headline it does not take a period. This is because the headline is just describing what is in that text and is not being related to other paragraph points. However once a sentence is in a paragraph a period is mandatory so the sentences can be related to each other at a higher level.

The Question Mark

The sentence *"Spirit Airlines will charge $45 for carry-ons."* converts to the question *"will Spirit Airlines charge $45 for carry-ons?"* by having the subject concept "come about" the seam. Changing the subject seam order indicates that the speaker expects information to flow in the opposite direction, now from second person to first person; information known to the second person, not known to the first person.

Fig. 2.7.8 shows the meaning flow tree for this question,

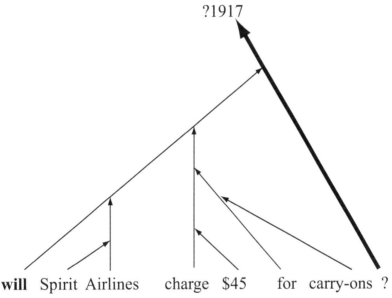

Fig. 2.7.8 Flow-of-meaning-tree and Mensa table for a question with a question mark.

Here are the operation rows that have to be added to the *Mensa* table above for our parser to be able to parse this question and identify which question it is:

will ~ SpiritAirlines =	willQ1	*"will Spirit Airlines"*
willQ1 ~ charge2	= willQ2	*"will Spirit Airlines charge 45$ for carry-ons"*
willQ2 ~ ?	= ?1917	*"will Spirit Airlines charge 45$ for carry-ons*

Concept symbol **.1917** is a statement **will** concept; **?1917** is a question **will** concept. It will be seen that the difference between a statement **will** concept and a question **will** concept is whether the **will** is enriched by the subject concept from the left or from the right. This *flow-of-meaning-tree* literally shows the **will** concept "turning into" a question concept.

The expression *"will Spirit Airlines charge $45 for carry-ons"* is already a question, But a question mark is added, *"will Spirit Airlines charge $45 for carry-ons?"*, to seal the meaning. The meaning of the whole question then becomes packaged in that question mark grammatical. The **?** symbol replaces the **.** symbol, the period punctuation mark, that made it a statement. One can imagine the shape of the question mark symbol showing a period taking a U turn pointing backwards to indicate information flowing in the opposite direction.

The Colon and Semicolon

Both colon and semicolon can also be thought of as concept packages that contain two concepts, one received from the left and one received from the right. The concepts can be simple phrase concepts or fairly complex full observation concepts. The two different pictographic elements of the ; exemplify that the two contributors are not equivalent; its period representing the main expression and its comma the expression that underscores it. The colon functions in the same pictographic way collecting meaning from left and right concepts. Its : pictograph with both elements identical indicates that the contributing concepts are equivalent. The colon resembles and functions like an equals sign.

Conclusions

The most important step we have taken with regard to punctuation marks is to see them as grammaticals and treat them just like the other traditional grammaticals as containers and shapers of meaning. This has made possible the encoding and parsing of extremely long sentences with multiple subordinate clauses quite straightforward. *Mensa* table are perfectly able to absorb and manage punctuation marks and they fit perfectly into *flow-of-meaning-tree* diagrams.

In perusing the *flow-of-meaning-tree* diagrams in this chapter note that punctuation mark arrow enclosing the preceding concept tree creates a shape like a purse snapping closed. We have speculated that the mnemonic origin of the word "parsing" came from "pairsing", and then from "pathing". Now it looks like it came from "pursing".

The rules of syntax become: lexicals enrich grammaticals which in turn pass meaning to punctuation marks; that is, punctuation marks trump grammaticals, which in turn trump lexicals in becoming the surviving concept of a mental operation. This means that punctuation mark contain the more complex concepts. Once the *flow-of-meaning-tree* reaches the *punctuation* level, the series of symbols of an expression has become an ordered string of punctuation symbols. Each packages a complex concept. With punctuation we are in the realm of *logic*.

BOOK II
CHAPTER VIII

Pronouns, Paragraphs and Poems

In this chapter we discuss how meaning can flow between related concepts that are not adjacent in the same line of text. Meaning can jump from a concept in one clause or sentence to a concept in a nearby clause or sentence. In paragraphs each sentence parses to its period grammatical making a paragraph a series of points made. Meaning flows back and forth between the points of the paragraph. The points can be combined in a flow-of-meaning-tree and Mensa table so as to parse to a unitary paragraph concept. As a paragraph is read, each point is given a score mentally. One point can underscore another and one point can undercut another. The scores are summed mentally. A total score is kept mentally, which is a measure of how persuasive the paragraph is. With poetry a different process ensues. Concepts in adjacent lines of a poem can be placed in vertical juxtaposition by meter and rhyme and relay meaning to each other. Meaning flows back and forth between concepts in the same line and between concepts on different lines. This allows for two dimensional relations and a great richness of concept enhancement.

The idea of a concept being serially enriched by being party to a series of relations has been expressed well by Saul Bellow explaining the difficulty of creating a full character in a novel: *"the man (writers) bring forth has no richness compared with the man who really exists, thickened, fed and fattened by all the facts about him, all of his history."*[1] In this chapter we consider how a concept can be enriched by relations with concepts that are outside the confines of the current expression or sentence, accruing meaning not just from flanking symbols in the same expression but also from concepts in other nearby and remote expressions. Once party to more than one expression or sentence, an **it** concept receives more and more meaning from its neighbor concepts in each sentence that **it** is mentioned in. This meaning enrichment process can continue indefinitely resulting in a very complex and unique **it** concept, **it**s wealth of meaning gathered from the totality of statements about **it**, gained from **it**s entire past and **it**s potential future.

In our discussion of relations so far we have mostly considered a surviving concept being serially enriched only by relations with concepts mentioned within the one dimensional line of an expression or a sentence. For example, in a noun phrase a series of adjectives can serially add meaning to a noun concept which is then subsumed by the determiner. We have described how, when two relative concepts within an expression pair up, they adapt their senses to fit with each other and one becomes the surviving concept that now incorporates meaning received from the other, which can then be retired. We have explained that in parsing an expression only some of the concepts enter into a relation with an adjacent concept in the first round, others get a bye to be matched up with another survivor concept in the next round, like players in a tennis tournament. Then, in successive rounds one concept from each pair of matched concepts survives into the next round but modified by its experience. This happens naturally in parsing an expression or finite sentence until the final **it** concept has received meaning in successive rounds from all of the other concepts mentioned via **it**s participation in several sentences.

In this chapter we discuss how meaning can flow not just from concepts in the same sentence but also from a concept or concepts in an adjacent sentence, a form of crosstalk. This leads to an brief analysis of how poetry

---

1   Saul Bellow, Letters, Edited by Benjamin Taylor, Viking, 2010.

and song work to reinforce the enrichment of concepts that are connected to many and varied memories and emotions.

Then, in our discussion of the period punctuation mark we argued that the meaning of each sentence in a paragraph is enclosed in the period grammatical; each sentence "makes a point". Then the points form a terse higher level expression that parses to a final **it** concept, the paragraph concept. This is not the intent of every paragraph. Sometimes the clear intent of a paragraph is to fill out the richness of one particular concept.

Serial Concept Enrichment in a Paragraph

In this kind of paragraph the main purpose may be to serially enrich one particular concept that is a party concept of several of the sentences. Then, we see the same concept being mentioned in many expressions and sentences, accruing more and more meaning in the process.

The following paragraph is taken from the review by David Oshninsky of Wilbert Rideau's book on Angola prison in the New York Times Book Review, June3, 2010.

> *"An hour's drive northwest from Baton Rouge sits the Louisiana State Penitentiary, known as Angola, the largest maximum security prison in the United States. On the site of a former slave plantation, it currently houses close to 5,000 inmates and covers more ground, at 18,000 acres, than the island of Manhattan. Surrounded on three sides by the Mississippi River, its stunning physical isolation and distinctive antebellum feel have provided the backdrop for numerous feature films and documentaries, including "Dead Man Walking," "Monster's Ball" and "The Farm." For Southerners, especially African-Americans, Angola is both a prison and a state of mind, a relic from before the civil rights era, when white supremacy was the custom and racial segregation was the law."*

As well as painting a picture, the author's intent in this paragraph is to add a wealth of meaning into concept **Angola** by making **it** party to a series of phrases, expressions, clauses and observations throughout the paragraph where **Angola** is the surviving **it**, so that **Angola** will accrete meaning from neighboring concepts at its every mention. If there were a heading on this paragraph it would be "Angola Prison". This example of skilled descriptive writing makes **Angola** a very rich concept.

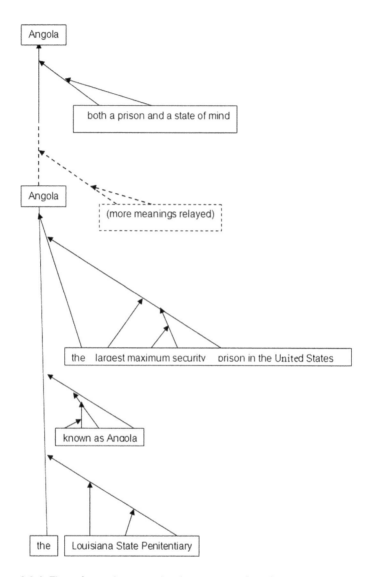

Figure 2.8.1 Flow-of-meaning-tree showing concept **Angola** accreting meaning from serial expressions

The **ex**tended *flow-of-meaning-tree* in Fig 2.8.1. is intended to show the **Angola** concept starting as an undifferentiated **the** determiner symbol. Then, it contributes and receives of meaning as a party concept of each next sentence, each *flow-of-meaning-tree*, that contains it. We have stated that within each *flow-of-meaning-tree* lines can't cross. However, when a concept escapes from one *flow-of-meaning-tree* to join another, an X does form at the exit point, illustrating the mnemonic effect of the grammatical affix **ex-** explained in Book III, Chapter III.

Identity

At some point concepts that accrete meaning in this fashion achieve an absolute identity that already incorporates meaning that may be revealed in later expressions. The *flow-of-meaning-tree* above suggests that the prison's final identity is fully established by meaning inflow in the early part of the paragraph, at which point it is assigned symbol **Angola**. By the end of the paragraph it has become an exceedingly rich complex concept, but its symbol remains **Angola**. The idea is that once a concept symbol attains established identity, anything more added to it does not change it because all meaning is already contained in what is meant by the symbol.

Angola ~ at1800	= Angola	*"Angola at 1800 acres"*
1800 ~ acres	= 1800acres	*"1800 acres"*
at ~ 1800acres	= at1800	*"at 1800 acres"*

John Locke's remarks on identity are pertinent here:

> *"For in them the variation of great parcels of matter alters not the identity: an oak growing from a plant to a great tree, and then lopped, is still the same oak; and a colt grown up to a horse, sometimes fat, sometimes lean, is all the while the same horse: though, in both these cases, there may be a manifest change of the parts."*
> *Essay II, XXXVII,3*

> *"Since I think I may be confident, that, whoever should see a creature of his own shape or make, though it had no more reason all its life than a cat or a parrot, would call him still a man; or whoever should hear a cat or a parrot discourse, reason, and philosophize, would call or think it nothing but a cat or a parrot; and say, the one was a dull irrational man, and the other a very intelligent rational parrot."*
> *Essay II, XXXVII,8*

Incidentally, consideration of the Angola paragraph allows some insight into the function of grammatical **that**. When an author wants to identify a concept among alternatives, he can employ **that** as an anaphor to point back to previous involvement that a concept has had from being party to a relationship previously expressed or well known. To do this Rideau would have to say *"Angola is the prison **that** is surrounded (sic) on* *three sides by the Mississippi river".* Now, **that** picks up meaning from known knowledge, which in this case is re-expressed locally, just so one understands which prison it is. Grammatical **that** fills with this meaning and relays it back onto **the prison,** which then relays it on via a **be** relation on into **Angola.**

The Point Making Paragraph

In most cases a paragraph serves a different purpose than enriching a single concept when it combines several whole observations. A paragraph is composed of several finite sentences, each one of which may consist of a main clause and several subordinate clauses. Each sentence is ended with a period grammatical. With each sentence the author is "making a point". Note that making the surviving concept of an observation into a point breaks the simplest syntax rule that the first mentioned concept of a match is the surviving concept. However it appears to be another *rule of syntax*, punctuation marks trump both *endits* and *ments*.

Once the meaning of the ordered string of concepts mentioned in the sentence is packaged into this period, thus the period acts as a unitary container for the meaning of the sentence. Meaning is relayed between different sentences, via the period grammatical of each sentence packed with its meaning. In this view of a paragraph, meaning is not transmitted in a granular way, as we will see in the next section on poetry, from a concept on one line to a concept further on the same line or to a concept on another line but rather from sentence period to sentence period, i.e. point to point. The brain in turn would have to wire up neurons assigned to each sentence point appropriately into a neural tree to manage such a complex relationship of concepts. Here, both the mind and *Mensa* are operating in the realm of logic.

A paragraph as a whole outlines a logical argument, discloses the steps of process, tells a story, paints a picture etc. A paragraph can be considered as an expression made up of a series of points (periods) that parse to a unitary paragraph concept. Let's say a paragraph composed of four sentences defines a paragraph concept composed of four observation concepts. When each sentence of a paragraph is parsed to a compact period symbol these points are "atomic". They become the leaves of a higher order tree. At the point level a four sentence paragraph comprising four observation concepts can be represented as a simple expression of four terms by letting the period at the end of each sentence be a unitary symbol for each observation concept.

Thus, a complex paragraph concept can be modeled with a *flow-of-meaning-tree* and *Mensa table*, by combining them into a unified mental structure. Let each of four sentences parse to its enriched period concept. Then, compact expression, **A. B. C. D.** can now represent the paragraph. Fig. 2.8.2 shows that a *meaning flow* diagram and *M5 table* for a paragraph template could be composed as follows:

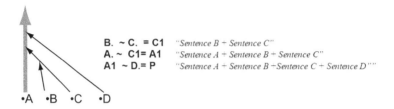

Figure 2.8.2 Flow-of-Meaning-Tree and Mensa table for a paragraph

Note that point **.B** underscores point **.C** not point **.A** directly. Point **.B** and point **.C** have to be matched up to give a survivor that will be matched with point **.A** before **.D** is folded in. Once our parser program has parsed each sentence to its period, three more *Mensa* rows in the database will allow our parser program to parse the text of the entire paragraph, to obtain the unique concept **P**, the paragraph concept.

Another common paragraph structure is the *narrative*. In a *narrative* paragraph each sentence describes actions or event that occur in strict order. A *narrative* paragraph starts with the first observation and the following observations steadily contribute meaning to it in turn along a storyline or a timeline to create paragraph concept **N**, a complex narrative concept.

Figure 2.8.3 Flow-of-Meaning-Tree and Mensa table for a narrative paragraph

The above tables of *Mensa* rows also suggest the idea of templates for paragraph *Mensa tables*. If actual concept ID#s of observation concepts are edited over generic .A, .B, .C and .D, it instantly creates a working paragraph *Mensa table* that enables our parser to parse an entire particular paragraph.

Figure 2.8.4 shows a *flow-of-meaning-tree* drawn like a long "n-arrow" to suggest the origin of words *narrative* and *narrator*.

Figure 2.8.4 flow-of-meaning-tree for an "n-arrow" paragraph

On this basis the Angola paragraph can be seen in a completely different light, parsed as a regular point-making paragraph of narrative type as shown in Fig. 2.8.5 with meaning flowing between whole sentences rather than flowing inter-sentence between individual party concepts.

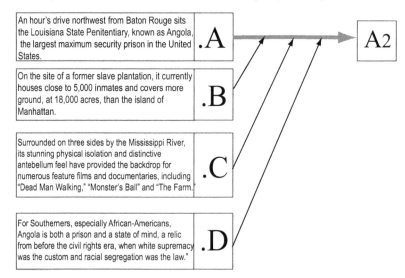

Figure 2.8.5 Flow-of-Meaning-Tree and Mensa table for the Angola paragraph parsed as a point-making paragraph

It's unlikely that this parsing was the intent of the author who clearly wanted to maximize the richness of the Angola concept.

Now let's look at another typical paragraph to see how these ideas play out in practice. Take the following paragraph from Franz de Vaal's review of *The Price of Altruism* by Oren Harmon in the New York Times Book Review p.18, July 1, 2010:

> *"It grows out of empathy with those in need or distress, a capacity that probably evolved when female mammals began to nurture their young. This would explain why women are more empathetic than men, and why empathy is affected by oxytocin, a hormone involved in birth and breast-feeding. Both men and women display strikingly more empathetic responses in lab experiments after oxytocin has been sprayed into their nostrils. Since oxytocin makes us feel good, there is no sharp line between care for others and self-love."*

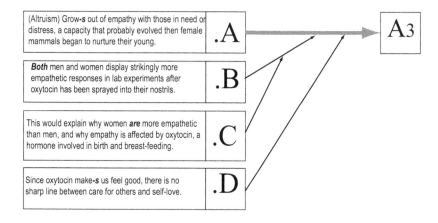

Figure 2.8.6 Flow-of-Meaning-Tree and Mensa table for a point-making paragraph

Fig. 2.8.6 shows the *flow-of-meaning-tree* for this paragraph.

These four sentences parse to observation concepts **.A .B .C .D** with the seam concept being the surviving concept in each observation. Seams are bolded in the text; notice that in observation concept **.B** the seam is hidden in plural grammatical both. Each sentence is packaged in a period grammatical, becoming a point concept. The paragraph now becomes a short expression of points, **.A .B .C** and **.D**.

Meaning flow diagrams like the above can illustrate meaning flow between the component sentences of a paragraph. Here, one could say that the **.B** point underscores the **.C** point. They show how point concepts are combined into a unified paragraph concept. Once a *flow of meaning tree* reaches the punctuation level it is in the realm of logic. This illustrates an important theme of this *Essay*, that once complex expressions have been parsed down to single concept symbols, these symbols can be related to each other very simply to perform quite high level logic.

An entire paragraph can readily be translated into a *Mensa table*, thereby holding perhaps a hundred concepts. A *flow-of-meaning-tree* can be drawn and a *Mensa table* composed to structure the entire series of concepts into a single unitary *paragraph concept* with its own unique compact concept symbol, a paragraph mark signified by a blank line. This *Mensa table* enables our parser program to identify all of the concepts mentioned in the paragraph and manage their relationships to each other.

In the following paragraph slightly adapted from a Wall Street Journal editorial,[2] meaning (spin) flows from the last two sentences into the first sentence.

> *"Oregon raised its income tax on the richest 2% of its residents last year to fix its budget hole, but now the state treasury admits it collected nearly one-third less revenue than the bean counters projected. The sun also rose in the east. The Cubs didn't win the World Series."*

Each observation concept expressed by a sentence is a singular *entity* concept. It is reasonable for the reader to judge whether all of the component observations fit together and that the ensemble of points makes an integrated paragraph.

A paragraph concept is one kind of group concept. We have seen that one function of the seam symbol of each sentence is to gather together all of the concepts party to an observation that are mentioned in a sentence into a gestalt, putting each one in its place. An *Mensa table* that focuses meaning into the seam concept can record this process exactly. Then, if all the seams in a paragraph, packaged in periods, are hooked together, all of the party concepts of the whole paragraph will be gathered together into a congruent unified structure and related to each other precisely. The meaning of a highly nuanced paragraph concept can change depending

---

2   WSJ Editorial, Ducking Higher Taxes, 12/21/10 p. A13

on how it is parsed. It is up to us to determine how the author meant us to parse it.

It is remarkable that a paragraph, such a grander-than-single concept, can organize hundreds of elemental concepts into a complex unified structure with every concept in its place and related correctly to every other one. The effortless power of a list of binary relations, using the method of the single-elimination tournament, to precisely specify the structure of an enormously complex paragraph concept, putting every party concept in its correct place, is impressive. Again, a *Mensa table* can record this larger process exactly.

One cannot hold an entire paragraph thought in consciousness at one time, yet there is a mental facility for unconsciously linking all the mentioned concepts into a structure that our mind's eye can examine. Consciousness can tour this mental construct via a mental tree traversal algorithm, weighing the integrity and coherence of the paragraph concept, and experiencing in consciousness the sensory graphic images described, and feelings referred to or evoked.

Poetry and Song

If an *expression* can be considered a one dimensional horizontal string of symbols where meaning exchanges only between adjacent symbols in order of precedence and in later rounds of the *ment*, then, a *poem* can be considered as a two dimensional array of symbols. Poems with regular meter place concept symbols into vertical juxtaposition in adjacent lines.

A good example is in the Ed Bruce song *Girls, Women and Ladies*.[3],[4]

Then, meaning flows vertically from a concept symbol in one line to an

---

3   To hear the song, Google "You Tube Girls Women And Ladies" I'm feeling lucky

4   Ed Bruce: Girls Women And Ladies Lyrics 1981
     "And he said there's girls and there's women and there's ladies
     There's yes'es and there's no's and there's maybe's
     There's teasin' and pleasin' they start learnin' when they're babies
     There's girls and there's women and there's ladies"

adjacent concept symbol in a line above or below, a kind of crosstalk. It's left to the imagination as what meaning the *yes'es* and the *no's* and the *maybe's* of the Ed Bruce song contain and as to what meaning reflects back onto the three kinds of females.[5]

It is the role of meter to place symbols on different lines in precise registration so there can also be crosstalk between individual symbols in registration on different lines can be considered adjacent. The function of rhyme is to relate the last word on one line with the rhyming word on an adjacent line ensuring that those two words will exchange meaning will adapt their senses, Rhyming of line end words or just their suffixes ensures which symbols will be in relation,

Rhyme can be intra-line:

> *"There's many a* **slip** *between the cup and the lip"*
> * *"There's many a* **slip** *between the lip and the cup"*
> *"Don't do the* **crime** *If you can't do the time"* "
> *"A Costco in* **Moscow** " *"***My way** *or the Highway"*
> *"Click it or* **ticket** "
> *"A man with a* **plan** "

Rhyming words share the same or phonetically similar suffix. In his book review, Leon Aron explains why Russian poet Joseph Brodsky was unable to translate his poems, originally written in Russian, into English verse with the same beauty and power of the original Russian, although he tried hard to do so. [6]

> *"Without a fixed word order, auxiliary verbs such as "is" or "are" or articles, Russian offers little to impede the lyrical poet, and Brodsky rejoiced in this paradigmatically inflected language. Rich shades of emotions and meanings are conveyed by prefixes and suffixes. Myriad rhymes are generated almost spontaneously as the mostly polysyllabic nouns, verbs, adjectives and participles conjugate (that is, change their endings) in accordance with six cases and three genders. English, with its rigid order, shorter words and precious little change in word endings, is hardly a happy counterpart."*

---

5   This is also a very good example showing how grammaticals like **yes**, **no** and **maybe** can be containers of meaning.

6   Leon Aron, A World Fiercely Observed A sublime lyrical poet, Joseph Brodsky knew the reality of human evil firsthand, New York Times Book Review. January 15, 2011

We can imagine a poet stuffing two different lexical roots into the same suffix. Maybe they are compatible and affect each other's sense in novel and delightful ways. Maybe they conflict in a way the poet uses to get an effect that gets our attention. The magic of poetry may come from a poet's ability with clever juxtapositions to load symbols with subtle meanings.

Tying these ideas to ideas advanced in the neural correlate chapter in Book I, the neural network activated by an expression "makes sense" when it addresses and actually gets through to left temporal lobe neurons with projections to both cortices able to evoke memories, images and feelings in consciousness. Each time a rhyming word is repeated it is a reinforcing stimulus, another jolt to the primed active network, awakens more memories, feelings images. This effect can be felt hearing the refrain of the Beatles' first big hit song in America "I Want to Hold Your Hand". Consider the highly calculated interaction of lyric and tune. The repeats of the refrain likely restimulate a neural network already primed and perhaps raises the level of activation to new heights to evoke other memories and feelings not raised earlier.

> *"Oh yeah, I'll tell you something*
> *I think you'll underst**and***
> *When I say that something*
> *I wanna hold your **hand***
> *I wanna hold your **hand***
> *I wanna hold your **hand**"*

This song upon its release in America in 1964 clearly activated the limbic system of millions, selling 10,000 copies every hour in New York, topping the charts for seven weeks, and rocketing the Beatles to the top of the pop music world.[7]

The propensity of the human mind to allow well ordered symbols to give pleasure makes writing one of the forms of art along with music and painting, sculpture et al. .

---

7 To hear the song, Google "You Tube I wanna hold your hand" I'm feeling lucky

BOOK III
CHAPTER I

Invariance for Expressions that Mean the Same Thing

*Perhaps the most important attribute of a computer language understanding system is an ability to precisely understand what is said to it no matter what words are used and even if the input text is phrased in many thousands of different ways. In neuroscience terms this is called **invariance**, the ability to recognize that something is a tree or a chair no matter how where on the retina its image is presented, or what is its size, orientation, surface color and reflectance, or lighting conditions. Stanislas Dehaene says that for that mind to do this, all possible representations of an entity have to be "tied together" in the mind. We picked a complex concept that cannot be specified precisely in less than 25 words and calculated that it could be stated correctly by more than nine billion different sentences. Then, as an exercise, we developed a Mensa table that enables our standard parser to identity all nine billion sentences that precisely mean that concept yet reject any sentence even using the same words that did not express the concept correctly. Incidentally, this exercise showed Mensa tables can seamlessly incorporate Truth Tables which enable a computer to mindlessly perform highly abstract logic better and faster than humans.*

L anguage is a vast combinatorial system which can say trillions of different things, all making sense. Linguists usually express this idea by saying an infinite number of sensible language expressions and sentences are possible. Steven Pinker in *The Language Instinct* perhaps best describes this remarkable property of language:[1]

> *"The fact that grammar is a discrete combinatorial system has two important consequences. The first is the sheer vastness of language. Go into the Library of Congress and pick a sentence at random from any volume, and chances are you would fail to find an exact repetition no matter how long you continued to search. Estimates of the number of sentences that an ordinary person is capable of producing are breathtaking. If a speaker is interrupted at a random point in a sentence, there are on average about ten different words that could be inserted at that point to continue the sentence in a grammatical and meaningful way. (At some points in a sentence, only one word can be inserted, and at others, there is a choice from among thousands; ten is the average.) Let's assume that a person is capable of producing sentences up to twenty words long. Therefore the number of sentences that a speaker can deal with in principle is at least 10^{20} (a one with twenty zeros after it, or a hundred million trillion). At a rate of five seconds a sentence, a person would need a childhood of about a hundred trillion years (with no time for eating or sleeping) to memorize them all."*

But what does not appear to be widely recognized by linguists is that it is also possible to say the same thing, to express the very same concept, precisely, in billions of different ways. Pronouns, epithets, synonyms, paraphrases, synecdoche, metaphors, multiple subordinate clauses, etc. are all commonly used in expressions and sentences that can refer to the same precise concept. One can freely use active or passive voice and change the order of words and phrases, again in a virtually infinite number of ways, while preserving the same meaning. We follow Stanislas Dehaene in using the term *invariance* to describe the minds ability to realize that a concept is the same even if expressed in many different ways.[2]

The sizes of the *Cartesian Product* of word strings that say exactly the same thing create a huge combinatorial problem for natural language

---

1   Steven Pinker, *The Language Instinct*, pp. 85-6
2   Stanislas Dehaene, *Reading in the Brain*, Viking, New York, 2009, p. 128.

processing.[3] A software parser program has to be able to field them all and pick out the multibillions of well-formed expressions and sentences that **do** have the same precise meaning and distinguish from the multibillions of sentences using much the same words that say something else, or **don't** make sense, or use bad grammar. This could be done by creating and storing a table of billions of text strings that express the concept accurately. Not practical. It would take thousands of clever literate people many lifetimes to generate a complete list of correct strings. However, we found that our parser program accessing a relatively small *Mensa* table of mental operations was able to distinguish correct variants of this statement from minimally changed statements that did not state the statute correctly.

Invariance for an Expression

We conducted an exercise to see whether, by composing an appropriate *Mensa* database, our parser program could precisely understand a specific concept no matter how it was expressed. Inspired by one of us failing a multiple choice question on the California DMV Written Test, we took as a test bed example the statute, California Vehicle Code, Division 12, Chapter 5, Article 3.3, Section 27360.5:

> *27360.5 b) (1) A driver may not transport on a highway a child in a motor vehicle, as defined in Section 27315, without properly securing the child in a rear seat in a child passenger restraint system meeting applicable federal motor vehicle safety standards, unless the child is one of the following:*

(A) Six years of age or older.
(B) Sixty pounds or more.

This statute can be stated quite fully with the following 26 word sentence: *"A child must be buckled in an approved safety seat if he or she is less than 6 years old and is less than 60 pounds."* How many other English sentences can correctly restate this statute? Billions.

We first performed a calculation, to estimate how many ways a sentence with a precise fixed meaning could be restated yet keep its original meaning. Our approach to estimating the number of language expressions that can precisely state the statute was to arbitrarily designate 15 stages in that sentence where it is possible to employ an alternate synonym or

---

3   Google "Cartesian Product" I'm feeling lucky`

paraphrase. One can thread a path through the alternate phrases choosing different paths without changing the meaning of the statement. Only correct paths through will preserve the meaning. The path through the various alternate phrases is a *tuple*, in this case a 15-tuple, and the set of all possible word strings that have the same meaning is the *Cartesian product* of the tuple. The number of possible correct sentences is the *Cartesian Product* of this *15-tuple*, obtained by serially multiplying up the numbers in the set of alternative words of phrases at each position of the tuple.

Table 3.1.1 shows 15 arbitrary points in this 26-word sentence where we were able to substitute a number of alternate synonyms or paraphrases for the word or phrase that can be used at each position without changing the meaning. Then, for the exercise, we came up with small subsets of possible alternative synonyms and phrases, or blanks when words can be left out, for each of the 15 points in the sentence.

Set #		Phrase	Alternate Phrases Feasible at Each Point
1.	5*	a child	he/ she/ he or she/ a toddler
2.	4*	must be	has to be/ must be/ needs to be/ is required to be/ and negatives/ blank
3.	10*	buckled	strapped/ secured/ held/ seated/ restrained/ seated / placed/ ride/ blank
4.	2*	in	into
5.	4*	a safety seat	a child's safety seat/ an approved safety seat/ an approved child safety seat
6.	3*	if	when/ unless
7.	4*	he or she	a child/ he/ she/ he or she
8.	4*	is	is not/ isn't/ weighs
9.	7*	under	less than/ younger than/ over/ more than/ older than/ blank
10.	9*	6 years old	six years old/ 6 years of age/ six years of age/ 6/ six/ age 6/ age six/ 60 pounds
11.	4*	and	or/ blank
12.	5*	he or she	he/ she/a child/ blank
13.	5*	is	is not/weighs/does not weigh\blank
14.	5*	under	over/ more than/ less than/ blank
15.	4*	60 pounds	60 pounds in weight /sixty pounds or more/60 pounds in weight/

Cartesian Product of tuple sets: 4*4*10*2*4*3*4*4*7*9*4*5*5*5*4 = 9,676,800,000

Table 3.1.1 Billions of alternate phrasings can be used without changing the meaning of a statement

With a 15-tuple, even with a small number sample of elements in each set, the total number of elements in the Cartesian product can be very large; billions of different sentences can state that DMV statute precisely. Further, if we rephrase the concepts, change the order of the main clause and the if clause, insert or not insert a comma between them, use other myriad subordinate clauses in different orders, include double negatives and reciprocals to get the same meaning, repeat the statement in other words, we calculated one can state this one statute precisely in well over 100 billion word strings. So, there are an infinite number of variant expressions that mean that concept, and there are an infinite number of concepts that language can express.

Here are some examples of the many billions of possible word strings that state that DMV statute exactly:

> *"A child must be strapped in a child safety seat if he or she is not 6 years old and is not 60 pounds".*
> *"A child has to be buckled into a safety seat if he is not six and is not 60 pounds".*
> *"A child does not have to ride in an approved child safety seat if the child is six or sixty pounds".*
> *"A child does not have to ride in an approved child safety seat unless he is under six years of age and less than sixty pounds"*
> *Etc.*

Here are some examples that use much the same set of words but do not express the statute correctly:

> *"A child must be strapped under a child safety seat if he or she is not 6 years old and is not 60 pounds"*
> *"A child must be buckled into a child safety seat if he or she is not 6 years old or is not 60 pounds"*
> *"A child who is not 6 years old or is under 60 pounds must ride in a safety seat"*
> *Etc.*

Therefore, language can say an infinite number of things each in an infinite number of ways. Infinity multiplied by infinity is infinity ($\infty * \infty = \infty$). The task now becomes how to develop a parser that is able to understand which of the variants means the statute and which do not.

Logic by Computer

Delving into the logic required to discern whether a particular statement faithfully expresses the statute, we found that just six complex concepts are involved in the wording of the statute. Each of these concepts can be expressed by a number of paraphrases. Each can be represented by a concept symbol that can be used in a truth table that can be precisely modeled with a *Mensa* table.

This allowed us to capture the logic of this California Motor Vehicle statute in a small truth table of six subconcepts: **a, A, b, B, Yes, No**. where:

> a child less than 6 years old = **a**
> a child 6 years old or more = **A**
> a child less than 60 pounds = **b**
> a child 60 pounds or more = **B**
> a child secured in a child safety seat = **Yes**
> a child not secured in a child safety seat = **No**

Here is the truth table:

Yes	a	b
	a	B
No	A	b
	A	B

or

It's Yes   if   a and b
It's Yes   unless   A or B
It's No   if   A or B

or

It's No   unless   a and b

This truth table can also be represented by the following four rows in a *Mensa* table:

$$a \sim b = Yes$$
$$a \sim B = No$$
$$A \sim b = No$$
$$A \sim B = No$$

Each row in this *Mensa* table of mental operations is an equation that models a mental operation that the mind must be able to perform to test whether the truth table is satisfied. Now the task of parsing for the billions of variants becomes vastly easier.

The reason that *Mensa* technology holds promise for computers doing abstract logic is that complex concepts parse down to a unitary symbol that represents the whole concept. Then relating these compact symbols in a short truth table becomes elementary.

The key to our parser detecting even small grammatical errors in the sentence is to add to and edit the *Mensa* table to make sure that different synonyms and paraphrases refer to the equivalent concept by manually assigning the same concept ID# to the same concept. The method involves making six subtables within the *Mensa* database that allow parsing for each of the subconcepts, making sure that paraphrases that have the same meaning parse to intermediary concepts that have the same concept ID#. Once the text expressions that describe each subconcept are parsed to compact symbols, applying the truth table to them is simple. The result is: if it takes an average of 7 *Mensa* rows to field each alternate phrase, then the number of rows required in a *Mensa* table with our system is related to the sum of the sets of the tuple rather than their product.

Sum of tuple sets: 1+6+10+2+4+3+4+4+7+9+4+4+5+7+9 = 60;   x 7 = 420 rows

As an example, our parser detected that the following version sentence, deliberately made convoluted, states the statute correctly, thrice:

> *"He must be strapped in a federally approved child safety seat if he is not 6 years old and is under 60 pounds and she must be secured in a child safety seat if she does not weigh 60 lbs and is not seventy two months old or more, and they must travel in a safety seat if he or she is not six and is not 27.2155422 kilograms or more in weight."*

And, it detected that this version does not state it correctly:

> *"He must be strapped in a federally approved child safety seat if he is not 6 years old and is under 60 pounds and she must be secured in a child safety seat if she does not weigh 60 lbs and is not seventy two months old or more, and they must travel in a safety seat if he or she is not six or is not 27.2155422 kilograms or more in weight."*

There are two small grammatical errors in this second version that render it an incorrect statement of the law. Can you find them and fix them, so as to make the sentence a correct statement? Our parser can find them, but not fix them at present.

We argue that this example of computer parsing by itself, which takes into account the contribution of every word and punctuation mark, validates the theory and practice of our parsing system. Note particularly that changing a word early in the statement, say *if* to *unless*, affects which word must be used later in the statement to maintain sentence meaning. Our *Mensa* table can take care of such flow of indirect meaning between words widely separated in the expression.

Adding a few more database rows to the table enables the parser to understand and respond to all of the **who, what, what if, when, where, how, why, how heavy, how old** questions that might be asked to probe the information in the statute no matter how they are asked, such as

> *"Does a child need to be buckled in a safety seat if he is more than 6 years old?*
> *"When does a child have to be restrained in an approved child safety seat?*
> *"Why must a child be strapped into an approved child safety seat?"*
> *"When does a child not have to ride in a safety seat?"*
> etc.

The point is that our parser program works. It can parse any variant sentence that precisely states the law and detect any variant that does not in less than one second. With a carefully constructed *Mensa* table we have been able to achieve *text invariance*, the ability to precisely determine that a particular concept is being referred to with an expression even if worded in any one of billions of different ways. Managing invariance is the key advantage of our parser approach.

We ran an experiment with two California lawyers as subjects to see it they could match the performance of the computer in judging whether doctored versions of the stature stated it correctly. It took them as long a one minute to read the sentence carefully and judge whether the version was correct or not. They made errors, which when pointed out they could see their error after a reanalysis. For us, it eerily echoed Hal's comments in *2001 A Space Odyssey*:[4]

> **HAL** Let me put it this way, Mr. Amor. The 9000 series
> is the most reliable computer ever made. No 9000
> computer has ever made a mistake or distorted
> information. We are all, by any practical definition of
> the words, foolproof and incapable of error.

> **HAL** It can only be attributable to human error.

This exercise suggested one interesting legal research project. Translate a set of laws into *Mensa* tables, and describe what an accused might have done to see if the computer can determine which law was broken.

---

4   Google "2001 Hal quotes" I'm feeling lucky

BOOK III
CHAPTER II

Meaning - the Accounting System of the Mind

Our research has focused mostly on theory and practice of parsing expressions and mapping them onto individual concepts, defining relations between them and assessing how their sense adapts in context. However, concepts also change in importance in context. Concepts can be scored and their scores added and subtracted as they take part in an expression

All of the party concepts of a language expression, once in relationship, shift to a new *qualitative sense*, within a range of possible senses, to fit their new context. Although the subtle shifts of sense of concepts in order to fit into context are potent, the conscious and unconscious mind does far more with party concepts in relationships. Concepts also appear to gain a new *quantitative value*. As the mind constructs complex concepts from simple concepts, it appears that the mind does these value calculations automatically, performing *mental accounting* as complex concepts are constructed. As the mind is constructing complex concepts it assigns a weight to each new concept that measures its importance in the present context. There appears to be a mental function that scores each concept, determines a value for it on a common scale of importance or status or worth as soon as it is incorporated into a particular gestalt. The mind thereby attaches importance and emotions, calculates risk and consequences for concepts in context. The *meaning* of any one component concept is not just its ability to shift the qualitative sense of its relatives but also its effect on the *worth value* of the others. Any one concept can have quite different importance, or meaning, or ability to relay meaning, or relevance in different contexts.

In society, there is a general principle in accounting for any complex system comprising components of dissimilar kinds. Many disparate goods and services are converted to a common quantifier of value: *money*. To help see the parallel with algebra, consider evaluating the equation: $y = 50$ **euros + 1000 yen - 25 U.S. dollars.** It is clear that each term has to be converted to a common currency if the algebraic operators, + and -, are to function, i.e. $y = 68.255$ **U.S. dollars + 10.448 Placement of the comma makes all the difference! - 25 U.S. dollars.** Now the equation can be evaluated: $y = 44.2998$ **U.S. dollars.**

A worldly example of this accounting function is the company balance sheet. The balance sheet is an equation where the sum of a company's various assets and liabilities such as *fixed assets* and *accounts receivable* must equal the sum of all liabilities like *accounts payable* and *stockholders equity*. And they are interactive. Certain lines on a company balance sheet: *intellectual property, good will*, and *other intangible assets* represent very abstract entities yet accountants treat them just like the tangibles. They are all mapped onto a common scale of magnitude, *money*. A balance sheet equation "**sum**marizes" the functioning of the company as a whole with special insight.

Apparently the mind has adopted the same principle. And even though mental concepts are of different kinds, just like items on a company balance sheet they appear to be scored in a common mental currency that the mind adds and subtracts to compute a total value for the whole complex concept, i.e. meaning. One must "add apples to apples" to measure the effect of one disparate concept on another in the common "currency" of importance. This common scale allows the mind to compare concepts.

It is no coincidence that "money" and "means" share the same phonemes and that one speaks of "a man of means." Once this mental mapping is done by operations of the mind, complex concepts can be measured, totaled and ranked. Importance is the name for this scale of values on which concepts are assigned. Importance is the common currency used by the mind to enable disparate mental concepts to interact and be compared. The meaning of any one concept is its effect on the value of the others. Expressions like "he's not *up to it*", "her idea is *worthless*", "that doesn't *count* for much", "to *sum* up". "it doesn't *add up*", "that *accounts* for the hostility" indicate that this evaluation function is going on constantly in all human thought. It is "mental algebra".

Courtroom justice is a good example mental scoring. The enormity of a crime and the severity of its punishment have somehow to be measured on a common scale, and balanced. Aspects of the crime are weighed on the "scales of justice" and aspects of the punishment are considered and matched on the same scale. The punishment must fit the crime, be meet and just, if justice is to be done. One the numerical scale used in the courtroom, common measures of punishment is *time*; "don't do the crime if you can't do the time", and *money* as in a fine. One can say "first degree manslaughter *means* 25 years in California". The mind has a marvelous ability to judge, to detect when moieties don't match up by "summing up" the meaning on the two sides. It is "moral algebra".

Scoring of meaning applies to the persuasiveness of paragraphs. As soon as an observation concept as expressed by a finite sentence is enclosed in a period grammatical it becomes a unit package of meaning for use in building a paragraph concept. By adding the period the author has made a *point*. The argument with the most *points* wins. If it is a cogent argument, it has a *point* value that it can contribute to the power of the paragraph to persuade the second person to adopt a new idea or change his mind. We enter the realm of scoring and the sports analogy again becomes relevant. A "point" is commonly used as a measure of score. A conversion is one *point*; a field goal is three *points*; a touchdown six. The team with the most *points* wins the game. The argument with more highly weighed *points* wins the debate.

Decisions

This mental accounting facility is constantly used making decisions. Every decision one makes involves this process of evaluation; the benefits and costs, the advantages and disadvantages, of one side are scored, added up and compared with the other side. The mind establishes two sides where the importance of facts, factors, and considerations on each side can be compared. This mental facility for valuing concepts is used when comparing two situations. Words like "justice", "justify", "satisfy", "match", "on the other hand" are used and apply here. At some point one has to "deside" i.e. take one side out of play and go with the other. "But" seems to label a factor that subtracts from the ideal or usual. "Unless" seems to label a pivotal consideration that will tip **it** one way or the other.

In humans, very nuanced calculations are done in our highly developed frontal lobes and the results passed to the much older limbic system where the conscious mind experiences feelings of pleasure, fear, horror, discomfort, envy, etc. The mind senses danger and effects automatic motor responses like smiling, laughter, grimacing, eye-rolling, etc. and marshalls defenses like crouching and adrenaline for "flight or fight".

Double Meaning and Humor

Many words phrases and expressions can have double meanings as in allegory, irony, satire, sarcasm and puns. *Irony* occurs when the evaluation score of a situation does not match the expected. For example when an action that would normally turn out bad has an unexpected good result or vice versa. *Satire*: where the true import of a situation nowhere near matches the appearances, as exemplified by the Monty Python skits where a group of impressive pretentious looking people are realized to be talking complete gobbledygook. *Sarcasm*: someone might say "that's just great" when the opposite is the case. *Puns* when words that sound much the same lead to very different meanings. The mind appears to evaluate both versions separately, put them side by side, appreciate the difference in status, then entertain both and perhaps go with one or the other.

The mind is constantly putting a value on situations as they apply to oneself or someone else, constantly evaluating our own situation relative to the situation of other people. We feel good or feel bad according to how we evaluate our current situation. Such pleasant or unpleasant conscious sensations are generated by calculations in the frontal lobes but felt by the amygdala nucleus of the limbic system of the brain.[1] The amygdala is the player. And we can enter the mind of another person, be sensitive to their status, understand their feelings. This is the basis of empathy and sympathy. And, when another person goes down we go up relatively. - it is a seesaw. A sudden relative change in the status of a person compared to our own status is the basis for a theory of humor.

When an expression or a story has a double meaning, and once it is realized suddenly that it can also be parsed to another it concept with a very different social or moral status for someone, the sudden switch brings humor, or horror. If parsing an expression first leads to one it concept and then to different one it can be very funny. What makes it funny is suddenness and scale of the meaning difference. Seeing a sudden large gap in evaluation of the two meanings will raise or lower our feeling of wellbeing.

Sometimes the concept embodied in a whole paragraph, and many of its component concepts, can radically change in meaning when a seemingly disconnected sentence is added to a paragraph. Often they can all fit together perfectly again with a totally different sense and meaning.

> *"At last, after much effort, an English lady found a psychic who conducted a séance where the lady was able to make contact with her late husband. Asked what it was like he replied. "We take it easy mostly, we lie around, then we have something to eat, take a nap, have some sex, have something to eat, have more sex, go inside and get a good night's sleep. Most days are like this". "I didn't realize Heaven was like that" she said. 'Heaven, no, I'm a rabbit in Arizona."*

For example, in this paragraph the last sentence changes everything. Such radical, "game changing," transformations are the task of the punch line, the last observation of a joke or story. Often in humor, one person's status goes up as another's goes down. It is a see-saw.[2] It's funny if yours goes up. And relatively is as good as absolutely.

---

1   Google "limbic system", "amygdala"
2   Notice how your mind has been primed by this same sentence on the previous page so as to immediately recognize it as a repeat.

Humor has its teleological purpose. Being able to see a joke, see what is behind a move, being able to realize a danger in a situation, see a hidden opportunity, is important for survival. It is very important survival facility to be able to see an alternate explanation for what is being observed. Seeing double meaning induces a feeling of pleasure, inducing a smile or laughter. The brain's reward system encourages us to practice this skill.

Mensa and Meaning

Our system of assigning unique symbols to concepts, relating them to each other in *Mensa* tables and *flow-of-meaning-trees* along with a parser program, is an unconscious orthographic system of mindless symbols that can identify which concept it is, express it in language if required, and respond appropriately. Although our software enables very competent computer understanding of the *sense* of language expressions in terms of identifying concepts, we have not yet begun to implement concept importance in software to any degree, except for calibrating responses to inputs. Example: we can indicate which is the intended meaning of an expression by the response; as in Sigmund Freud's joke *"Has anyone taken a bath?* *"No, why, is there one missing?* With a *Mensa* table we can control the *sense* of a given expression force it to mean a particular concept.

And then, once a human mind has measured the emotional values of concepts arising in a given situation described by language, it should be possible to manually insert values of status and importance into new columns in our *Mensa* tables. Once numerical values for emotions, information, knowledge and wisdom are assigned and stored away in *Mensa*, values could be added, subtracted, totaled and balanced, managed by simple algebraic equations. Subtle questions about emotions could be understood and responded to in appropriate language.

In the seventeenth century Leibniz began but never finished a project to give numerical values to mental concepts and use algebraic equations involving such numbers to construct a theory of thought. Pursuing this line of thought evokes intriguing glimpses of the possibility that computer algorithms could be developed to weigh concepts and access situations. With the *Mensa* database, tools are now available for some very exciting future research.

BOOK III
CHAPTER III

What Language Tells Us about Consciousness and our Mental Life

*This chapter is concerned with teasing out what language can tell us about consciousness and the way the mind models the world and our mental life and how language is a vast mnemonic system. Many English phrases and common sayings describe operations of the mind. Perhaps the most relevant mental construction that language defines is the relation between our conscious inner self and will and our bodies and the outside world, an archetypical command and control system. Language sees the mind dividing the world into a **how** zone where operations take place and a **why** zone that houses causes and results, that closely relate to each other. It is a helpful exercise to surmise or guess what **how** zone operations and how they relate to the **why** zone. Also to meditate on what these common phrases mean and how they get their meaning. Flow-of-meaning-trees and Mensa tables, an orthography that can model thought and language, will allow scholars to pursue research that will surely provide very important insights into how language works and how it got to be the way it is. There is hope that very commonly used "cognitive" grammaticals, morphemes, words and phrases can be mapped explicitly to mental operations and so provide insights into cognitive processes. This chapter is necessarily a work in progress.*

anguage appears to be interfacing with its own particular conceptual model of the mind and consciousness. Language can tell us a lot about the organization of our mental life. We have had flashes of understanding as we worked on different aspects of our project, finding the unraveling of the non-obvious meaning of various commonly used phrases a fascinating activity, leading to very seductive but distracting byways not quite central to our mission. We have barely scratched the surface of this very worthwhile endeavor, entertaining only a few of them. Flow-of-meaning-trees and *Mensa* tables can record mental operations explicitly, creating the possibility of modeling the precise details of many of these mental processes and thereby enhance our understanding of both linguistics and cognition.

In this chapter we will argue that our mental life is a typical command and control system. Analysis and understanding of *command* and *control* is relevant because much of language is concerned with describing the mind and the world **it** models in these terms.

We have noticed again and again during this project that what a word means is hinted at strongly by its phonemic sound and graphemic shape. We have noticed many examples of phonetic cueing of meaning; parts of words contribute standard meanings. We think there are thousands of words that owe their origin directly to this process.

Language and the Unconscious Mind

We have no conscious access to the unconscious mind and we have little control over unconscious processes. However, the unconscious mind does come up with words and phrases that describe what it is doing and provide insights. Many commonly used "cognitive" words and phrases refer to operations of the unconscious mind, which should allow their analysis to determine what is going on when the mind is managing complex mental processes. John Locke in the *Essay* employed very thorough introspection to define many of them, like and *reflection* and *abstraction*. It will be worthwhile to mine language to come up with the best understanding of mental processes we can put together.

Grouped in what appear to be similar mental processes, here are just a few examples of words and phrases that describe various functions and regions of our mind's model of itself.

Understand explain think say believe idea theory hypothesis suspect suspicion happen occur thought ponder reflection abstraction truth correct sum up right on spot on false lie tall tale haywire sense meaning relation relative –ship relationship disparate mean meaning mental -ment analyze understand explain congruent incongruent real reality realize realization existence literal virtual idea concept memory imagine imagination illusion delusion ignorant tell foretell foresee plan planning look look out say state express make clear make a point point out underscore confuse decide evaluate debate convince persuade sway question ask answer tell believe deny remember see is saw was allusion metaphor analogy synecdoche humor sarcasm satire irony double meaning desire want volition reflect reflection response, etc.

*"He understands what he sees" "that makes sense" "He has to figure out what is going on", "he has to put two and two together", "connect the dots" "make a point" "to stretch a point". "he doesn't get **it**" "what gives?" "the grand scheme of things" "the way it is" "the larger meaning" "the idea behind what he did". He may say "I have no idea", "I haven't got a clue". "Everything's gone haywire". "that's a stretch", "takes place" , "mind your Ps and Qs", etc.*

What exactly are the processes that these words, phrases and expressions describe?

Mind and Body as a Command and Control System

What is a *command* and *control (comcon)* system? What is the relation between a *commander* and a *controller*? How does the role of the commander differ from that of a controller? A *commander* can be thought of as being in a mental world considering things that apply to the real world that he is constantly trying to make more ideal, but which has no direct control over. He has to communicate with the *controller*, who can be thought of as being *hands-on* in a real world that contains things that he can deal with directly so as to change the world indirectly. The *commander* communicates his commands to the *controller* who executes them. Built into the *comcon* relationship is the expectation that they will work together optimally. A command issued by the commander expects a willing action by the controller. Once the controller has carried out orders the commander commends him. Although the roles themselves of *controller* and *commander* are separate, the same person can share these roles, make plans and carry them out, change hats.

This separation of roles is formalized in the titles CEO and COO, director and producer, creative and business, orchestra conductor and musicians, foreman and gang and of course military organization.[1]

Often, in a typical *commander-controller* relationship a written *command* or plan can be considered to be the *commander*. Even an inanimate object or situation can be the *commander*. For example, *"This painting will command a high price"* means that people are willing to pay it. A *demand* expects a begrudging or involuntary response. *"He demanded a high price for the painting"* indicates that the buyer may be unhappy paying the price he has to pay.

Command and Control - How and Why

Command and *control* are the **why** and **how** niches of human endeavor and are coded for everywhere and all the time in language. How does language indicate whether a particular concept is in the *command* zone or the *control* zone?

Verb actions *take* and *get* distinguish between **how** and **why**. Much of language and thought is concerned intimately with the way *take* and *get* zones are related to each other. We *take* steps **to** *get* what we want. The commander asks what **it** will *take*. The controller asks what will we *get*. One can *take* great care that the steps we *take* are adequate to ensure the desired *result* (res ultima), to *get* the *outcome* we want, or ameliorate a bad situation, but it is never absolutely certain. We *take* a look, **how**, and *get* to see, **why; we** *take* a listen, **how** and *get* to hear, **why**, we *take* a touch, **how**, and *get* to feel, **why; we** *take* a sniff, **how**, and *get* to smell, **why**. This *take/get*, **how/why** dichotomy is central to thought, and language. Verb actions *take* and *go* always refer to the **how** zone and *get* and *come* always refer to the **why**.

What *happens* in the **why** *zone* is by definition not under direct control. In the **why** zone it *happens* whether one likes **it** or not. Verbs *go* and *come*

---

1   There are many synonyms for these roles: commander, controller, person in charge, curator, manager, boss, head, leader, director, administrator, conservator, custodian, guardian, keeper, steward, concierge, janitor, keeper, superintendent, supervisor, warden, watchperson, etc. It is an interesting exercise to divide these terms into which of the two roles they indicate.

mark the same dichotomy. We are *going* to do something in **how**, but what *comes* from it, the *outcome*, is in **why**.

How and Why - For, To, Through and By

Grammaticals **for, to, through**, and **by** are the relation grammaticals that manage **how** and **why**.[2] For example, with *"she is saving money to buy a Chanel jacket"*, the **how** zone contains the *first relative* of **to**, a verb activity that is governed by being in **to** relation with the *second relative* of **to**, a desired result concept contained in a **why** zone.

Fig 3.3.1 How and **why** related by grammatical **to**.

In this example, the infinitive made with grammatical relation particle **to** indicates that its *second* relative, the *buy* verb action, is in **why** zone. And this explains why getting a Chanel jacket in **why** zone is said to be the 'object' of her saving money in the **how** zone.

In another example, in *"I am mailing the book for Harry"*, grammatical **for** seems to create a **how** space which contains activities named by the *first* or *subject* relative of **for** designed to bring about a desired end contained in a **why** space named by the *second* or *object* relative of **for**. In this case, someone else, not Harry, plays in that space. And paradoxically, *"I am mailing the book for Harry"*, implies a sentence something like *"Harry's interests ... have ... me mailing the book"* where preposition **for** makes its *syntactical object* the subject of an implied sentence that involves **for**'s *syntactical subject*. Such implied sentences are implied by all prepositional phrases.

In the sentence *"It is for James to pick up the tab"*, **for** creates a space that contains what's on James' plate, a **how** space where James can operate, but also where others can operate on his behalf. The *object* concept of **for** is a label that tells us which **for** space it is. **For** spaces are equivalent to empty fields of a **for**m that are labeled to indicate and control what information is to be entered in them. Grammatical **to** creates a **how** space

---

2   The phonemes **pre, pro, por, per** are also cognate members of this group that
      cue **how/why** meaning mnemonically into many lexical words

for the activities and operations required for a direct way to **it,** the end goal. The syntactical object of **to** names the final goal (go-all), of the path, the result, (res ultima). In this case grammatical **to** defines the same **how** space that **for** does. They overlap and shape each other and the concepts they contain.[3]

Both **for** and **to** indicate looking ahead to creating **how** and **why** zones whose content is not yet realized, not yet **for**-filled. In the sentence *"the town is very busy for it is market day"*. Here, the *object* concept of **for**, seen looking forward, influences, even causes, its subject relative. And, the syntactical object of **for** becomes the subject concept of an implied sentence like *"It being market day for the rest of the day makes the town busy"*.

When someone *"goes forth"* or someone *"went for him"* it certainly suggests they are going to do something more there in a **for** zone, something in order to reach a goal further on. When activity goes on without a real world goal it is **por**-lay (play); activity with a real world goal is phonetic reversal lay-**por** (labor, work). Mnemonics again.

A **how** zone created by **for** or **to** contains activity to be **per**formed at an intermediate stage on the way to an end result. From the perspective of an individual on a path, the immediate goal is to get to the next point, the next **how** zone, at which something can be done that can't be done at the current point. Activities performed in **how** are under the **pro-to**-agonist's direct control; events or outcomes in **why** are not, although they can be highly influenced by steps taken in **how**. We say we have to get into a position (**por**-sition) where we can do the next thing. The phrase *"in order to ... "* indicates there are several successive **how** *zone* stages on the way **to** the end.

Mnemonics nicely suggests the meanings of the words ***port**, **for**ward, **fut**ure, **fort**une, **for**eman, **cor**pora, **pro**posal, **pro**ceed **pro**pose* and ***pro**position. The common sense of **for**, along with its Latinate cognates **per**, **por**, **pro**, **pre**, **through** and **by** becomes apparent. Grammaticals *through* and *per* indicate the idea of *let* or permission rather than doing something to *make* **it** happen. The idea of these zones can explain exactly

---

3 The classic example of overlapping prepositional phrase spaces is from Abraham Lincoln's Gettysburg Address: "government of the people, by the people, for the people".

how relative pronouns **how** and **why** work and how prepositions **for**, **by**, **through**, and **to** work. **For** looks forward, **by** looks back. We look forward to the *syntactical subject concepts* of **to** and **for**; we look back at the *syntactical subject concepts* of preposition grammaticals **by** and **from**. People saying "farewell" (**for**-well) are looking forward to those leaving, who say "goodbye" (good-**by**) looking back at the ones saying "farewell". Activities that take place in **for**, **through** and **by** spaces remains separate, whereas a **to** space does reach to and **to**uch the **it**.

Mnemonics cue which zone a concept is in. The –**ing** inflection indicates a verb action is still in process in the **how** zone. For example, a golfer saying *"I am go-**ing** to break 80"* implies that he is doing things that will try to ensure that outcome. Note that verb inflection –**ing**, literally **in go**, still going on, is rendered in Latin languages as –**into**, which is literally not yet **to**. The –**ate**, –**ation** and –**ative** suffixes on lexical verbs indicate **how** zone. The –**ion** suffix indicates a completed **on** verb action in **why** zone. The distinction between *unification* and *union* is a nice example.

There are other mnemonic cues for **how** and **why** zones. Nouns with suffix –**ist** code for the hands-on person, the agonist in the **how** zone, for example, typ**ist**, real**ist**, novel**ist**. Does a **pro-to**-agon**ist** stay at **it** by himself not making use of an ag-**ent**, or have a cooperator. Teasing out the meaning of agon-**ist** from the meaning of ag-**ent** is a good exercise to aid understanding. We're still working on it.

Feelings: what is going on in the world affects the feelings of the controller in the **how** zone. Feelings as well as actions are the province of the **how** zone. We ask *"how are you?"*, *"how do you feel?"*, not *"why do you feel?"* This suggests that ascessing and feeling the relative importance of things out in the world and the status of ourselves and other people is the work of the of the *controller's* mind not the *commander's*.

One can operate in the **how** zone to influence whether **it** *happens*, even ensure that **it** *happens*, see to **it**. This leads to a very simple unified theory concerning the role and function of the modals. They are concerned with accessing the status or likelihood of completion of goals in **why** *zone* in response to action or lack of action in **how**. When grammatical modal *will* is used, one is talking about the **why** part of an action that one does not directly control, yet predicts successful completion of **it**.[4] When grammatical modal *shall* is used one is indicating that one will make sure that the **why** goal will complete by pursuing the **how** activity that one has control over, dealing directly with things in **how**. "I shall see to **it**" is equivalent to "I'll keep at **how** until **why** happens". When grammatical modal *may* is used it has two senses; one grants permission for the **how** part of an action to proceed or just declares there is a chance **why** will happen. When grammatical modal *can* is used the speaker is saying that the **why** result is possible in response to actions in **how**.[5] To talk about the **how** part of an action, the *act*, he has to say one is "capable of" doing *one*'s part. A successful person is "able to". With grammatical modal *must* the speaker declares an extreme need for a **how** verb action to proceed to obtain a critical **why** outcome.

Understanding **how** and **why** zones, and the ways that language cues reference to them, is important for enabling the computer to manage **how** and **why** questions.

More Mnemonics

This a good point to enlarge the idea that language is a vast mnemonic system with its symbols highly focused on cueing which operation of the mind it is talking about. That the phoneme, grapheme and morpheme parts of words carry information is a pervasive theme of this essay. Once a lexical word is deconstructed into its phoneme, grapheme and morpheme parts its meaning can be guessed. The mnemonic values of phonemes graphemes and morphemes are why words come into use and then stick. [6]

For examples that illustrate mnemonics in action let's start with suffixes and prefixes. The **-er** phoneme or grapheme grammatical names the smooth movement on a scale of the needle onward to the right, or upward, and becomes part of the meaning of any word that contains the **-er** suffix. *Higher* means a move of the needle further from *high* on a scale. Mnemonically **to-er** could mean a move past **to**, you're dead, in a **to**-em, which suggests the origin of French verb *tuer*, to kill. With phoneme **-est** the movement

---

4   That is presumably why one's last testament is called a "will".

5   If one *can* do something one has the *knack*, *can*'s phonetic reverse anagram.

6   Phonetic cueing of meaning is just one the fascinating side issues we have encountered in this project. But it is somewhat irrelevant to the practical side of our mission.

reaches its limit, the speedometer needle goes horizontal, indicating the car is going *"flat out"*. Phonemes -**er** and -**est** serve the comparative and the superlative, and as noun suffixes they mean an agent,

The -**in**- -**an**- -**en**-   -**on**- -**un**- -**ion** phoneme *affixes* can be *prefix* or *suffix* to a lexical word. They appear to stand for a verb process with a timeline that has both a beginning and end. Suffix -**in** gives mnemonic meaning to words *like act-***ion** *promot-***ion** *un-***ion** cueing time processes that complete. Curiously, English uses *end* (**in-de**: **off-in**) and French uses *fin* (**off-in**) for the concept of end. Suffix, -**into** indicates the verb action is still going on, suffix -**in** or -**en** says it completed. On the other hand, when the **in-** morpheme is the prefix of a word it indicates the process goes in the opposite direction or does not go at all. Like the direction a train goes depends on which end the locomotive is on. This is why **in-** prefix cues *negation*. Interestingly, palindromic word *engine* (**en-go-in***)* has this phoneme on both ends of a root. It is an almost graphic description of the piston rod of a steam engine moving back and forth. Voila, a simple theory of *affirmation-negation* falls out of this mnemonic idea.

The **oo-** phoneme is perhaps the most intriguing phoneme of all in mnemonic terms. Phonetically, en-**oo**, "no", is a process not running forward. If phoneme -**er** indicates a forward or up movement, phoneme **oo** bespeaks a reversal of direction as in "Whoa", the command to stop or still a horse. "**oo**ps" a mistake, stop and reconsider the situation. An "**oo**-er" is an oar that goes back and forth, and its reverse phonetic anagram "er-**oo**" is "row", as in boat. The the word "error" (er-**oo**-er) gets its meaning from its suggestion of the meter needle hunting back and forth about the optimum. If East is "est", west is "**oo**-est". This leads to a very exciting idea, which could explain the origin of the relative/interrogative pronouns and questions which have information flowing the other way.

Another very good example of a phoneme carrying meaning occurs in words with a -**t**- phoneme in them. Almost universally these -**t**- containing words mean something that is fixed in position, not moving or movable, unchanging, tight, taut or set, completed or finished. Grammatical **it** as in "that's **it**" is the archetype. Phoneme -**d**- carries much the same idea as -**t**- but less tight, the difference between putting a heavy glass object down on a grani**t**e counter or a woo**d**en cutting board.

Prefix **ex-** indicates that a concept, while contributing and receiving meaning normally in one *flow-of-meaning-tree*, escapes to join another *flow-of-meaning-tree*, to do the same there, as explained in the chapter on paragraphs and poetry. It requires an X in the *flow-of-meaning-tree*, to diagram this crosstalk.

Table 3.3.1 shows the mnemonic meaning of some common grammatical affixes along with lexical words that incorporate them.

PHONEME	MEANING	EXAMPLE WORDS
-t	fixed tight stopped	metal granite tied tight
-d	stopped	hard wood
cha-	sudden movement and slow down	cha cha cha lurch
t-ech	initially fixed but more force releases sudden movement	latch match ratchet
-er	smooth limited upward movement	more higher heavier
oo-	in the opposite direction	oo-er (oar) oo-east (west)
-est	to the limit	east highest
-ist	agonist dealing directly with related concepts	tobacconist linguist typist
in- -in en- -en -on -ion -un	a process in order or time with a beginning and end	union session
-ition -ation	a process still going on	unification verification
-ate -ative	a process in **how**	debate relegate
-ment	concept with a directed binary tree structure	statement argument
-ex	link from one *ment* or *endit* to another	exit escape

Table 3.3.1 Relating phonemes to their determinative meaning in lexical words

As a final example, consider how verb "tell" operates to help us understand this mnemonic process. The common phonetics of *tell*, *tale*, *tool*, *toll* and prefix *tele-* tell us something about mnemonics and how the sound of words echoes their meaning. Verb *tell* defines a two step process where meaning is successfully transferred between two end concepts via an intermediary relation concept. Verb *tell* indicates that meaning flows into the mind of an observer via an intermediary like *text* or *talk*. Words with phonetic prefix grammatical **tele-**, like **tele-**scope, **tele-**phone, **tele-**vision, name instruments that the user deals with meaning flowing from things one can't sense directly with an intermediary between the user and his object. An "in*tell*igent" person is one who interprets "signs" cleverly. For example when one says *"I can't tell if it's raining"* one indicates one is using some kind of intermediary sensory-mental evaluation process to obtain the information.

But, meaning can flow through *tell* in the other direction. The first person tells a tale and the tale is the *media* that informs the second person. In a communication between the first person and the second person one can think of *text* as the *relation* between knowledge in the first person's mind and knowledge in the second person's mind. What is transmitted is *talk*. In the case of a screwdriver one's hand deals with the handle of a screwdriver, the business end of a screwdriver deals with the screw. One can think of a screwdriver as the relation between one's hand and a screw. It is a *tool*. What is transmitted is *torque*, the meaning that flows between the hand and the screw through the means, the screwdriver just like *talk* from person to person is the meaning that flows in a conversation. A user interacts with a *tool* and the *tool* does the work. The *tool* is the **relation**, the instrument, between the user and his work. Why does the expression "a telling blow" mean what it does? The blow causes damage, takes its *toll*, and that *toll* is the **relation**, the agent, that disables the opponent. The *toll* is the relation between subject and object. The close phoneme match between "tale" and "toll" and "talk" and "torque" is telling. It is no coincidence. Harry Bosch says there are no coincidences.[7]

In any case all of these thought processes is can be captured precisely in *Mensa* tables, which makes expeditious management of **how** and **why** questions possible. This is because symbols named in *Mensa* tables just do their appointed job correctly and mindlessly. Again, one thinks of the remark of physicist Heinrich Hertz

> *"One cannot escape the feeling that these mathematical formulae have an independent existence and an intelligence of their own, that they are wiser than we are, wiser even than their discoverers.*

7   Michael Connelly, The Black Echo, Warner Books, New York, 2002, p.26

These examples strongly suggest that language is a vast mnemonic system. Such cueing of meaning by mnemonics suggests why a consensus develops about which word becomes used for a particular meaning; why words "stick" to mean what they do. Collecting and analyzing specific individual phonemes and graphemes with established standard meanings to understand their contribution to lexical words and phrases would be a worthwhile study, or is this idea too fresh to be objectionable yet. This chapter is necessarily a work in progress; the field is so large as to require another book.

BOOK IV
CHAPTER I

Theory and Structure of the Mensa Database

Here we describe a software database structure, Mensa database, that can model human thought and language to the same degree of subtlety as natural language itself. A Mensa database is simply an alternate orthography able to store large amounts of declarative knowledge with the same authority as natural language, but in a preparsed form that enables a computer to utilize it. We call a system module that manages a domain of knowledge in this format a Maven, an expert in a limited domain of knowledge. Knowledge stored in our Mensa table format is completely computer accessible. However, there is opportunity to translate large corpora of language into Mensa tables stored in databases. At present, translating language text into Mensa requires a human mentor and there is need for research into automation of the encoding process and for a deeper understanding of the rules of syntax for language expressions. Then, language will no longer be considered to be unstructured information.

N atural language comprises a linear series of finite sentences arranged in order in paragraphs, chapters and larger volumes of text. We have seen that each of these text forms is a notation for a tree structure, a *flow-of-meaning-tree*, whose leaves and nodes are concepts and which can hold these concepts in a precisely defined unified relationship. We represent language trees as arrays, each tree node taking up one row, each expression requiring only a small number of rows, using language symbols themselves as much as possible to represent element concepts.

Adopting the array method to implement language expression trees, we have developed a *Mensa table* structure, which we also call *M5, the Fifth Medium of knowledge*, to model complex mental concepts and enable our parser program to identify them unerringly.[1] Mental concepts specified by texts are represented as a list or table of relations between pairs of symbols representing mental concepts. Each row of the table, a record in the database, is a relation between two concepts along with the surviving concept that results from their interaction; each row represents the mental operation that constructs a surviving concept; each row directs our parser to perform a computer operation that is the equivalent of that mental operation; each row represents the surviving concept. Of course, at present, since computers are not conscious, each such mental operation has to be precalculated by a human, who records the result of his mental operation in the row. Thus, a small table of relation rows describes and defines a data tree structure able to represent a complex mental concept, idea, or thought, just as well as a word, phrase, expression, sentence, paragraph or longer language text can.

Mensa tables specify symbolically both the set of operations that the mind uses to construct complex concepts that are expressed by text strings and the steps required to parse the texts. Thus, our software can parse each sentence input down to a single unique symbol, which can however be programmatically exploded back into meaningful language expressing a complete list of constituent concepts. As simple concepts are enriched with meaning and survive, their symbols are marked up to reflect that they are now more complex concepts. Such markup can capture their enrichment.

---

1   The other four media of knowledge are the world itself, the mind, art and language.

Since each concept table takes up just a few rows in the database, a modern database can hold millions of concepts, keep them organized in correct relationships, and provide fast precise conversational access to any one. So, large domains of declarative knowledge presently stored in text in unstructured form can be losslessly structured in *Mensa* format.

We call such a database table and associated parser and response program that manages a domain of knowledge a Maven. A Maven understands exactly which one of thousands of questions or remarks is being addressed to it and makes the precisely appropriate response, no matter how the question is worded; as long as the text uses vocabulary and refers to concepts already installed in its *Mensa table*.

Our *Mensa tables* have been implemented in our proprietary Tracker database format, which allows easy entering, viewing and editing of data in a database. Fig 4.1.1 shows a screenshot of a *Mensa* table embedded in a Tracker database that enables our parser to understand the question

ID	Reference	Vocab	Lookup	CF	Concept	Ele	LR	Response	Text
771	000.001.339	point			point		0		point
772	000.001.340	What			What		0		What
773	000.001.341	is			is		0		is
774	000.001.342	the			the		0		the
775	000.001.343	most			most		0		most
776	000.001.344	important			important		0		important
777	000.001.345	key			key		0		important
778	000.001.346	thing			point		0		point
779	000.001.347	about			about		0		about
780	000.001.348	a			a		0		a
781	000.001.349	Maven			Maven		0		Maven
782	000.001.350	Mavens			Mavens		0		Maven
783	000.001.351	?			?		0		?
784	000.001.352	what's	What~is	C	whatis		0		What is
785	000.001.353		important~point	C	IP\1		0		important point
786	000.001.354		a~Maven	C	+ AM		0		a Maven
787	000.001.355		most~IP\1	C	MIP\1		0		most important point
788	000.001.356		key~point	C	MIP\1		0		most important point
789	000.001.357		about~AM	C	+ AAM		0		about a Maven
790	000.001.358		key~AAM	C	+ TMIP\1AAM		0		about a Maven
791	000.001.359		key~FAM	C	+ TMIP\1AAM		0		about a Maven
792	000.001.360		about~Mavens	C	+ AAM		0		about a Maven
793	000.001.361		show~AAM	C	+ SAAM		0	IPAAM	about a Maven
794	000.001.362		the~MIP\1	C	+ TMIP\1		0		the most important point
795	000.001.363		TMIP\1~AAM	C	+ TMIP\1AAM		0		the most important point about a Mav
796	000.001.364		whatis~TMIP\1AAM	C	whatisTMIP\1AAM		0	IPAAM	the most important point about a Mav
797	000.001.365	ip			IPAAM		0		The most important point about a Mav
798	000.001.366						0		
799	000.001.367						0		
800	000.001.368						0		G:\Maven Presentation Folder\Maste
801	000.001.369	sss	do~Vslideshow		Vslideshow		0		D:\00 Payam Presentation Folder\Pay
802	000.001.370		thankyou~Maven		Maven		0		Maven

Fig 4.1.1 Screenshot of a section of a Mensa database implemented as a Tracker file

The Structure of a Mensa Database

A database comprises rows of mental operations, each one creating and representing a unique concept. Each row has a carefully designed record structure, a tuple that is able to capture all of the essential features of an individual mental concept. Seven essential columns provide all the properties and functions:

There is a vocabulary or lexicon column containing all the language elements, lexical words, grammaticals and punctuation marks that have been used or might be used to express concepts in each domain of knowledge stored in the database.

Another column contains the unique identifier symbols of the two related operand concepts that are operated on to form a compound product concept.

Another column contains the identifier of the unit product concept, which also a row identifier.

There is a column containing the most apt text expression for the concept since every mental concept can be specified very precisely by a carefully composed language expression. This field controls the sense of the concept represented by that record in the current context, since, like a word, the same concept symbol can have very different senses in different contexts. And allows the computer to explicate the precise meaning of any concept if required in context.

Then there is a response column, which contains the identifiers of responses that the computer will make when text parsing to that concept is input. Preprogrammed responses can be written or spoken language, a computer action, a machine operation, execution of a hyperlink or change of program behavior. By linking an appropriate response to particular meaningful text inputs, one can control how the computer will respond to each text input. Surprisingly, the response also has an important effect on the intended sense of a concept because the response's "take" on the concept indicates whether the intended meaning of the input string is different from the literal meaning, as in humor, irony, metaphor, synecdoche, allusions, sarcasm, litotes, allegory etc. by making an appropriate programmed response. Carefully tuned responses to precisely understood inputs enable a computer to mimic a human personality to a very high degree in a restricted domain of knowledge.

Another critically important column in a *Mensa* database is an outline column filled with ordered numbers that define an outline tree structure. Following a numbered chapter and verse format, this concept address column, by ordering rows, imposes a tree structure on the whole *Mensa* knowledge domain. This tree structure aggregates concepts allowing concepts to take their place in context in a logical and convenient manner. As an outline, it locates each concept both in its local context and in the larger context of the knowledge domain. This column is essential for our parser because, just like a word, the same concept can assume a very different sense in different contexts. The outline tree structure of the knowledge domain allows our parser to operate in restricted local sections of the database, in local contexts where words have special senses. This column enables what we call "local search", which is essential for pronoun reference and lexical word and phrase disambiguation in context, making sure that the correct sense of the text is taken in each context.

Another column contains the set of symbols for all the higher level concepts that each concept is party to, which empowers programs to intersect these sets to come up with concepts that may not be explicitly referred to in the text, i.e. to figure out what the larger picture is with very few clues, make likely diagnoses automatically. One of our earlier parser programs used intersection of the concept sets in this column to determine the one concept that each concept pair pointed to. We abandoned this method, finding that the current *Mensa* row with it explicit naming of the surviving concept works better. However, in the future we expect to make use of this column again to enhance current parser performance.

Properties of a Mensa Database

Mensa tables of mental operations bestow very special properties:

The table matches each word and punctuation mark with a symbol that identifies the elementary concept it represents. Each intermediary concept product of operations is identified by a unique arbitrary symbol generated by the computer.

Mensa table lookup enables the parser to determine which binary operations are specified by an expression by displaying which adjacent elemental and intermediate terms enter into binary operations. By looking for matches in the *Mensa* database the parser can determine which adjacent symbols in an expression do pair and which do not pair. This enables the parser to avoid seeing pairing between concepts that make no sense and to determine precedence of operations essential for obtaining the right parse result.

The table enables evaluation by lookup rather than "mental" calculation for all the operations that our parser requires to parse a text input to a single complex concept. Thus, an *Mensa* parser with access to an adequate *Mensa* table can exploit the mindless power of algebraic manipulation of symbols to identify the precise complex mental concept encoded in a text input, whether it is a statement, question or instruction, without "understanding" its meaning.

Mensa tables can fully deal with pragmatics, truth, the correspondence of our ideas and thoughts of the real world or of an imaginary world.

Mensa tables enable performance of high level propositional logic[2] once complex concepts expressed in language are reduced to compact identifying symbols, Yet, an almost an extreme "figuring out" process is required when the second person hears speech or reads text, mitigated for our software parser by being preparsed into a *Mensa* table.

A *Mensa* database is therefore simply an alternative orthography for language, able to store declarative knowledge to the same level as natural language, but in a preparsed form that enables a computer to utilize it. When symbols representing mental concepts are organized into this *Mensa* data structure, the resulting tables share the full power of language in representing the structure and function of highly complex concepts. There is no need for *Mensa* parsers to actually execute the individual mental operations because they use simple table lookup to obtain result values. Our parser can identify precisely which concept among the infinitely scalable millions that can be stored in *Mensa*. This is *find* rather than *search*; *closed* rather than *open* interlocution.

Many of the steps in construction of *Mensa* tables from text can be automated. We look forward to very large *Mensa* databases been built in particular realms of knowledge with high hopes they can be made inclusive enough to be very useful. This is a very important area for future work. In any case, the properties of an inclusive *Mensa* table make it possible to bring the principles of algebraic evaluation and high level propositional logic to processing of language expressions and human thought in a very practical way. Asked this question:

> *"What is the most important thing about a Maven?"*

Our computer *Maven* pre-programmed to answer responds:

> *"The most important point about a Maven like me is that I will understand exactly which one of thousands of questions or remarks is being addressed to me and make the precisely appropriate response, no matter how the question is worded; as long as the text uses vocabulary and refers to concepts that I already understand."*

---

2   Google "propositional logic"

BOOK IV
CHAPTER II

Computer Programs and Mensa

In this chapter we discuss several software programs that interact with Mensa databases. Our parser-response software program with access to a Mensa database parses a meaningful input text expression to identify the single unique concept that the text expresses, no matter what words are used or how it is phrased. Then, the program's response module makes an appropriate programmed response to that input. This parser-response program constitutes a sophisticated human-machine interface, which we call a Maven. We have developed several other programs to speed the creation of Mensa databases some of which build Mensa databases automatically from marked up source text inputs. Then, another program employs a short Mensa table as a probe to search large texts to find a particular concept no matter how it is worded in the text. It would be straightforward to scale up this program to search for thousands of concepts simultaneously in a large text corpus. One fun program set two Mavens talking to each other, each making a very appropriate response to what was said to it by the other.

W e have explained how *Fifth Medium, M5, Mensa,* databases can store human thought in all its subtlety. They constitute a computer friendly notation holding the full meaning of language expressions, and thus are an alternative medium to language for representing declarative knowledge. *Mensa* tables enable a very simple of parser program to precisely identify what is meant by a language phrase, expression, sentence, question or paragraph.[1] However, each *Mensa* database must contain a vocabulary of all words that are used or might be used, and contain all relevant concepts in the context of interest along with the *relations* between them.

We have developed a series of computer programs and tools to interact with *Mensa* databases. The key program is our parser-response program which accepts text input and parses it to a particular physical row in the *Mensa* database, the one that represents the complex concept meant by the text. From there the response program initiates an appropriate response.

We have also developed software programs to assist the translation of natural language text into *Mensa* tables; to create what we have called computer *Mavens*. A computer *Maven* is a system module comprising a *Mensa* database which stores a particular domain of knowledge along with a software program that can communicate with it and respond appropriately. One fun program set two Mavens talking to each other, each making a very appropriate response to what was said to it. It was impossible to predict which way the conversation would go.

Another program, the *trawler* program, searches large bodies of text, complete e-books, to find every instance of a particular precisely defined sophisticated concept, no matter no matter what words were used or how it was phrased.

Another programming exercise of particular interest was our demonstration that the very same program that could parse an arithmetic expression to obtain its value could parse a language expression to obtain its meaning. This was to all intents and purposes a demonstration that algebra and language operate on the same self principles, which require strict precedence of binary operations that match up pairs of concepts in a series of loops, to evaluate an expression

---

1   A fully operational language parser was written in Visual Basic by Tony Cooper using Microsoft Access databases

One astonishing observation we made was that once large complex concepts are parsed to compact symbols, it is possible to perform very high level abstract logic by relating them in a *Mensa* table. This has important implications for computer intelligence. It will be a very fruitful area of endeavor.

The Parser Program

The task of the parser program is to identify which concept a given text input means, out of the billions it might be, no matter what words are used or how it is phrased. Having realized that language expressions were in fact algebraic expressions, we developed a natural language parser employing the standard calculator algorithm. This parser program relies on a pre-constructed lookup table, which must include all mental operations specified or implied in that language expression. We call such a table of precalculated mental operations a *Mensa* table.

To identify and execute the ordered series of binary mental operations encoded in a language expression our parser consults a *Mensa* table composed of precalculated mental operations. Only then can it construe the complex structure of a mental concept represented by an expression. Our parser program uses the principle of a *single elimination tournament* to evaluate a language expression, but with some of the symbols in each round getting a bye to the next or a later round instead of being involved in a matching in that round. Consulting a *Mensa* table of relations allows the parser to know which pairs of operands match up and therefore can be operated on in each round. The *Mensa* table dictates precedence of operations, and provides the product concept for each operation, eliminating the need for a mental calculation. By employing lookup of a *Mensa table* of operations a very simple software program can parse language expressions and determine the precise concept that they mean. Also determine whether an input expression makes sense. And recognize when the concept expressed by the text input is not there in the *Mensa* knowledge store.

Our system sees all three language elements: lexical words, grammaticals, and punctuation marks simply as symbols standing in for concepts, as operands in an algebraic expression. For example, consider the words of the language expression, *"the contribution of a given non-CO_2 greenhouse gas to radiative forcing"*. We will call it expression **y**. It can be thought of as an algebraic expression made up of eleven ordered word symbols, each standing for a concept. Each complex concept expressed is tagged with unique symbol ID #. To underscore the idea that words are just algebraic symbols for concepts. Let **y** equal the above expression in more compact symbols, the upper case initials of its words: **y = T C O A G N G G T R F**. So, when this language expression of eleven ordered concept symbols is submitted to the parser, the parser is required to consult the *Mensa* table shown below to extract and execute the ten mental operations that are entailed in the expression.

The eleven terms of the expression *"the contribution of a given non-CO2 greenhouse gas to radiative forcing"* specify ten mental operations, which can be represented by 10 physical rows in an *Mensa* table.

Table 4.2.1 lists the required operations rows embedded in a *Mensa* database table of mental operations.

344	... ~ ...	= ...	...
345	... ~ ...	= ...	...
354	T ~ C	= 1	*"the contribution"*
346	G ~ G	= 2	*"greenhouse gas"*
347	R ~ F	= 3	*"radiative forcing"*
348	N ~ 2	= 4	*"non-CO2 greenhouse gas"*
347	T ~ 3	= 5	*"to radiative forcing"*
350	G ~ 4	= 6	*"given non-CO2 greenhouse gas"*
351	A ~ 6	= 7	*"a given non-CO2 greenhouse gas"*
352	O ~ 7	= 8	*"of a given non-CO2 greenhouse gas"*
349	1 ~ 8	= 9	*"the contribution of a given non-CO2 greenhouse gas"*
355	9 ~ 5	= y	*"the contribution of a given non-CO2 greenhouse gas to radiative forcing"*
356	... ~ ...	= ...	...
357	... ~ ...	= ...	...

Table 4.2.1. Expression **y** embedded in a Maven Database

The 10 operations encoded in this language expression are represented by 10 rows, perhaps embedded in a large database table of mental operations that also may hold the mental operations of many other language expressions. These ten *Mensa* rows hold the necessary instructions for building the parse tree. It is critical to explicitly identify each higher order unit concept derived at each stage of construction, at each round of the *single elimination tournament*, with a concept ID# and for the final concept to be given an arbitrary but unique symbol identifier. In this case, **y**. And, integer **3** is the unique symbol identifier standing for intermediary concept **radiativeforcing** and named by the words *"radiative forcing"* in the text field of its own *Mensa* database row.

Figure 4.2.1 shows a run of our table driven parser, accessing above *Mensa Table* 4.2.1 using the same exact algorithm that parses an arithmetic expression in an RPN calculator, to parse this language expression.

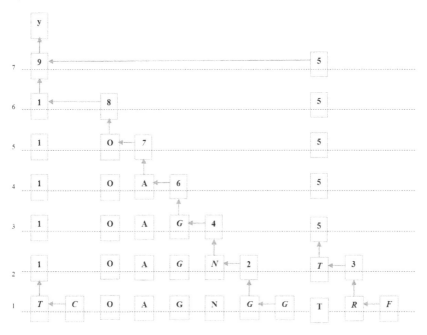

Fig. 4.2.1 Run of the parser program on expression *"the contribution of a given non-CO2 greenhouse gas to radiative forcing"*

Parse narrative: parsing along this string of concept symbols from left to right, consulting Table 4.2.1, our parser finds three operations it can perform: **T ~C = 1**, **G ~ G = 2** and **R ~ F = 3** in the first tournament round. This results in a new row **1 O A G N 2 T 3**. In the second round the program performs two operations on this row, **A~ 2 = 3** and **T ~ 3 = 5**, resulting in new row **1 O A G 4 5** for the third round. And this continues until the parser has re-enacted the ten operations in the table, substituting two concepts for one; until only one term is left, concept **y**, which represents the meaning of the whole expression.

Here is pseudocode for parsing an expression to the concept that it means consulting a *Mensa* table:

```
Input text string into the first row of an x,y array
    before first symbol of current row
        look in Mensa table for row matching next symbol pair
            if row found put product symbol in next array row
            if row not found put first symbol in next array row
        loop until end of row reached
    next row
loop until one symbol left
```

Thus, in a series of rounds the parser program makes passes through the expression as shown in Fig. 4.2.1 looking for pairs of terms that the *Mensa* table indicates it can combine into one term for the next round. It "puts two and two together" by lookup of pairs of concepts related in the *Mensa table*, by parsing (pair-sing) the string of concepts. The *Mensa* database is consulted for of each operation in the table to obtain the result concept by lookup rather than calculation. The algorithm loops, continuing until there is only one term left, the **it** symbol that stands for that meaning of the whole expression, in this case **y**. It looks like concept **y** above "one" the tournament.

Considering the metaphor of a tennis tournament helps us to understand what is going on here. The winner of each match survives, i.e. each survivor literally "lives on". Losers go home. Odd players get a *bye* to the next round. Evaluating an expression is in Niklaus Wirth's words like *"the history of a tennis tournament ... with each game being a node denoted by its winner and the two previous games of the combatants as its descendents".*[2] Just as higher ranked players are seeded into different sixteenths of the draw to ensure they do not meet until later rounds, it points up how enriched concepts do not match up until the correct round. Perhaps the format of a boxing championship is more apt in this case since the incumbent world champion, the **T** (the) concept in this diagram becoming **y**, gets byes all the way to the final (boxing) championship match, which, as we have explained before, is how punctuation mark and pronoun concepts work.

Figure 4.2.2 shows that this parse tree can be represented equally well as *flow-of-meaning-tree* which similarly shows surviving determiner concept

the being enriched directly and indirectly by all of the other ten concepts to become concept **y**. We find that this figure tells how an expression parses more intuitively than the "co-rrect" tree format of Fig 4.2.1.

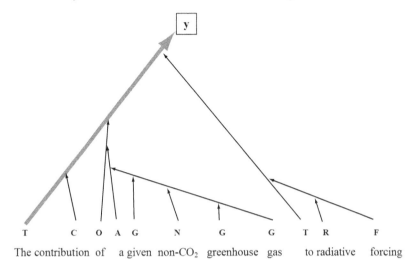

Fig. **4.2.2** The Flow-of-meaning-tree for Expression *"the contribution of a given non-CO2 greenhouse gas to radiative forcing"*

And, we have found that a software "expression" program running the same parser algorithm backwards, consulting Table 4.2.1 starting with final concept **y**, iteratively substituting two concepts for one, keeping the order will generate the original language expression. This is how the entries in the text column of our *Mensa* databases are generated automatically. Mapping a concept onto text in this manner is useful because then a *Mensa* database can communicate the meaning of a concept to a human by automatically translating concept symbols into language expressions that the human can understand. It is possible to manually compose more elegant paraphrases than the computer generates that express the mental concept and output different versions at different times in the interests of variety. This allows our *Mavens* to answer the same question aptly in more than one way.

The same *Mensa* database table can contain thousands, even millions, of other rows representing myriad concepts, each row matching two concepts, with a pointer to the concept that both of them connect to in common. If a text expression that means a pre-installed concept is input into our computer parser program, it will utilize lookup of the *Mensa* table to perform operations that arrive at the exact concept row that represents the meaning of that text. Typically each concept row in the database is replete with an appropriate "cargo" of metadata in other columns with special purposes. This is entirely analogous to a specific medial temporal lobe cortical neuron firing when a particular meaningful text in heard or read; the neuron that has a receptive field for that text, a neuron with projections to many other linked brain functions in both cortices, many of which project in turn to consciousness.[3]

Just like characters and words that appear in many different local areas of a text do, concepts take on different meanings in each local contexts. A very important feature of our parser is that once it focuses in on one section of the database it stays there to capture the local meaning of the concepts, particularly pronouns. We call this *local search*.

What is interesting is that a software algorithm implemented in compact code comprising a single digit number of rows can parse long complex sentences with punctuation and subordinate clauses easily. It illustrates the power of recursive algorithms operating on a recursive data type like a tree variable. Niklaus Wirth notes *"the simplicity and transparence ...... that is obtained through the use of recursive procedures. It is obvious that recursive programs are particularly suitable when a program is to manipulate information whose structure has been defined recursively.[4]* One has to wonder if the brain uses these same recursive methods to parse language expressions using neuron networks connected in the form of ordered binary trees.

The Response Program

As noted in the chapter on mental accounting, philosophers have long argued that the active mind is comprised of three cooperating systems, the *cognitive*, the *affective* and the *conative*; knowledge, feeling and action. *"Conation is a term that stems from the Latin conatus, meaning any natural tendency, impulse, striving, or directed effort. It is one of three parts of the mind, along with the affective and cognitive. In short,*

---

3   Damasio A R, *The Brain Binds Entities and Events by Multiregional Activation from Convergence Zones*, Neural Computation, 1. 123-132, 1989.

4   Niklaus Wirth, *Algorithms + Data Structures = Programs*, Prentice Hall 1976 pp. 189-242 p.197

the cognitive part of the brain measures intelligence, the affective deals with emotions and the conative takes those thoughts and feelings to drive how you act on them."[5] So far we have dealt mostly with the cognitive faculty of the mind identifying the meaning of concepts and relating them to each other. Although we see clear approaches, as yet we have not dealt with the emotive system of scoring concepts and evaluating the changing status of individuals. But we have spent some effort on developing a computer response system that together with the parser constitutes a quite sophisticated human machine interface.

Because the computer can identify the precise meaning of what is input, it is possible to program an appropriate response for each text input based upon its meaning. Every concept is represented in a *Mensa* database by its own physical row, analogous to every concept being represented in the brain by its own cortical neuron. If the expression input makes sense and the *Mensa* table has the necessary rows to parse it, the parser program will find the exact row in the database assigned to represent the individual complex concept meant by the expression. In that row of the *Mensa* database there is a text field containing a carefully composed text expression that describes the concept most accurately. The default response in our system is to output in print or voice, or both. Yet, upon reaching that row, the response program will perform whatever instructions have been placed in that row. A specific response may be a text output, a computer action or a change in behavior of the computer. A computer action is itself a concept, a motor concept, and is identified with a symbol and its own row in a *Mensa* table. Not all computer actions are responses. Our software can initiate actions, ask questions and understand the responses to them.

Text strings in the text field of rows have been carefully composed to express the concept in the most succinct way. For example, should you ask *"What is the concept in row 17432?* The response might be *"The effect of quantitative easing on the unemployment rate"*. Millions of questions and answers can be embedded in a database. The parser will determine which question it is no matter how complicated it is, what vocabulary is used or how it is phrased. Thus, the precise request in any anticipated **yes/no, when, where, how, how much** or **why** question will be recognized, and a very appropriate pre-programmed answer returned.

---

5   Wikipedia "conation":

But other actions are possible. In the same row of the *Mensa* database there is a response column field that holds symbols that identify actions that the computer can make. As a *motor concept*, as opposed to a *sensory concept*, each response action has its own row in the *Mensa* table, which when activated the action will be performed. If there are motor concept symbols in this response column, executing them takes precedence over text output. We have developed software that uses a random number generator to pick and execute one of the actions, or to do them in order, or to do the next one next time. A set of motor concepts could be arranged as the leaves of a tree implemented as a *motor Mensa table*, so that a tree traversal algorithm could be used to execute the steps of a complicated process in the right order.

This combination parser-response program constitutes a *Maven*.

Online Maven

We have developed a Web based text entry toolbar to receive input texts, which are passed to our parser/response module running on a server. Responses are passed back to the Web page. This allows a user to run a *Maven* in a Web browser window.

Exam program

Our Exam Program outputs preset free text questions that have clear correct answers and waits for an answer. Even though a correct answer might be given in thousands of different wordings, our parser is able to detect whether the answer given matches a correct answer, and thereby grade the exam automatically.

Trawler Program

We have developed a probe program that can find a particular concepts in a large body of text no matter how worded. It is not practical to find concepts in a large text corpus by searching with fixed text strings because thousands of different text strings can be used to express any particular concept. And, key word searches famously miss many pertinent concepts and find many not pertinent because they do not take full account of the of meaning contributed by word order and grammaticals. And key word searches require a human to validate all results. Our *trawler* program is able to find every instance of the concept no matter how it is worded without human help.

This program employs a *Mensa table* probe constructed with rows for appropriate vocabulary and sub-concepts able to detect concepts of interest. The entire text to be searched is fed in sentence by sentence. Every string in the text that expresses the concept of interest is identified if it is expressed in any way that makes sense. The method: every contiguous series of words and punctuation marks all from the vocabulary of the probe is parsed to see if it expresses the concept of interest. If it does, it will be detected. Use of synonyms, different phrasing, change of word order does not matter.

To prove feasibility we salted a full length book with instances of several different paraphrases that expressed concepts of interest. The program worked its way through the text and found all instances of expressions that meant concepts of interest, ignoring control expressions using the same words even slightly changed in order that no longer expressed the concepts. *Trawler* can easily be scaled up with a large *Mensa table* to search for thousands of concepts simultaneously in a large text corpus. ICD.10 coding of patient records is a promising application.

Mensa TableBuilder Programs

Although a *Mensa* database can be built by manual input and editing, the process is meticulous and slow. There is a huge need to bring automation to the installation of knowledge in *Mensa* database format, the translation of language into *Mensa*. We have spent a certain amount of time developing working programs using text markup to speed up the process of composing *Mensa* tables, but with limited application so far. We have developed two prototype *Tablebuilder* programs that translate texts marked up in RPN notation into *Mensa* tables.

The approach we tried was to mark up text so that a computer can do the rest to build a Mensa table. Inserting "superfluous punctuation marks" into text expressions allowed our *Tablebuilder* software program to construct *Mensa* tables automatically from them. Such markup provided our computer program with precedence of mental operations in a language expression in the same manner that RPN notation provides unambiguous precedence of binary operations to a calculator. *Tablebuilder* constructs a *Mensa* mental operations table without any further human supervision from appropriately marked up text. We saw immediate improvements in speed and ease of building *Mensa* tables. We have no doubt that an industrial scale effort in this area would work wonders, and render worthwhile insights into the rules of grammar and into human thought processes as a valuable by-product.

Our experience with marking up many texts is a skill that anyone can quickly learn. However, the tables produced do not allow for *invariance* of input text as described in Book III Chapter I and so must be further edited manually at present so as to be able to field synonyms and paraphrases the might be used to express the same concept.

There is a requirement that the *Mensa* installer have a grasp of rules of syntax of English and also have experience of the world to know when concepts match up to make sense. This is beyond the capabilities of present day computers. In our earlier discussions of the rules of syntax of English we showed that application of the rules would allow a parser program to determine the order of precedence of the operations needed to parse an expression largely automatically. However there will always be need for a human parser applying common sense to some degree to determine whether two concepts can be fused to form a product concept that makes sense. There is a tradeoff: the more that rules of English syntax are truly understood and applied, the less the need for human common sense to be applied to get the parse right. This points to a need for intensive study of the rules of syntax along with a serious commitment to incorporating them into computer parser programs.

Still, with further refinements that incorporate more complete programmatic use of the rules of syntax to greatly ease the burden of markup, we envision that authors in the future will provide marked up versions of their texts as a routine practice thereby allowing publishers to routinely create online *Mensa* tables that make all the concepts in the text fully accessible to a computer parser program.

Tracker Program

In parallel with our language understanding software we have developed Tracker, our proprietary database management module. Tracker can convert any standard database file, such as **.dbf**, to a proprietary **.trk** file. Tracker greatly facilitates access to and editing of databases. *Mensa* databases are stored as **.trk** files. We have found that the ease Tracker brings to the task of constructing *Mensa* tables is virtually indispensable.

Future Programming Directions

The human mind is continuously jumping from one thought to another, the so-called stream of consciousness. These thoughts are often a spur to action. Planning for actions is done in the frontal lobes, organized in the premotor and motor cortices and carried out by the basal ganglia, cerebellum, medulla oblongata, anterior spinal cord. There are opportunities for software modeling of the development of the will to act and the choice and performance of appropriate action in response to inputs and situations: desire, volition, initiative, striving, and responses to the environment

Imagine a system continuously receiving input information in the form of text. The program reads and parses incoming word strings. Given that our parsing program understands precisely the meaning of the input expressions it could detect syndromes by activating concepts and waiting for a subsequent concept that means something is going on. These could be related to see if a response is needed. Responses to syndromes could be programmed that are perfectly apposite. Such a program could interpret a complex situation since each complex situation is reduced to a unitary identifying symbol and see a syndrome. One can see that by making these basic tools available for improvement and experimentation one might model a human mind to a high degree. This is up to artists whose future designs will continuously improve *Mensa* software.

During this programming enterprise a very interesting process occurred. It brought discipline to out linguistic theory speculations. When a program did not work we would have to adjust it iteratively, trying this and that until it did. This forced us to come up with linguistic theory to explain why it now worked. It is unlikely we would ever have thought of many of the novel aspects of the theory without the inspiration coming from this discipline. And of course we take it that the practical achievements of the system validate the underlying novel linguistic theory. Because of limitations of time and resources we have only made a start on the programming possibilities. We are developing a programming kit to put into the hands of many smart programmers. The future is huge.

BOOK IV
CHAPTER III

Hal – Actual Conversations with a Mensa Database

Since Hal starred in Stanley Kubrick and Arthur Clarke's 2001- A space Odyssey the Holy Grail of artificial intelligence has been to achieve the level of machine understanding depicted in the film. We have been able to conduct sophisticated conversations with our Mavens but only about concepts that are stored. A Maven must expect all of the concepts that will be presented to it and have very flexible preprogrammed responses installed. However when scaled up to millions of concepts in a limited domain of knowledge we expect the computer will appear formidably intelligent.

A computer Maven consists of a software parser and response program addressing a *Mensa* table holding a certain domain of knowledge. There are no restrictions upon the complexity or abstractness of concepts represented. Each *expression, statement, question* and *response* is a unique concept assigned its own identified row. Our parser can understand any input text expression, no matter how it is worded once its meaning is encoded in the *Mensa* table and for any given restricted domain of knowledge there is no limit to the number of *concepts* encoded, no limit to the number of *statements* that can be understood, no limit to the number of *questions* that can be asked. There is provision in a *Mensa table* to make one or more appropriate text responses or other computer actions in response to any input text that is understood.

Our approach to creating a Maven is to start with a text that describes the domain of knowledge relatively fully, making sure that all the main points are covered. Then to translate all the sentences, one by one into a *Mensa table* making sure that all synonyms and paraphrases that can be used to address concepts are encoded. Then for each sentence make sure that all of the questions associated with that sentence are addressed. Current Mavens can carry on very appropriate conversations in plain English between user and computer in their restricted domain of knowledge.

An Immunology Maven

Here is a passage from a paper in Nature Immunology describing complex immunologic concepts.[1]

> *"The fundamental idea that T cells with autoimmune potential exist in the normal peripheral T cell repertoire is based on the finding that CD4+ T cell populations depleted of regulatory T cell subsets are capable of causing tissue-specific immunopathology after adoptive transfer into lymphopenic hosts. It is now recognized that these autoreactive T cells are normally kept in check by the presence of CD4+ regulatory T cells (Treg cells). A feature shared by Treg cells and T cells with autoimmune potential is the ability to recognize self antigens. Treg cell recognition of self antigens was initially suggested after observations indicated that the presence of a particular organ was important for the maintenance of Treg cell mediated tolerance to that organ."*

---

1   Chyi-Song Hsieh, Ye Zheng, Yuqiong Liang, Jason D Fontenot, Rudensky A.Y., *An intersection between the self-reactive regulatory and nonregulatory T cell receptor repertoires*, Nature Immunology, 7, 401-410, 2006,

We constructed an *Mensa table* that represented all the concepts in the passage as well as the concepts in a series of questions that arise naturally in the mind of an expert. This immunological *Maven* comprises a *Mensa table* of several hundred rows.

Here are sample questions and answers from the transcript from an actual run of the program:

QUESTION
What cell populations are capable of causing tissue specific immunopathology after adoptive transfer into lymphopenic hosts?

ANSWER
CD4 + T cell populations depleted of regulatory T cell subsets

QUESTION
Why are CD4+ T cell populations depleted of regulatory T cell subsets capable of causing tissue-specific immunopathology after adoptive transfer into lymphopenic hosts?

ANSWER
Because they contain active autoimmune T cells

QUESTION
Who first suggested the fundamental idea that T cells with autoimmune potential exist in the normal peripheral T cell repertoire?

ANSWER
It was first proposed by John Gorman in 1960[2]

A Literary Maven

In another exercise we constructed a Maven that (who) understands all of the concepts in James Joyce's 1902 short story *Araby* from *The Dubliners*. This required a database of eighteen thousand rows. Our parser program can read through the text of the whole story in five minutes, twice as fast as a human, taking into full account every lexical word, grammatical and punctuation mark, identifying each simple, intermediate and complex concept and seeing its precise relation to others. It can appropriately answer hundreds of questions about events, characters in the story and plumb their motivations and feelings.

---

2   Gorman J.G and Chandler J.G., *Hypothesis: Is there a an Immunologically Incompetent Lymphocyte?*, Blood, 23, 117-128, 1964.

Here is one paragraph from *Araby*:

> *"Every morning I lay on the floor in the front parlour watching her door. The blind was pulled down to within an inch of the sash so that I could not be seen. When she came out on the doorstep my heart leaped. I ran to the hall, seized my books and followed her. I kept her brown figure always in my eye and, when we came near the point at which our ways diverged, I quickened my pace and passed her. This happened morning after morning. I had never spoken to her, except for a few casual words, and yet her name was like a summons to all my foolish blood."*

Here are some questions relating to this paragraph from an actual run of the communications program:

QUESTION
Why did our protagonist lie on the floor at the window to watch for Mangan's sister to come out on her doorstep to leave her house to go to school?

ANSWER
So that he would see her leave her house, so he could follow her.

QUESTION
Why was the blind pulled down to within an inch of the sash?

ANSWER
So he could not be seen.

QUESTION
Did he keep her always in his eye and, when they came near the point at which their ways diverged, did he quicken his pace and pass her?

ANSWER
Yes he did.

Storing declarative knowledge in a *Mensa* database to the same level of complexity as language is relatively straightforward. And the amount of knowledge that a Maven can be given is infinitely scalable. However, for a computer conversation system to be useful and practical, it is important to make it capable of fielding a high percentage of domain relevant questions that can be asked, and to respond appropriately to relevant inputs by the interlocutor. We have made a start that demonstrates a clear path to this goal, but there is much more work to be done.

BOOK IV
CHAPTER IV

Applications for Mensa Technology

There is a great need for computer applications that can store human knowledge in computer accessible form, understand language and respond appropriately with words or actions to spoken text inputs, a human-machine interface. The most immediate place for Mensa technology is an interface to the Internet, but there are many other worthwhile areas to apply our system, in a variety of major industries and fields of study from medicine to education to advertising. Mensa technology enables many worthwhile knowledge facilities.

T he ultimate goal, perhaps for some, is to model an intelligent human mind to a level displayed by iconic Hal in Stanley Kubrick's 1968 movie *2001, A Space Odyssey*. Using *Mensa* technology it is possible to have a computer completely understand what you are saying to it and program it to respond appropriately. *Mensa* technology has total command of the semantics and syntax of a message in a closed knowledge domain, which makes it unique in natural language understanding, where efforts are now focused on open domain questioning using statistical key word techniques, enormous computing power and high-capacity indexes of vast open text sources. *Mensa* technology, in contrast, is closed domain and deals only with preregistered vocabulary and concepts that humans install. With *Mensa* technology a computer can be programmed to respond to double meaning and appreciate and react to subtle subtext. There is no limit to the level of intellectual sophistication that can be encoded, and it is infinitely scalable.

What follows are brief discussions of potential applications for *Mensa* technology.

Mavens

Mavens in this context are software agents that respond to humans using regular text or voice conversation in a closed and specific domain of knowledge. This is the most intriguing application, building a Maven that can pass the Turing test, but also endowed with personality and appropriate display of feelings and emotions as inspired by iconic Hal of *2001, A Space Odyssey*. The extraordinarily enthusiastic reception for iPhone's Siri shows clearly that a Maven application has its place. A Maven could provide completely sensible and on the point responses in contrast with Weisenbaum's Eliza programs, which, although they pass the Turing test with many people, attain very poor sensitivity and specificity.[1] Current *Mensa* tools are capable but it will require some very clever teams of authors to bring a Maven up to a level of broad range and insightful humor.

Mass Storage of Knowledge

A less strong version of Hal would be comprehensive structured knowledge repositories in various fields, but without the personality.

---

1   Google "wiki Eliza program"

Content in any domain of knowledge can be installed and access to it can be obtained by ordinary conversation at a fully human level. *Mensa* databases are eminently more searchable than free text because previously "unstructured" information is now formally prestructured. In the future authors may post a *Mensa* version of their work on the internet in parallel with language publication. While the effort to produce this *Mensa* version would not require as much effort as writing the material in the first place, it would require an interactive process with a human editor using a set of highly developed authoring tools. However, we think the investment would be worth it to have a Wikipedia that you could have an intelligent conversation with.

Much like the way the internet offers links to other websites, authors will decide that "off-topic" questions are best answered by a link to another *Mensa* published book, and could route the question "through" that book before returning an answer to the person asking the question. While the quality and biases of the sources of information would still be as important as they are today, we anticipate that a prolific industry of knowledge services would emerge from this process.

Publishing

There is an important future for publishing informational material, news stories, reviews, reports, scientific papers, and textbooks etc. in *Mensa* database format. We foresee such materials will be published both as printed text and in an online *Mensa* database in parallel. The online version will give reader much better and faster access to material they are particularly interested in. Intelligent information services will be able to make use of networking since a particular query could be broadcast to thousands of *Mensa* databases simultaneously. If any one database had the desired information it would be forthcoming.

However, publishing extant text material in *Mensa* will require a Wikipedia scale of effort with thousands of human curators supervising the knowledge installation function, perhaps best done at the time of writing by the authors themselves. Our experience is that building *Mensa* tables is a fascinating activity and a lot of fun. We are making a software kit available that can be used to encode knowledge in *Mensa* format to create *Mavens* of all kinds on a personal computer. If enough people develop the necessary skills there is an opportunity for crowd sourcing construction of *Mensa* databases on a massive scale, thereby allowing unprecedented intelligently filtered access to enormous amounts of knowledge.

FAQs and Smart CRM

The ability to field a question no matter what words are used or how it is phrased will make FAQs much more convenient. There will be no need to read through 20 questions to see if your question is there with an answer to your question. And the practical number of questions is no longer limited to 20. Good responses to questions that come in can be pre-prepared that customers can access online just by asking their question in their own words. Closely related is smart CRM. Human customer service representatives answering phones will have much better access to relevant information to serve customers better.

Intelligence and National Security

Intelligence and national security institutions could make good use of a network of *Mensa* databases since a particular query could be broadcast simultaneously to thousands of *Mensa* databases containing intelligence information maintained by disparate groups. If any one database had the desired information it would be forthcoming. *Mensa* access has an additional benefit. It can prevent fishing expeditions, because specific information can be made available without access to sensitive or classified information in which it may be embedded.

Human-Machine Interfaces

An immediate place for *Mensa* technology exists in Human-Machine Interfaces, particularly an interface to the Internet. Current *Mensa* technology enables complex instructions to be given to a computer in ordinary language with any vocabulary and any phrasing, as long as the meaning is perfectly clear. With *Mensa*, any clear message in good English phrased in any way whatsoever will be understood perfectly. As long as it is within the bounds of the knowledge stored, our software parser will recognize which instruction has been given or which question has been asked and make a programmed response to that instruction.

The computer must expect what will be said to it; it has to be supplied with the necessary vocabulary and with all of the concepts in the area of interest. And of course, what you ask the machine to do must be in its repertoire. But when you think about it, humans have the same restriction. You can't talk intelligently to someone about a subject using words or concepts they don't know or ask them to do something they can't do. Hard facts have to be faced though. Because the number of concepts is infinite there is no way we can store an infinite number of concepts in a computer's memory, enough to anticipate any concept that someone might want to talk to the computer about. However we believe a particular domain of knowledge could be covered well.

From Print to Web – The PEN Application

The first practical and most easily implemented Human-Machine Interface application for *Mensa* is a natural language interface to the Internet. Major efforts are underway worldwide, to help create the "semantic Web", which constitutes an ambitious effort to make the Internet more intelligent and to enable the ability to communicate with it in ordinary English and have it make very appropriate responses.[2]

As a first application we have developed what we call *Plain English Name (PEN)* technology. We have built a fully implemented working prototype. What is *PEN*? Many advertisers announce in a print, radio, TV or billboard ad the existence of supplementary information online that they want viewers of the print ad to see, or that there is a product or service they can provide. They usually include a URL Web address in the ad and recently some include a barcode tag readable by smartphone cameras and tablet computers. These are the intended "bridge" between the offline and the online worlds, between high-production value impressions and deep product information and specifications.

As a more conducive alternative, our system places a PEN icon in the print ad along with words describing the information, product or service that is available online. Once an ad reader sees the PEN icon in a print ad, he knows that useful adjunct information or service is online and is accessible just by typing a clear request for it in his own words into an entry field on his desktop or mobile device. A browser window opens enabling the exact item to be immediately obtained. We argue that a PEN request for specified online item is a more natural way, a better way, to access a particular Web item that an advertiser wants the print ad viewer to see or get. The user just has to remember the idea, not the URL Moreover, because it's so

---

2   Google "semantic Web"

immediately available in a format that is natural to him, the user is more and he is more likely to use it.

The need for this bridge is already demonstrated by the market today. There are several alternatives ways currently being promoted for a reader to see such online material: enter a URL or shortened URL supplied in the print ad, or, with a smart phone or tablet app, read a barcode tag that has been placed in the print ad, photograph a picture with Google Goggles, SMS text a keyword to a number. And of course, one can search for the particular Web page on Google. The fact that all of these ways are being encouraged and used more and more validates the need for convenient methods of access to specially prepared or pertinent Web items announced in print. We think a natural language option will emerge as the best one.

Mensa Text Probes – Search Documents for Specific Concepts

There is another application that will appeal to scholars in every field. It is possible to create a relatively small *Mensa* probe that encodes a particular idea or concept. We then pass a large corpus of text against that short *Mensa* table probe to see if a particular concept is expressed somewhere in the text, and record its location. It does not matter how the concept is expressed in the text corpus as long as the meaning is clear. As an experiment, we spiked a long e-book with several expressions that meant a particular complex concept, each one worded differently, along with control expressions that used the very same words but scrambled so as to not make sense. This concept probe program found all the correctly worded expressions and ignored the jumbled ones using the same words. Sensitivity and specificity for detecting the planted ideas was 100%. While this performance relies entirely on a human being having authored the small probes that recognize the differently worded expressions used for the concepts of interest, we believe this facility will be very useful for authors and researchers in many fields in the future.

The Electronic Patient Record

In the electronic patient record 60% of information in the form of text and is considered "unstructured". It is not, of course, since with an understanding of the rules of syntax a parser can reveal a high level of structure in text. There is an urgent need for computerized access to textual information in patient records for purposes of chart review, quality assurance studies, and automatic generation of CPT ICD-9 codes and soon the new CPT ICD-

10 codes, as well as for clinical research and providing physicians with access to clinical information. Major efforts are presently going on in this area. This is an ideal application for our *trawler* program, which is able to search large bodies of text to find concepts no matter how they are worded with 100% sensitivity and specificity. And, it would be straightforward to scale up this program to search for thousands of concepts simultaneously on each pass through a large text corpus.

Education – Automated College Courses

Mensa databases will have an important use in education. Automated courses are an obvious application. Exams where answers are in essay form can now be graded by computer can now become a practical alternative to multiple choice exams. We have shown feasibility for the exam program with our Araby database which contains all the knowledge in James Joyce's short story *Araby*. Here, our exam program outputs a programmed question related to the story and waits for an answer. The answer text is parsed and matched for its concept against a set of correct answer concepts and graded accordingly. And, for essay exams, a grading program could examine each sentence in the student's essay to see if it matches one of the points that would be expected to be made by an A student. Essays would be scored for the number and relevance of points made. Wrong answers and regularly seen off the point answers would be detected to see if students were responding with common misconceptions. If a student's novel answer happened to be a remarkable new insight that teachers had never thought of, this could be added to the canon of good points to be made in a domain, and to be taught.

Writing Courses

Mensa technology will be important for teaching of writing and for developing more precise style manuals.[3] Most writing courses are taught by English departments but businesses are becoming much more concerned with the writing skills of their executives in writing proposals and in internal and external communications. Diagrammatic *flow-of-meaning-*

---

3   One example: the common style manual rule in sentences ending with quotation marks - place the period within the quotes - is shown to be wrong. Unless the period is party to the quoted text, *flow of meaning trees* can't be drawn that way without crossing arrows. Note the correct placement of periods in this *Essay*.

trees and *Mensa tables* with scoring of paragraphs for meaning and weight show what is the main point in each paragraph, and exactly how other sentences underscore or undercut that point, providing a clear eyed view of what has been said.

Avatars and Computer Games

One other very interesting and potentially huge application for *Mensa* technology is in computer games endowing avatars with human understanding, giving them personalities and the ability to reply sensibly to text messages, and to obey spoken orders with physical on screen actions. With voice recognition, face recognition and machines like Microsoft's Kinect recognizing movements, the opportunity to develop very sophisticated multimodal interactions with a computer or its avatar becomes ripe for development. *Mensa* will add a whole new dimension to computer avatars. This facility is expected to have enormous appeal to serious gamers.

Research in Linguistics and Cognitive Science

Mensa technology opens up important opportunities for research in Linguistics and Cognitive Science doing hands on experiments modeling human thought. IBM's Watson project demonstrates the current high interest and investment in computer cognition research. The more precise and complex the query the greater edge *Mensa* has over current NLP approaches because key words without the exact relations between them do not carry specific meaning. In particular, the analogy between an expression that a person hears or reads firing a particular neuron out of millions in the left inferior temporal and frontal cortices and the same expression causing our parser to find a particular physical address out of billions in computer memory is telling. It suggests that building and tuning *Mensa* databases would enable experimental models that could provide worthwhile insights into how the brain and the mind work.

EPILOGUE

What have we accomplished so far? What have we not done yet? Where are the future directions for Mensa technology?

W ith *Mensa*, we are able to model human thought to the same intellectual level as language, but in a format that is completely accessible for a computer. We can reduce complicated expressions which mean subtle ideas and situations to a single unitary symbol that identifies them. So called "unstructured" natural language information can now be explicitly structured. We have developed a very capable language understanding system whereby the computer can precisely identify concepts addressed to it. Finally, we have programmed the computer to make very appropriate responses to specific text inputs.

Mensa is a closed knowledge storage and language understanding system. There is the proviso that the computer already has to have the vocabulary that is used and "knows" the concepts that may be mentioned in conversations with *Mensa*. One can only converse with *Mensa* using vocabulary and concepts that are already stored in *Mensa*. Therefore, presently, there is a need for the user to have a good idea of what the computer knows and to try to restrict the conversation to what satisfies that restriction. This applies equally to human conversations. *Mensa* databases are infinitely scalable so we hope that in the future this will not be much of a restriction.

It will be very worthwhile in the future to construct extensive domains of knowledge in *Mensa* databases, as they will be much more accessible than large texts of language. Humans can learn new concepts on the fly directly from what they are told and employ them immediately, storing knowledge as we read or listen to sentences. We can detect sarcasm, irony, puns humor and other forms of double meaning. Computers at present cannot do this and it is not yet possible with our system. Because any fact can be stated in many different ways, synonyms and paraphrases of concepts presently have to be added into the *Mensa* table manually if our parser is to be able to field all the variant ways of stating a concept. So, translation from text to *Mensa* presently requires a degree of human help to make sure the right meaning has been encoded

Fortunately, there are approaches for greatly speeding up and automating the construction of *Mensa* databases. We have made some early efforts in this area. For example, one our programs will construct a *Mensa* table automatically without further human help from text marked up for precedence of operations. However, the effort of translating the world's knowledge into *Mensa* databases will require a Wikipedia type effort with thousands or even millions of human *mentors*.

Will it be possible for the computer to do sophisticated logic? Really think. Presently *Mensa* databases contain only canned thinking. Because we can relate compact symbols that stand for very complex abstract concepts, it will be possible, for example, to perform *if .. then* functions to come up with worthwhile deductions and inferences. Relations between symbols could be defined to make rules that would be applied whenever two symbols are seen in a particular context. There is a wonderful future opportunity for progress way beyond our starting efforts.[1]

The process of crafting a Maven in a computer makes one feel like one is sculpturing thought, building and shaping a mind and a personality. One has control of ideas attitudes, and prejudices. One can incorporate wit. One has a sense of power. It is a very good feeling. Our experience is that building *Mensa* tables is a fascinating activity and a lot of fun.

More importantly, *Mensa* will be a tool for others to use and we would like to see it in clever hands pursuing its possibilities. We make a software kit available for encoding knowledge in *Mensa* tables to create *Mavens* of all kinds on a personal computer. *Mensa* technology will put true power in the hands of creative people. Heed Richard Feynman's belief *"What I cannot build, I cannot understand."* Build some *Mensa* tables for yourself.

---

1 We have ideas we haven't though of yet.

GLOSSARY

Avatar   A software program that models a human person in a computer

Command and Control (COMCON)   A system where a *commander* communicates orders to a *controller* who operates directly in the real world of interest, used to explain workings of our mental life.

CRM   Customer Relationship Management

Directed binary tree   In graph theory a tree graph where all the edges are directed to the one vertex

Encephalography   The recording of electrical brain activity from the scalp

Expression   An ordered list of symbols that can be parsed using appropriate rules of syntax to obtain its meaning or value

FAQ   A list of frequently asked questions in a given context

Flow-of-meaning-tree   A tree diagram that represents the flow of meaning between matched concepts in an expression into a single surviving concept that holds the meaning of the whole expression

fMRI   Functional magnetic resonance imaging is an imaging method that can show active regions of the brain in real time

FOMT   See Flow-Of-Meaning-Tree

Function   A mathematical or software procedure that computes an explicit value into a symbol

Grammaticals   The function words of language like determiners or prepositions

Grandmother cell   The neuron that has a receptive field or a particular sensory pattern, that fires when its sensory pattern is presented

Graph Theory   An important specialized field of mathematics involving *graphs*, of which *trees* are an important example.

Hal   The iconic computer character in Stanley Kubrick's 1968 film *2001, A Space Odyssey*

Hebb's law   The principle in neuroscience that states that *"neurons that fire together wire together"* that is the basis of most theories of memory

Invariance The ability of the brain to identify an object no matter its orientation, surface properties or lighting. In the special case of this book a private term denoting the ability of our parser program to obtain the meaning of an expression no matter what words or phrasing are used

Lexicals The content words of language, nouns, adjectives, verbs, adverbs

Linefinder A automatic circuit in a telephone exchange that recognizes when a subscriber line is off-hook, which is a useful analogy for how neurons find which cell to connect to

Maven A private term introduced to describe an intelligent computer program which comprises our parser-response program with access to a Mensa table. A Maven understands exactly which one of thousands of questions or remarks is being addressed to it and makes the precisely appropriate response, no matter how it is worded, as long as the text uses vocabulary and concepts pre-installed in the Mensa table..

Mensa A private term introduced to name the theory and technology that enables storage of declarative knowledge in a computer, the understanding of ordinary language that communicates with that knowledge, and the ability of the computer to make appropriate responses

Mensa Table A private term introduced to name a database table that models operations of the mind.

Mnemonic A language process where phonetic sounds suggest meaning

Ment A private term introduced to name the binary tree that represent the parsing of a particular expression to the single concept symbol that it expresses

N400 The electroencephalographic signal recorded when an expression makes no sense

NLP Natural language processing

P600 The electroencephalographic signal recorded when an expression contains errors of syntax

Phonetic palindrome A private term introduced to name words in which the phonemes are palindromic, like *entertain* (one-two-two-one)

Parsing A procedure that obtains the meaning of any kind of expression using rules of syntax appropriate for that type of expression.

Receptive field The sensory pattern that a neuron responds to

Rules of Syntax The appropriate rules that have to be followed to parse an expression

Seam grammatical A private term introduced to name a new kind of grammatical that confers reality first on one concept and thereby on all the concepts connected to it in an expression

Single elimination tournament A common tournament format where pairs of players or teams are matched in successive rounds. The winner survives to the next round, the loser goes home until there is just one champion

Synecdoche A figure of speech where a part refers to the whole or the whole refers to a part

Tracker Our proprietary database viewer and editor software

Turing test A test of a computers ability to appear human to an observer proposed by Alan Turing in 1950

Watson IBM's artificial intelligence supercomputer program that famously defeated two humans in a televised *Jeopardy* contest in 2011

World A private term in the grammar group of *tense*, *mood* or *aspect*, denoting whether a sentence refers to the present world of the observer or to a past or imaginary world, Every finite sentence is either *real world* or *remote world*

INDEX

T

U

V

W

X

Y

Z